Solving Identity Management in Modern Applications

Demystifying OAuth 2, OpenID Connect, and SAML 2

Second Edition

Yvonne Wilson
Abhishek Hingnikar

Apress®

Solving Identity Management in Modern Applications: Demystifying OAuth 2, OpenID Connect, and SAML 2

Yvonne Wilson
San Francisco, CA, USA

Abhishek Hingnikar
London, UK

ISBN-13 (pbk): 978-1-4842-8260-1
https://doi.org/10.1007/978-1-4842-8261-8

ISBN-13 (electronic): 978-1-4842-8261-8

Managing Director, Apress Media LLC: Welmoed Spahr
Acquisitions Editor: Susan McDermott
Development Editor: Laura Berendson
Coordinating Editor: Jessica Vakili

Distributed to the book trade worldwide by Springer Science+Business Media New York, 233 Spring Street, 6th Floor, 1 New York Plaza, New York, NY 10004. Phone 1-800-SPRINGER, fax (201) 348-4505, e-mail orders-ny@springer-sbm.com, or visit www.springeronline.com. Apress Media, LLC is a California LLC and the sole member (owner) is Springer Science + Business Media Finance Inc (SSBM Finance Inc). SSBM Finance Inc is a **Delaware** corporation.

For information on translations, please e-mail booktranslations@springernature.com; for reprint, paperback, or audio rights, please e-mail bookpermissions@springernature.com.

Apress titles may be purchased in bulk for academic, corporate, or promotional use. eBook versions and licenses are also available for most titles. For more information, reference our Print and eBook Bulk Sales web page at http://www.apress.com/bulk-sales.

Any source code or other supplementary material referenced by the author in this book is available to readers on the Github repository: https://github.com/Apress/Solving-Identity-Management-in-Modern-Applications. For more detailed information, please visit http://www.apress.com/source-code.

Printed on acid-free paper

Table of Contents

About the Authors

 **Yvonne Wilson** has had many roles in the software industry related to security and identity management as a security and identity architect; enterprise architect; director of developer success working with identity customers; senior director of security governance, risk, and compliance (GRC); chief strategy officer; and founder of cloud identity services. Yvonne was responsible for IT security strategy and architecture at Sun Microsystems, founded and designed the identity management services offered through Oracle Managed Cloud Services, and founded a developer success team for Auth0, working with customers and overseeing the creation of an identity management training program for customer-facing support and professional services engineers. Yvonne currently serves as an advisor on cybersecurity and identity management to startups in the lending, healthtech, financial, and cybersecurity consulting sectors.

In working with business teams at Sun, designing and deploying identity systems for customers at Oracle, and while founding a developer success team at Auth0, Yvonne had the opportunity of working with many customers, from small startups to large enterprises. Her experience spans the implementation of SSO, identity federation, directory services, adaptive knowledge-based authentication, and identity provisioning as well as multilevel authentication systems with certificate-based authentication and enterprise security architectures. She founded training programs for professional services and support staff on identity and access management (IDAM), including OIDC, SAML 2, WS-Fed, and OAuth 2. From this depth of experience, Yvonne realized the growing need for a basic overview of identity management concepts that is understandable to business application owners as well as architects and developers.

Abhishek Hingnikar is a staff engineer at Okta, in the Auth0 Product Unit. He has seven years of experience designing and demonstrating identity management with open standards like OAuth 2, OpenID Connect, and SAML 2. His current focus areas involve identity for SaaS applications, Consumer IoT, Device Identity, and designing solutions that apply web-based identity in peripheral domains.

About the Technical Reviewers

Artiom Ciumac is a Senior Solutions Architect at Okta / Auth0 Product Unit. He has 12 years of Software Engineering experience, including over 5 years of IAM with open standards like OAuth2, OpenID Connect, and SAML2. During his career he fulfilled various roles like developer, team lead, software architect, and solutions architect. Currently, the main focus is to consult customers in order to integrate with SaaS IDP in the most secure and optimal way possible to get maximum benefit out of the used services.

Sumana Malkapuram is a Staff Solutions Architect Auth0 (Okta's Product Unit). Sumana is CISSP certified with 15 years of experience in building innovative services within Cloud Security and IAM.

Carlos Mostek is a Principal Solution Architect for Okta. Carlos has more than 20 years of experience working in software development and security. He loves challenging problems and enjoys dealing with the complexities of identity management. Previous to his time at Okta, he held engineering and leadership roles at Auth0, Thomson Reuters, and BAE Systems. He has a Master's in Software Engineering and undergrad degree in Aerospace Engineering. Identity isn't rocket science, but it could be! For fun Carlos likes to juggle fire and play soccer, generally not at the same time.

ABOUT THE TECHNICAL REVIEWERS

Jared Hanson is a software engineer with experience across the full stack of desktop, mobile, and server-side application development. Jared is the developer of Passport.js, the popular Node.js authentication framework, and a contributor to the OpenID and OAuth family of specifications. He has worked as an architect at both Auth0 and Okta, leading companies in the identity and access management industry.

Acknowledgments

The best way to find yourself is to lose yourself in the service of others.

—Mahatma Gandhi

This book would not have been possible without the generous help of many friends and coworkers who have graciously shared their expertise and knowledge to review and improve the original draft. It has been a pleasure working with each of them over the years, and we are fortunate and much indebted for the knowledge, wisdom, and insights they have shared with us as well as, on occasion, the laughs.

We owe a huge debt of gratitude to Artiom Ciumac for his review of, and many helpful comments and suggestions on, the entire second edition of this book. His comments, based on a depth of experience from helping many customers with identity and access management challenges over the years, led to the addition of many clarifications, use cases, and explanations that will be beneficial to readers.

We are also very grateful for Sumana Malkapuram's review and suggestions for improving portions of the second edition of this book. Sumana's insightful feedback contributed to many clarifications and additions drawing on her significant experience working with customers to solve identity and access management scenarios.

Our massive appreciation and heartfelt thanks to Carlos Mostek for careful reviews of the first and second editions of this book and contributing many corrections, insightful additions, and helpful advice from his trove of development and IAM wisdom as well as his experience helping many customers solve their IAM challenges over the years.

Immense, heartfelt thanks also to Peter Stromquist for thoroughly reviewing the original draft version of this book and adding many corrections, suggesting additional ideas we'd left out, and adding wisdom from his valuable store of development and IAM expertise developed while designing solutions for many, many customers.

Huge, sincere gratitude to Amaan Cheval for careful reviews of the original draft for this book and contributing many corrections, clarifications, and suggestions for additional content from his keen knowledge of IAM topics, customer challenges, and broad development experience.

ACKNOWLEDGMENTS

Enormous and ardent thank you to Nicolas Philippe for thorough reviews of the original draft of this book from his extensive identity, security, and development experience; suggesting clarifications and additional topics requiring explanation; and adding wisdom from his years of experience with IAM as well as application development.

Titanic, sincere thanks also to Nicolás Sabena for excellent, careful reviews and contributing much valuable guidance to the original draft of this book on troubleshooting from his extensive expertise in IAM and development, as well as his keen ability to solve even the most puzzling customer issues.

Huge, grateful thanks to Jared Hanson for generously answering many questions and for reviewing and contributing corrections to many chapters of the original edition of this book from his deep knowledge of identity protocols.

Massive gratitude and thanks as well to Vittorio Bertocci for graciously sharing his extensive IAM knowledge in many forums, from which we and others have learned a great deal, and for reviewing portions of the original edition of this book with an eagle eye, providing valuable critique on errors in content, logic, and flow as well as suggestions for improvements and kind advice about writing.

Immense gratitude is due to Erin Richards for careful reviews, corrections, and additions to the original edition of this book on compliance matters, adding wisdom and practical advice from her long experience in this field as well as content on privacy and security frameworks.

Huge appreciation also to Adam Nunn for thorough reviews, corrections, and suggestions for the compliance chapter of the original edition based on his wisdom and experience in technical audits and compliance.

Sincere gratitude to Bill Soley for commiseration during the project as well as review and contributing suggestions and advice to the original draft from his immense knowledge of security matters.

Much appreciation also to Subra Kumaraswamy for reviewing a portion of the original draft of this book and contributing suggestions from his experience in both IAM and security.

Immeasurable and heartfelt gratitude to Laura Hill for insightful editorial reviews, finding the logic disconnects in early drafts, and making numerous suggestions for how to cut out extraneous fluff and clarify explanations in the original draft. Many thanks as well for patiently listening and providing encouragement as this project took shape!

Colossal thanks to Terence Rabuzzi for his razor-sharp editorial reviews of the original draft and advice on everything from graphics to structure and approaches for evaluating the logic of many sections.

Tremendous thanks to the creative eye, graphic talents, and technical knowledge of Liliya Pustovoyt for creating diagrams to illustrate several of the concepts discussed in the book.

We are also extremely grateful for the work of Vittorio Bertocci and the graphic design team at Auth0 for creating a library of identicons, a visual library for use in illustrating identity management concepts, which we have incorporated into many diagrams in this book.

We also owe a huge debt of gratitude to Rita Fernando, Susan McDermott, Laura Berendson, Liz Arcury, Jessica Vakili, and the rest of the Apress team for their patient advice, answering numerous questions, clear guidance, help with promotion, as well as editing on the text and graphics for this project.

A final massive and heartfelt thank you is due to our dear friends and family for their patience and support during this very long project. The kind words and voices of encouragement throughout meant a lot during the long hours of research, writing, development, and editing.

We are incredibly grateful to all who helped make this project possible by reviewing early drafts and contributing suggestions, advice, corrections, and additions. The text has been immeasurably improved by our reviewers' careful attention and many insightful comments. We could not have done this without them. That said, a line by Albert Camus is appropriate here: "The only real progress lies in learning to be wrong all alone." Any errors in the final text are solely ours. Any errata we discover after the book is published will be noted in the Apress GitHub repo for the book, accessible via `https://github.com/Apress/Solving-Identity-Management-in-Modern-Applications`.

Introduction

Every day you play with the light of the universe.

—Pablo Neruda, Chilean poet, politician, and diplomat, from *Twenty Love Poems and a Song of Despair* (1925)

There is a significant and growing cybersecurity workforce gap. A Global Information Security Workforce Study[1] predicts a cybersecurity workforce gap of 1.8 million individuals by 2022. At a time when the number of online services and devices that need security is growing rapidly, this is nothing short of alarming. In order to fill this gap, it is imperative to encourage more people to learn about this field and provide adequate resources for them to efficiently come up to speed. Identity management is an important component of security which is critical to protect the rapidly expanding array of innovative online services, smart devices, bots, automated agents, and the like that are being created.

The authors of this book are fortunate to have been a part of this field for some time. Between the two of us, we have created and deployed a variety of different types of applications, single sign-on, identity federation, provisioning systems for various access control models, directory services, and various forms of strong authentication. We have had the pleasure of working closely with many customers to understand their unique requirements and help them design and deploy identity and access management systems in both cloud and enterprise environments. We've learned many lessons from these projects, some of them the hard way through the school of hard knocks!

We wrote this book to share what we've learned from our experiences. We hope to provide others a head start based on the lessons we've learned. Our intent is to provide an introduction for those who are new to identity management and inspire them to continue learning more about this topic. We provide an overview of three identity management protocols, namely, OIDC, OAuth 2, and SAML 2, that will be useful for application developers who need to add authentication and authorization to their

---

[1] www.prnewswire.com/news-releases/global-cybersecurity-workforce-shortage-to-reach-18-million-as-threats-loom-larger-and-stakes-rise-higher-300469866.html

applications and APIs. We've covered the problem each protocol is designed to solve, how to initiate basic requests, and how to troubleshoot issues. A sample program accompanies the book and illustrates some of the concepts. We've also provided information on typical identity management requirements to help you identify what to include in your project plan, things that can go wrong that should be planned for, common mistakes, and how to approach compliance. These chapters will be valuable for developers as well as architects, technical project managers, and members of security teams involved with application development projects.

In terms of scope, the book is designed to provide an introduction to identity management. We cover how the three identity protocols can be used to solve common use cases for authentication and authorization that you will encounter in creating an application. We don't have space to cover every protocol, corner case, or every nuance of the protocols. We also can't cover every detail in the specifications for the protocols. Our intent is to give you an overview that will help you get started and provide sufficient background to help you more fully understand more in-depth materials.

We are extremely grateful to numerous colleagues who've generously contributed to this book through reviewing original drafts and providing corrections and feedback on what we missed, what might be misunderstood, and what is most valuable for people to know. This project would not have been possible without their assistance and expertise, as noted in the acknowledgments. That said, any errors are completely our own. Any errata we discover after the book is published will be noted in the Apress GitHub repo for the book, accessible via `https://github.com/Apress/Solving-Identity-Management-in-Modern-Applications`.

We hope this book and the sample code are useful to you and wish you luck and security for your application projects!

CHAPTER 1

The Hydra of Modern Identity

Wisdom is not a product of schooling but of the lifelong attempt to acquire it.

—Albert Einstein, theoretical physicist, from a letter dated March 24, 1954

Throughout our experiences helping customers implement identity management solutions for their applications, we have seen two common paths that lead a company to focus on identity management-related issues. In many cases, this focus even leads to a dedicated identity management division or project within the company.

Some companies quickly recognize the challenge and build identity management as a component separate from their applications from the beginning. This is common in larger organizations starting new projects, often after they have experienced significant challenges. Another common pattern we have observed is an organization taking a reactive approach, usually triggered by having to resolve blockers in product sales, reduce unexpected downtimes, solve challenges associated with continuous investment of time and effort required for building and maintaining identity management services, or, in the worst case, having to face identity-related crises like data breaches that need immediate attention.

On both paths, we have often seen application developers start by cataloging a laundry list of to-dos involving what the user journeys such as sign-up, login, and account deletion should look like, what account management and analytical requirements are needed, if multi-factor authentication is required, and so-on. There is an expectation for all of this to work smoothly across multiple devices, several versions of browsers and operating systems, all while satisfying many constraints in terms of user experience and of course cost.

© Yvonne Wilson, Abhishek Hingnikar 2023
Y. Wilson and A. Hingnikar, *Solving Identity Management in Modern Applications*,
https://doi.org/10.1007/978-1-4842-8261-8_1

The result is usually an identity service built using in-house engineering and DevOps teams, often with commodity off-the-shelf or open source tools. As one or more applications connect to this service, it quickly becomes obvious that this identity service needs to be fault-tolerant and highly available, to avoid becoming a point of failure for the applications. It also needs to be secure and protect user data against many types of attacks.

Over the course of time, the teams maintaining the in-house identity service start to feel like they are fighting a Hydra – the mythical beast from Greek mythology with nine heads. When any one of her heads was cut off, two more grew back in its place. In the same way, solving one identity management challenge can give rise to more without a well-planned strategy.

In this book, we'd like to give you a high-level introduction to identity management and provide you with as much knowledge as we can to better equip you on your quest toward delivering successful identity management in your application and avoiding a Hydra.

Identity Challenges

While identity management may initially seem to require little more than a form with a username and password, many factors need to work together for it to work well in practice. It requires careful planning, design, and development to implement identity management for an application while balancing the myriad expectations stemming from business requirements and security, not to mention the need to provide a great user experience.

Unfortunately, identity management isn't a one-size-fits-all proposition. There isn't a master solution we can provide that fits every use case. However, we believe that our combined experience may help you navigate through the landscape better, equipped with an overview of the challenges that you'll face ahead.

As an example of these challenges, here are a few of the most common decisions to consider when developing your applications.

Who Are Your Users? And Will They Authenticate?

A consumer using an app on their phone to book a restaurant will probably want the ability to log in quickly, perhaps using an existing identity like Google or Apple, often referred to as social logins. Users may even expect to use more than one way to authenticate and still be recognized as the same person. We have seen this happen often as a result of a user forgetting the original "account" they signed in with, resulting in confusion and a drop-off in application usage because users can't remember how to log in.

Employee users of an application at their workplace want easy access via a single work account. This is usually referred to as single sign-on, enterprise federation or enterprise login. For an increasing number of organizations, this is a mandatory requirement when purchasing a workforce application.

You may also encounter requirements to offer passwordless authentication or username-password authentication for first-party accounts that are stored in your system.

Level of Authentication Strength

Which authentication mechanisms will adequately protect your application? It depends. An application with sensitive content like a banking application is a clear scenario where you'd want to ensure you know who the user is, in the most secure way possible. For other, less sensitive, applications, you may need to determine how to provide adequate security while still being convenient for users.

There are many options to consider for authentication. Today, the most common means of implementing authentication are based on something the user knows, such as a password. While passwords provide basic security, they are prone to being stolen. For more secure applications, there are additional means to verify a user's identity, which may be used on their own or with a password. These strategies typically rely on something the user possesses like a one-time password generated on a device or a hardware security token with a cryptographic key. Alternatively, other approaches rely on who you are, leveraging biometric scans or user behavior, such as typing, to authenticate a user. You need solutions that are easy for users to adopt and use because cumbersome solutions may result in users circumventing the solution or simply abandoning the application entirely.

Unfortunately, your problems don't end once the user is authenticated. After authentication, a user's password may be compromised or their authentication device stolen. Applications need to accommodate for additional threat vectors, such as authentication tokens being lost or stolen, credentials being breached, and scripts that mimic user activity in order to brute-force their access into user accounts.

Simplifying Access for Users

How do you provide simple but secure access for your users? Your users will likely want single sign-on so they can log in once[i] and access their account at multiple applications easily, such as your application and your application's support center. Single sign-on provides convenience to users, but it is also considered great security hygiene as it offers a single place to control authentication policy, reduces the number of passwords that users have to remember, and allows you to focus efforts on simplifying identity.

It is important to keep in mind that authentication requirements will often change depending on the platform or device the user is using to access your product. Authentication on the Web is very different from apps running on a smartphone or a Smart TV. It can be even more different if you want to support devices like Alexa. Identity management can easily become a limiting factor if your solution does not accommodate the possibility of easily supporting diverse future platforms and devices for users.

In addition to authenticating users, your application will also need to enforce access policies. For some applications, such as a platform to stream movies, access policy may be simple, based solely on whether a subscription fee has been paid. For other applications, such as enterprise systems for manufacturing and inventory control or sales management, access policies can become complex and might need to take into account a user's profile attributes, the time of day, the method of authentication used, and the specific data involved.

Migrating Users from Legacy Applications

Will you need to migrate any existing user accounts from elsewhere? A part of simplifying access is the integration challenge if you need to migrate users from legacy in-house applications that have highly specialized user stores and third-party apps like support centers and community forums that also have their own user stores. Mature legacy application projects may offer a means to connect single sign-on, but in other cases, it is largely left as an open problem to solve for the application builder, with minimal support for industry identity standards like SAML, OAuth, or OpenID Connect.

The migration of existing users from legacy user stores, however, is not covered by those standards and is often a very time-consuming and expensive process to solve. This involves migrating existing users along with their credentials, merging duplicate users in a secure manner, ensuring uptime for the existing applications during the migration, and migrating some apps while ensuring other systems can stay in place. This is a challenging part of many identity projects and can severely impact the likelihood of success due to scope creep!

Regulatory Requirements

How will you satisfy regulatory and compliance requirements? Privacy is a hot topic among developers, companies, and legislators. Modern users are concerned about identity data breaches, identity theft, and about being continuously tracked, in many cases without their consent, by third-party marketing analytical websites. These issues raise several ethical and technological challenges.

Many governments see the privacy of their constituents as a fundamental right and have been working on regulations for the handling and protection of sensitive identity data. These are topics of increasing interest among global legislators. With legislation like the GDPR (General Data Protection Regulation) in the European Union, California's CCPA (California Consumer Privacy Act), and similar legislation being drafted, debated, and enacted in many jurisdictions, applications that collect or process user data must comply with privacy requirements, as noncompliance may incur severe penalties in the event of a breach.

User Experience Constraints

How do you create a good onboarding experience for your users? Bad identity decisions can negatively impact a user's perception of an application. Imagine you just installed a brand-new application to look at pictures and the sign-up process asks for a scan of your passport and a selfie video. This would doubtless seem a bit suspicious because it's hard to imagine why a picture browsing application needs your passport information. A bad sign-up and login experience can hurt the usability and adoption of your application.

On the other hand, for a financial application, the need to provide a passport for identity validation would seem more reasonable. Recording a video to verify your identity is, in fact, part of an innovative onboarding experience for a challenger bank application like Monzo.[ii]

The challenges outlined here are just a sample of what you may face in designing identity management for your application. Additional challenges involve when and how to collect user profile information, how to manage user sessions, and even what to do when a user logs out. The design of identity management for your application needs to answer all these questions and more while considering the sensitivity of your application and satisfying all the relevant business and legal requirements. You'll need to weigh different approaches and design for a user experience appropriate for your application's delivery platforms.

Objective

Our objective in writing this book is to provide you with an introduction to the topic of identity management, based on our experience building and deploying applications. The focus is particularly on aspects of identity management for software applications, such as creating accounts, authentication, API authorization, single sign-on, account management, logging users out, and deprovisioning accounts. To set realistic expectations, identity management is a huge topic. One book cannot make you an expert or cover everything there is to know. The specifications for the identity protocols we'll discuss total over 800 pages, and they represent only a portion of the information that you need to know. We cannot hope to cover every aspect of these protocols or every identity management use case. What we can reasonably do is provide an introductory overview that helps you understand common aspects of identity management needed by a typical application project, how three standard identity protocols solve basic use cases for you, and how a sample program solves some real-world scenarios.

We will cover three popular identity protocols, namely, OAuth 2, OIDC, and SAML 2 – specifically, what problem each is designed to solve, how they work, how to implement authentication and authorization requests for simple cases, and how to troubleshoot issues. We can't cover every parameter or use case, but you should get a basic understanding of what each protocol does and how it works. We hope the text and sample program that accompanies this book give you a helpful overview of identity management for your application development projects. We also hope you are inspired to explore this topic further to learn about more advanced use cases and solutions.

Appropriately designed, an identity management solution can simplify your overall architecture. It can allow your application to delegate some identity-related responsibilities to other components, and it can provide a single view of the user and unify access control to simplify access issues, provide critical auditing capabilities, and more.

We've organized the content around the events in the life of an identity. We start out with a discussion of account provisioning and several options for getting users set up so they can use your application. Then we dive into API authorization and authentication and provide an overview of three popular protocols in use today, namely, OAuth 2, OpenID Connect (OIDC), and Security Assertion Markup Language (SAML) 2. These chapters cover authenticating users and handling authorization for applications and APIs. After covering the basic mechanics of the protocols, we have a chapter that explains the sample program that accompanies this book and how it uses these protocols.

The subsequent chapters cover additional scenarios, with introductory information about single sign-on, stronger forms of authentication, account management, logout, and deprovisioning. In case your application doesn't work perfectly the first time, we've included a chapter with guidance on troubleshooting. We've also shared information on problematic scenarios that may arise and some more unusual use cases we've come across. We close with a quick overview of compliance as well as some mistakes that have led to some very unfortunate breaches.

We recommend reading the chapters in order, at least through Chapter 15, as many of these chapters build on previous chapters. For the rebels in the crowd, we especially recommend at least reading Chapters 4 through 10 in order as they have the most dependencies on earlier content. The chapters after Chapter 15 can mostly be read in any order. Chapter 16 on troubleshooting will be most relevant when you need to debug an issue. Chapter 18 on less common requirements might be valuable to read early on in a project as it may help you identify items to include in your project plan. Chapters 17 and 19 cover different types of issues and will help you plan for, or avoid, many mistakes.

In the chapters on OAuth 2 and OIDC, we've provided samples of HTTP requests to be made by an application. We realize you may use a library or SDK to facilitate such calls, and in fact we heartily encourage this. If so, the call syntax will differ for your chosen implementation. However, while every library or SDK will be different, the underlying calls should be in alignment with the standard specifications. When it comes time to troubleshoot your implementation, you'll likely use a browser tool or debugger to analyze the calls made, and at that point, an understanding of the underlying HTTP requests such as we've shown in the book will be useful. Even if you are merely configuring a purchased application, an understanding of the basic requests and responses will be of benefit for troubleshooting.

One note about naming is in order. The protocols we cover have each used different terminology. This makes it difficult to use consistent terms for certain components. We debated between several approaches and finally decided that in a chapter discussing a specific protocol, we would use the terms used by that protocol, and in other chapters, we would use more generic terms. For example, in the OAuth 2 chapter, we refer to an authorization server; in the OIDC chapter, the OpenID Provider; and in the SAML 2 chapter, the identity provider. In the other, more general chapters, we use the term identity provider for a service that authenticates a user for an application. One exception is in our term for a client application. There are many names for a client application across these protocols – client, relying party, service provider, client application. The terms client and relying party mean different things in some specifications. To reduce confusion for beginners, we've chosen to use the term "application" throughout to refer to an application making authentication or API authorization requests via OAuth 2, OIDC, or SAML 2. This is not ideal as it ignores the fact that in more involved use cases, OIDC and SAML 2 clients may not be applications but rather can also be providers to other clients. Since our focus is on introductory, basic use cases, we decided to make this trade-off for the sake of simplicity and consistency across chapters. We occasionally use the term relying party where the entity referenced is a relying party which could in turn be an identity provider serving other clients rather than a simple application. We also refer to end users as simply users, as we don't need to differentiate between types of users.

A note on versions is also in order. Since the original publication of this book, there has been additional work on OAuth, resulting in the OAuth 2.1 framework specification document. This edition of the book is aligned with the recommendations made in the current draft of OAuth 2.1, and the versions of OIDC and SAML 2.0 published at the time of writing. For the sake of simplicity, we will refer to these identity protocols as OAuth 2, OIDC, and SAML 2, unless we are referencing a particular version of a specification document or a document title.

Sample Application

To complement the text, we've provided a sample application that uses the OIDC and OAuth 2 protocols. Chapter 10 explains the sample application and how it was designed to use the identity protocols as part of an identity management solution. We need to give the usual caveat here. As sample code, the code samples in the book and sample application omit various functions for the sake of simplicity. They are not production-ready code and should not be used as a basis for production applications.

Design Questions

To get started on your own identity solution, we suggest thinking about the following questions in preparation for reading through the following chapters:

- Who are your users: employees, consumers, or a business?

- How will users log in? Is there an existing account available to them that they would like to reuse?

- Can your application be used anonymously or is authentication needed?

- What kind of delivery – Web or native – does your application intend to provide?

- Will your application need to call any APIs? If so, who owns the data that your application will retrieve?

- How will your application interact with APIs, both public APIs and your trusted subsystems?

- How sensitive is the data that your application handles?

- What access control requirements are needed?

- How long should a user stay logged in?

- Is there more than one application in your system? If so, will users benefit from single sign-on? (Don't forget a support forum!)

- What should happen when users log out?

- Are there any compliance requirements associated with this data?

Summary

Modern users expect a frictionless, well-designed experience when using an application. Identity management should help them access an application quickly, not get in their way. In order to achieve that, developers face a lot of questions and need to sort through a wide range of options available to them when developing identity management solutions for modern applications. The next chapter will help you understand the components of an identity management solution by covering the events in the life of an identity.

Key Points

- Identity management poses many challenges to developers of modern applications.

- Identity management solutions must be appropriate for the sensitivity, desired user experience, and delivery platforms of an application.

- Identity management is a huge topic, more than can be covered completely in one book.

- We'll provide an overview of identity management and typical requirements for identity management for your application.

- We'll cover three protocols – what they are used for, how they work, and how to make a basic authentication or authorization request.

- We'll provide a sample program that illustrates some of the topics discussed.

Notes

i.   https://auth0.com/blog/what-your-customers-really-want-from-your-login-box/

ii. https://monzo.com/

CHAPTER 2

The Life of an Identity

That it will never come again is what makes life so sweet.

—Emily Dickinson in "That it will never come again" (1741)

To clarify the terms used in subsequent chapters, we need to describe what an identity is and how it is used, as well as the most common events in the life of an identity.

Terminology

The concepts of an identity, an identifier, and an account are closely related but subtly different. We use the term "identifier" to refer to a single attribute whose purpose is to uniquely identify a person or entity, within a specific context. Passport numbers, driver's license numbers, and employee numbers are all examples of identifiers used for people. Nonhuman entities, such as agents, bots, or devices, may be identified by an alphanumeric string of characters assigned at their time of creation or registration within a context where they will act. The context, for our purposes, is an application, online service, or a set of the same. Identifiers allow us to refer to a specific person or nonhuman entity within such a context and are essential to identity management.

The term "identity" is defined as a collection of attributes associated with a specific person or entity in a particular context. An identity includes one or more identifiers and may contain other attributes associated with a person or entity. Human identities may include attributes such as name, age, address, phone number, eye color, and job title. Nonhuman identities may include attributes such as an owner, IP address, and perhaps a model or version number. The attributes which make up an identity may be used for authentication and authorization as well as conveying information about the identity to applications.

Y. Wilson and A. Hingnikar, *Solving Identity Management in Modern Applications*,
https://doi.org/10.1007/978-1-4842-8261-8_2

A given person may have more than one identity. Just as a person might take on different personas in different social contexts, such as a parent, child, engineer, or coach, a person can have multiple online identities as well. One might have a work identity used to perform tasks for an employer. The identity attributes might include an identifier issued by the employer, a department name, building location, and manager. One might also have a variety of personal identities used for different purposes, including managing a youth sports team or running a side business. These real-world examples demonstrate the contextual aspect of our definition. An online identity consists of at least one identifier and a set of attributes for a user or entity in a particular context, such as an application or suite of applications.

An identity is associated with an account in each such context. We define an account as a local construct within a given application or application suite that is used to perform actions within that context. Identity attributes may be contained within an application's account object, or they may be stored separately and referenced from the account object.

An account is uniquely identified by an identifier. Usernames, email addresses, and mobile phone numbers have often been used as identifiers for online accounts. As we will see in Chapter 4, the selection of an appropriate account identifier requires careful thought because identifiers such as email addresses and mobile phone numbers can change over time or may be shared by multiple people in some contexts. An account may have its own, internal identifier in addition to that of the identity associated with it. Having an account identifier separate from the identity associated with the account provides a useful degree of separation. The internal account identifier can be used in application records, which makes it easier for users to change the username or other identifiers associated with their account without impacting all the application records.

An account typically has several attributes associated with the owner of the account. An account for a human being might have attributes for the person's name, home address, phone number, email address, age, and preferences, as relevant to the application. An account for a bot might have attributes such as the owner of the bot, the manufacturer, bot model, and version. This set of attributes will vary widely based on application needs and is often referred to as the user profile for an account. In addition, an account will typically have some attributes used for the purposes of authentication and authorization. These may include credentials, information to support multi-factor authentication, and attributes used in access control decisions.

We will use the term "identity" when specifically referring to online identities as the set of attributes about a person or entity. We will use the term account when referring to an account as a construct within an application or service that has an identity associated with it. It should be noted that an account can have more than one identity associated with it through account linking which will be explained further in Chapter 18. In addition, a user may establish many accounts using the same identity attributes. To summarize, a person logs in to use an account which has various identity attributes associated with it and which enables them to perform actions within a system.

Nonhuman actors can certainly have identities as well. Software components serving as agents or bots and smart devices can have identities and may interact with other software or devices in ways that require authentication and authorization just like human actors. In order to keep this book to a manageable size, however, we will primarily discuss human actors and their online identities.

As you might guess, an identity management (IdM) system is a set of services that support the creation, modification, and removal of identities and associated accounts, as well as the authentication and authorization required to access resources. Identity management systems are used to protect online resources from unauthorized access and comprise an important part of a comprehensive security model.

Events in the Life of an Identity

With basic definitions out of the way, we can move on to describe the primary events in the life of an identity, illustrated in Figure 2-1. We've shown this as a linear diagram for the sake of simplicity and to provide an organizing sequence for subsequent chapters. In real life, the events shown can repeat, branch, loop back, and in general are more complex than a single linear thread. We'll outline the events in this chapter in the order shown, to provide a high-level overview, and then go into each in more depth in subsequent chapters.

Figure 2-1. *Events in the Life of an Identity*

Provisioning

The first step in the life of an identity is its creation. The act of creating an account and associated identity information is often referred to as provisioning. Provisioning might be done by having users register, importing identity information from a legacy system or leveraging an external identity service. Regardless of the mechanism used, the objective of the provisioning phase is to establish an account with associated identity data. This involves obtaining or assigning a unique identifier for the identity, optionally a unique identifier for the account distinct from that of the identity, creating an account, and associating identity profile attributes with the account.

For example, a user named Alice wishes to use some online banking services. Alice might establish an online account at a bank by filling out an account registration form. Alice would provide identity information including a username, a password, her name, home address, phone number, email address, and some form of tax ID. This data would be used to provision an online account at the bank associated with Alice's personal identity.

Alice could create multiple online accounts at the bank for different identities. In addition to the personal account, Alice might establish a second identity as a small business owner with a second online account using her business identity and tax ID. The provisioning phase establishes an online identity and account, which are then used to access online services.

As part of the provisioning process, the identity information associated with an account may optionally be subject to a verification process. Identity proofing is the process of collecting, authenticating, and validating identity information to ensure an account holder is who they claim to be and the owner of the identity is a person who can be held liable for actions taken using an account issued to them. In-person identity proofing usually involves showing one or more government-issued identification documents. Online identity proofing solutions exist that ask a user to record a selfie video in real time for a "liveness" check and then verify a facial match with government-issued identification documents shown in the video.

Authorization

When an account is created, it is often necessary to specify what the account can do, in the form of privileges. We use the term authorization for the granting of privileges that govern what an account is allowed to do. The authorization may be based on a variety of factors, including identity attributes such as a team membership at work or the purchase of an application subscription level by the user.

When Alice creates her online account, the bank authorizes her account to access the application to view checking accounts. If she does not have a brokerage account at the bank, her account would not be authorized to access the bank's stock trading application. Needless to say, her account would also not be authorized to view account information for the bank's other customers! Alice's authorization indicates the privileges her account has been granted in the form of which applications she can access and what types of transactions she can perform. This type of authorization for an account is typically done at the time an account is created and may be updated over time.

Another form of authorization may happen later in a user's interaction with an application or service. One example is a more complex use case that involves more than one application domain. If a user invokes a feature in one application which requires data owned by the user in a third-party application in another domain, the user may be asked by that third-party application to authorize the first application to programmatically access the user's data in the third-party domain. In this case, the authorization grant is for an application to act on the user's behalf. This has become a common scenario in modern applications and will be discussed further in Chapter 5.

Authentication

To access online content that is not publicly available, a user needs to authenticate. A user provides an identifier to signify the account they wish to use and enters login credentials for the account. These are validated against credentials previously registered during the account provisioning phase. The credentials may involve something the user knows, something the user has, and/or something the user is. A password is something the user *knows*. A numeric code generated from a previously registered device, such as a mobile phone or hardware security key, involves something the user *has*. Biometric information such as a fingerprint or facial scan is something the user *is*. Authentication with one or more credentials which are validated against previously registered information demonstrates, to some degree of confidence, a user's right to use an account to access protected resources.

After Alice establishes her online identity and account at the bank, she can access the bank's online services. To access protected resources, such as her checking account balance, she will need to authenticate by entering the username and password established during the registration step. The username indicates the account she wishes to use, and knowledge of the password demonstrates her right to use the account. For sensitive applications and transactions, it is best to use additional, stronger forms of authentication, as described later in this chapter.

Access Policy Enforcement

Once a user has been authenticated and associated with an account, it is necessary to enforce access policy to ensure any actions taken by the user are allowed by the privileges they have been granted. We use the term access policy enforcement for the enforcement of access policy specified by authorization. In other words, authorization specifies what a user or entity is allowed to do in a particular context such as within a banking application, and access policy enforcement checks that a user's requested actions are allowed by the privileges they've been authorized to use and any other relevant policy.

When Alice logs in to the bank's online retail banking application and makes a request, the application will check she has the authorization to make the request. If she attempts to access the stock trading services, she would be denied as she is not authorized to access those services. In this case, the application might display a message indicating she is not allowed to view that service, perhaps with information on how to sign up for it.

Access policy enforcement may need to implement a variety of policies. For example, if Alice opens a savings account, she would typically be authorized to withdraw funds from the account. However, the authorization to withdraw money would typically not allow her to withdraw more money than exists in her account. Then again, if she has a checking account with overdraft protection, she might be able to write checks for more money than is in her account, up to a certain limit. Access policy enforcement in this case includes the privileges associated with her account as well as other bank policies around overdrafts.

Sessions

Once a user has been authenticated and authorized, they will perform various actions within an application. Some applications, typically traditional web applications and sensitive applications, only allow a user to remain active for a limited period of time before requiring the user to authenticate again. They do this by managing a session for the user. A session tracks information such as whether the user has been authenticated and, if so, typically also the authentication mechanism and/or strength level of the authentication mechanism used, when authentication occurred, and the IP address, in addition to a user identifier. This enables an application to decide when the user should be prompted to reauthenticate.

The length of time a user is allowed to remain active before reauthentication is known as a session limit or session timeout. The session timeout settings will typically vary by the sensitivity of the data in the application. Session limits help protect against users who walk away from their screen without logging off and identity information that may have changed since the session was created. A session limit that forces a user to periodically reauthenticate provides a check that it is still the legitimate user at the keyboard. It can also trigger a renewal of the user's identity information and account status.

Alice's retail banking application that provides access to her bank account may allow only a relatively short session, measured in minutes. Another, less sensitive service offered by the bank, such as an investment newsletter, may allow a longer session, measured in hours or days. Each time Alice makes a request of either application, it is necessary for the application to check if she has authenticated recently enough for the requested transaction. If so, she can continue without authenticating again. If too much time has elapsed since she last authenticated, she would have to authenticate again.

The previous example is a scenario where interactive reauthentication with the user is required. There are additional scenarios where security tokens obtained by an application during a user's session have expired. These tokens usually have a short expiration time to reduce the risk impact if they are compromised. When they expire, an application can request new tokens from the entity that issued the original tokens, and there are scenarios where this can be done without any interaction with the user. This is sometimes called silent reauthentication and occurs when the entity issuing the security tokens has sufficient knowledge about the user's activity and the security context to warrant issuing new tokens without requiring the user to actively reauthenticate.

Single Sign-On (SSO)

After a user accesses one application, they may wish to do something else involving another application. Single sign-on (SSO) is the ability to log in once and then access additional protected resources or applications with the same authentication requirements, without having to reenter credentials.

When Alice accesses her bank's website, single sign-on would provide convenient access to multiple banking services. If Alice signed up for the investment newsletter service at her bank, she could log in to access first the retail banking application to view her account balance and then access the investment newsletter without having to sign in again.

Single sign-on is possible when a set of applications has delegated authentication to the same entity. An authenticated session in that entity can be used to access multiple resources via single sign-on and is often called an SSO session. The use of single sign-on can result in multiple layers of sessions for a user because there may be a session for a user maintained in each application as well as in an entity to which the applications delegate authentication. In this case, the design of session handling is important for security and a good user experience.

Stronger Authentication

Step-up authentication and multi-factor authentication (MFA) both involve authenticating a user with stronger forms of authentication. Some forms of authentication, such as username-password authentication, are considered relatively weak because they involve a single factor, the password, which can be captured and easily used by others. Stronger forms of authentication involve other factors, such as something the user *has* and/or something the user *is*. Authentication that requires multiple factors at the same time is known as multi-factor authentication. Multi-factor authentication typically involves a password as well as possession of a device such as a laptop or mobile phone or possibly a biometric factor such as a fingerprint, facial scan, or voiceprint.

Step-up authentication is the act of elevating an existing authentication session to a higher level of assurance by authenticating with a stronger form of authentication. For example, a user might initially log in with a username and password to establish an authentication session. Later, when accessing a more sensitive feature or application with higher authentication requirements, the user would be prompted for additional credentials, such as a one-time password generated on their mobile phone or through the use of a hardware security key. Step-up authentication may be required when a user accesses a more sensitive application or when they attempt to perform more sensitive transactions, like withdrawing unusually large amounts of money.

Alice might initially log in with a username and password and be able to view investment newsletters on the bank's website. If she later attempts to access her bank account to transfer a large amount of money out of her account, she might have to step up her session and enter a stronger authentication factor, such as a special one-time use code generated by an application on her phone. This elevates her session to a higher level of authentication assurance which provides a higher degree of confidence that the user requesting access or performing a transaction is the legitimate account owner.

Logout

When a user is done with an application, they should terminate their session by logging out. At a minimum, the act of logging out should terminate the user's application session. If they return to the application, they would have to authenticate again before being granted access. In situations where single sign-on is used, there may be multiple sessions to terminate, and it is a design decision as to which sessions should be terminated when the user logs out of one application.

The act of logging out is slightly different than a session timing out. In the former case, the user explicitly requests that their session be terminated. When a session times out, an application may elect to keep the session in a suspended state and reconstitute the session if the user authenticates again.

In a scenario where Alice has logged in to her bank's website and viewed her bank balance as well as a recent investment newsletter, she would have a session in the retail banking application, in the investment newsletter application, and in the bank's SSO service. If she is idle for a few minutes to take a phone call, her session in the retail banking application may time out. When she finishes her phone call, she would have to reauthenticate to continue. When she finishes viewing her account, she would click a "Logout" link to terminate all of her open sessions.

Account Management and Recovery

During the course of an identity's lifetime, it may be necessary to change various attributes of the user profile for the identity. For example, a user may need to update their email address or phone number. A user may need to update their name in some circumstances or to periodically change their password or mobile device used in the authentication process. In a company, a user's profile might be updated to reflect a new position, office location, or privileges such as roles. In addition, many privacy laws around the world require that users have the ability to view, correct, transfer, and request the deletion of certain information held about them. Account management consists of features or processes which enable users and administrators to view and update user profile attributes associated with an account and to remove accounts, when appropriate.

In addition to user-initiated changes, administrators may need to modify or remove a user's account over time. Administrators may change the privileges associated with a user's account, especially in an enterprise when an employee moves from one team to another or when responsibility for a particular function is moved from one team to another in a corporate reorganization. Corporate compliance initiatives and governance audits that periodically review all user accounts and the access they've been granted may also trigger the removal of access or accounts that are no longer appropriate.

A user may forget their password or lose a device that is required for an authentication process. If this happens, a user needs to establish new credentials. This requires an alternate means of establishing the user's ownership of the account before allowing them to set new credentials. Account recovery is a mechanism to validate a user is the legitimate owner of an account through some secondary means before allowing the user to establish new credentials.

If Alice goes on a trip and forgets her password after being gone for a while, she would need a means of resetting her password. She may have to enter a code using an alternate authentication mechanism she set up previously, or she may be able to trigger an account recovery link sent to her email that will enable her to reset her credentials. Similarly, if Alice decides to move, she would need the ability to update her profile at the bank to reflect her new address. Throughout the lifetime of an identity, various changes may occur, requiring the ability to view and update the identity profile attributes as well as reset account credentials.

Deprovisioning

There may come a time when it is necessary to close an account. In this case, the user's account and associated identity information must be deprovisioned so that it can no longer be used. Deprovisioning may take the form of completely deleting the account and associated identity information or simply disabling the account, to preserve information for audit purposes.

If Alice decides at some point to terminate her relationship with the bank, she would request that her accounts be closed. The bank would close out her checking and savings accounts and terminate her online account so that she could no longer log in. The bank would, however, need to keep sufficient information to meet tax reporting and audit obligations. Deprovisioning can be challenging to design as it must balance numerous requirements including audit needs and privacy regulations.

Summary

This chapter has introduced the concept of an account and an associated identity and the most typical events that occur during their existence, from provisioning and authorization to authentication and access policy enforcement, all the way to deprovisioning. In the next chapters, we'll dive into more detail for each event, starting with a summarized history of approaches to identity management.

Key Points

- Provisioning creates an account and associated identity.

- Provisioning may include an identity proofing process to validate the owner of an account is who they say they are.

- Authentication validates a user is entitled to use an account.

- Authorization specifies the privileges granted for an account.

- Access policy enforcement checks that requests are within the privileges granted by authorization.

- A session and session limit are used to govern how long a user can remain active without reauthenticating.

- Single sign-on allows a user to log in once and then access additional protected resources without reentering credentials.

- Multi-factor authentication requires authentication by multiple forms of authentication, such as something the user knows (a password), something the user has (such as a device), and/or something the user is (such as a fingerprint or facial scan).

- Step-up authentication is the elevation of an existing authentication session to a higher authentication assurance level when a user authenticates with a stronger form of authentication.

- Logout terminates an authenticated session, requiring reauthentication to access a protected resource again.

- Account management features allow a user or administrator to update account and identity profile attributes.

- Account recovery is required when a user loses the ability to authenticate using previously established credentials.

- Deprovisioning is the removal or disabling of an account and associated identity information.

CHAPTER 3

Evolution of Identity

Progress is not an illusion; it happens, but it is slow and invariably disappointing.

—George Orwell, from *Inside the Whale and Other Essays* (1940)

Over the years, there has been an ongoing evolution in how identity information is stored and used to enable users to access applications and the functionality they provide. You'll see in this chapter that each bit of progress has solved some problems but given rise to new ones, as technology and security challenges evolved. We'll describe some past approaches that have been used to manage identity information and provide authentication and authorization. We've selected specific technologies to highlight specific advantages and disadvantages of each approach that may help you evaluate solutions for your project. We'll also discuss why you should use an industry standard protocol instead of inventing your own solution. Subsequent chapters will then cover specific protocols in more depth.

Identity Management Approaches

It's valuable to understand the advantages and drawbacks of approaches which have been used in the past for managing identity data, authentication, authorization, and access control. Many of these approaches are still in use today. This will not be an exhaustive list of every approach or technology, but rather a curated list to illustrate the practical, real-world benefits and drawbacks of selected approaches. As you read about each one, pay attention to the problems each solution was designed to solve as well as the benefits and shortcomings of each. Knowing the advantages and disadvantages of

© Yvonne Wilson, Abhishek Hingnikar 2023
Y. Wilson and A. Hingnikar, *Solving Identity Management in Modern Applications*,
https://doi.org/10.1007/978-1-4842-8261-8_3

each will help you evaluate alternatives for your projects and more effectively advocate for use of newer solutions. We'll start by going back in time to when applications each implemented their own authentication and user repository.

Per-Application Identity Silo

In the Stone Age, relatively speaking, of computer applications, each application often implemented its own identity repository, authentication, authorization, and access control. A large enterprise company typically had core business applications, such as finance and inventory control systems, and perhaps a few productivity applications. Each application often had its own dedicated database or other storage in which user identities, credentials, and user profile data were stored, and each application prompted the user to log in and then validated the user's credentials against its own repository of user information. This meant an employee might have a different username and password to remember for each application. It also meant that if some element of a user's profile changed, the profile change had to be made in multiple applications. Of course, this did not happen reliably if a company had many applications, so user profile data invariably became out of sync across systems. User exasperation with data integrity issues and having to remember numerous passwords was bad enough when there were just a few applications. As the number of applications in an enterprise grew, however, having every application implement its own siloed identity repository and authentication solution quickly became untenable for businesses.

This siloed approach is still used today in many consumer-facing scenarios where a user signs up by providing an application-specific username and password. If a user reuses the same password across multiple sites, a compromise at any one site could put the user's data at other sites at risk. If a user specifies a different password for every application, they have to remember or securely store the passwords or rely on the security of an account recovery process provided by the application. Either way, consumer users face some of the same inconvenience with this approach experienced earlier by corporate users.

Centralized User Repository

With time, more and more software was written for a wide swathe of business functions. This drove a need for a better approach to identity management. Many companies implemented directory services to house and centralize user identity information. Directory services are optimized for information that is frequently read but infrequently modified, which is often the case for user identity data. Applications were able to use a directory service to store user data and credentials. It was also possible for an application to prompt a user to log in and validate the entered credentials using information in a directory service. Large, on-site commercial business applications targeted to enterprise environments[1] often included support for this approach. This centralized approach offered a significant improvement over the siloed, per-application approach.

The centralization of identity administration and access with a directory service provided many advantages. Directory replication capabilities enabled applications hosted around the world to leverage the same identity information, eliminating data inconsistency issues. The same username and password could be used across applications. A centralized directory service also provided a single point of control at which to implement password policy or quickly terminate an identity if necessary. As a result, directory services became widely adopted, at least in larger companies.

For all their advantages, however, directory services also had some disadvantages. A directory service by itself did not maintain any sort of session for a user. The centralization of identity information in a directory service usually meant a user had only one username and password to remember, but the user still had to enter the credentials into each application's login screen because each application needed to collect user credentials and validate them using the directory service (in the absence of additional technology such as single sign-on servers and proprietary OS features). In addition to being an inconvenience, this exposed the user's password to the applications. A compromise at one application might put other applications at risk. This was bad enough when all applications involved were inside a trusted corporate network. As companies began using cloud applications, exposing directory passwords to cloud applications owned by others would have posed an unacceptable risk. Once again, a better solution was needed!

---

[1] Such as Oracle and SAP application suites.

Early SSO Servers

Several types of what became known as identity and access management (IAM) or single sign-on (SSO) servers provided further improvement. Early SSO servers leveraged the identity information in a directory service, but provided a layer on top of the directory service that maintained a session to remember users that had already authenticated. The way they worked varied, but in a typical approach, an application could redirect a user's browser to an SSO server to have the user authenticated there, and the application would receive the authentication results in a secure, predetermined fashion. If a user accessed a second application, shortly after they authenticated for the first application, the second application redirected the user's browser to the SSO server,[2] and the SSO server would detect the user's existing session and redirect them back to the application with a success status without prompting the user for credentials again.

The introduction of single sign-on servers offered many advantages over directory services. Users benefited from the ability to access multiple applications with a single authentication. Security teams appreciated that the user's static directory password was only exposed to the SSO server, instead of to each application the user accessed. IT departments were happy because it gave them a single place to implement authentication policy and stronger authentication mechanisms.

Unfortunately, there were some disadvantages with early SSO servers in practice. The interaction between applications and SSO servers was somewhat proprietary, and SSO products were often time-consuming to implement. This meant their adoption was more evident in larger companies with resources to integrate applications with SSO servers. A more significant limitation was that single sign-on relied on cookies which, due to browser restrictions on cookie access, meant the solutions worked within one Internet domain such as `www.mycompany.com`. As many companies were becoming interested in external Software-as-a-Service (SaaS) applications, this was a limiting restriction.

---

[2] As an optimization, an agent was sometimes installed in front of the application to check session state with the SSO server and only redirect the user to the SSO server if the session state could not be confirmed.

Federated Identity and SAML 2

The explosion of new SaaS applications created challenges for managing identities. In the blink of an eye, business teams everywhere could thumb their noses at backlogged IT departments and sign up for SaaS applications with a credit card. Unfortunately, there was often no good way to manage employee identities in SaaS applications. It was difficult for a company to track accounts its employees created in SaaS systems, and users once again had to remember a password for every application. The single sign-on they enjoyed across internal applications didn't extend to external SaaS applications in other domains.

Fortunately, a new industry standard, SAML 2 (Security Assertion Markup Language), had been published in 2005.[i] It provided a solution for web single sign-on across domains and federated identity. This happened to be perfect for enterprises with SaaS applications. Although the SAML 2 technical overview focused on a consumer-facing use case, SAML 2 provided an excellent solution for enterprises needing better control over employee identities in SaaS applications.

With SAML 2, SaaS applications could redirect corporate users back to a corporate authentication service, known as an identity provider (IdP), for authentication. Identity federation provided a way to link an identity used in an application with an identity at the identity provider. Companies could now have the advantages of single sign-on with both internal and SaaS applications. Users benefited by having a single username/password to remember. The enterprise had a centralized control point for both internal and external identities and could shut off access quickly at the corporate identity provider if needed. Password policy and multi-factor authentication could be implemented in a single place. In this way, SAML 2 solved many identity headaches for enterprises.

Despite being widely adopted, however, SAML 2 was no silver bullet. The protocol was designed to cover many scenarios, making it complex to configure and implement. While SAML 2 became widely adopted within enterprise environments, there was no viable business model for it to address consumer-facing scenarios. Users were unlikely to pay money for a consumer-facing identity service. As we'll see later, this was solved by making someone else entirely pay for the service! Another limitation was that SAML 2 only solved the problem of authentication. Applications were evolving to architectures based on APIs. As typically implemented, SAML 2 solved the problem of authenticating users but didn't help with API authorization.

WS-Fed

The Web Services Federation Language (WS-Fed) federation framework was created by an industry coalition as part of a larger set of protocols known as the WS-* specifications. The WS-Fed 1.2 specification was published as an OASIS standard in 2009[ii] and provided mechanisms whereby "authorized access to resources managed in one realm can be provided to security principals whose identities are managed in other realms."[iii] It was supported by Microsoft's ADFS server as well as many other commercial SSO products and provided similar functionality to SAML 2's web single sign-on and federation capability. It was taken up in many enterprise environments and, like SAML 2, is still in use today in many corporate settings.

OpenID

The original OpenID protocol[iv] is worth mentioning for its notion of user-centric identity. With SAML 2 only adopted in employee-facing scenarios, consumer users were still forced to register anew at each consumer-facing website. A new industry group formed to create a solution for what it termed "user-centric" identity, and this gave rise to a protocol called OpenID. In addition to organization-controlled identity providers commonly used with SAML 2 and WS-Fed, OpenID included the idea of user-controlled identity for the consumer use case. Consumer users could even set up their own identity provider and point applications to it for authentication. The original OpenID protocol didn't become widely used, but it did highlight the need for user-centric identity solutions and laid the groundwork for another protocol named OpenID Connect, which we'll cover shortly.

OAuth 2

With Web 2.0 and the rise of social media, many consumer-facing websites were created that allowed users to upload content such as pictures. This gave rise to use cases where an application needed to retrieve such content on the user's behalf. For example, a person who uploaded photos to a social media site might want to enable another website that printed photos (`www.photos.com`) to access their photos at the social media site. In the absence of a better solution, the user would have to share their social media credentials with the photo printing site. If the photo printing site were compromised, it would put the user's social media account at risk. The user also had no control over what the photo printing site could do once it had the user's password for the social media site. A solution was needed that would allow a user to authorize an application at one website to retrieve their content from another website's API, without the user having to expose their credentials to the first site.

The OAuth protocol provided a solution for this use case. The OAuth 2.0[v] version of the specification allows a user to authorize one application, known as a client (the photo printing site), to send a request to an API, known as a resource server (the social media site), on the user's behalf to retrieve data at the resource server owned by the user. To do this, the application interacts with an authorization server which authenticates a user as part of obtaining their consent for the application to access their resources. The application receives a token which enables it to call the resource server on the user's behalf. OAuth 2 solved an important API authorization use case. Given the lack of a consumer-facing authentication solution like SAML 2 and WS-Fed, and the fact that authorization servers might need to authenticate users as part of obtaining the user's authorization consent, it may have been tempting to some to want to use it for more than this.

By this time, there were several social media sites on the Internet, such as Google and LinkedIn, and they implemented OAuth 2 to enable consumer-facing applications to retrieve information from a user's Google or LinkedIn profile. The authentication step performed by an OAuth 2 authorization server as part of obtaining a user's consent might have seemed to some like it could provide a handy authentication solution. There had not been a viable business model earlier for general consumer-facing SAML 2 identity provider services. Neither the users, applications, nor anyone else were likely to fund such services.

The rise of social media, however, provided a new possibility for a solution. Social media providers already had to authenticate users for access to their site and when an OAuth 2 authorization request was received that required authenticated user consent. If they were to provide a general authentication service, it might attract more users to their platform, and a consumer-facing authentication service would effectively be paid for by the advertising that paid for the social media sites. There was one slight problem, however. OAuth 2 was not designed as a general authentication service and could not securely be used for this purpose, at least without proprietary additions to the pure OAuth 2 features. (Several social providers that support OAuth 2 have implemented such proprietary additions.) Another solution standard was needed.

OpenID Connect (OIDC)

OpenID Connect (OIDC) was designed to provide a key feature needed for an authentication service. Even if OAuth 2 authorization servers were capable of authenticating users, the framework did not provide a standard way to securely convey the identity of an authenticated user to an application. OIDC provided a solution for this need. OIDC was devised as a layer on top of the OAuth 2 protocol to provide information in a standard format to applications about the identity of an authenticated user.[vi] This provided a solution for applications for user authentication as well as API authorization. The implementation of OIDC by widely used social media/service providers like Google, PayPal, and Yahoo provided a solution for consumer-facing authentication services, but there was nothing in the protocol to limit it to consumer-facing scenarios.

OIDC offers benefits to users, application developers, and identity providers. Website developers can delegate the work of implementing authentication and password reset logic to an OIDC provider. Users benefit because they can leverage one account to log in to many sites without exposing their account credentials to those other sites. Users have fewer usernames and passwords to manage and enjoy single sign-on. Providers may benefit if OIDC support attracts more users to their platform. OIDC provides the web single sign-on benefits that were attractive in SAML 2 and, when combined with OAuth 2, provides a solution with authentication as well as the API authorization capabilities needed by modern applications.

OAuth 2.1

After the publication of the OAuth 2.0 specification in 2012, technology and applications continued to evolve. To address changes, several additional specifications and documents describing best practices were published. By 2020, application developers were faced with the prospect of finding and reading many lengthy OAuth 2–related documents, and then carefully reconciling the differences between them, to fully understand the current best practices for using OAuth 2 in different types of applications, such as browser-based applications, native mobile applications, and classic web applications.

At the time of writing, a new draft OAuth 2.1[vii] authorization framework specification document has been published to consolidate, reconcile, and merge several earlier OAuth 2–related specifications and best practice recommendation documents. The OAuth 2.1 specification document is meant to replace the OAuth 2.0 specification document. The new version includes updates for native applications and browser-based applications as well as several security-related updates. It also removes some elements included in the original OAuth 2.0 specification which are no longer recommended. This book is aligned with OAuth 2 as described in the draft OAuth 2.1 authorization framework specification. We will include a brief discussion of some features which were removed from OAuth 2.1, to help you understand how these features worked and why they are no longer appropriate. We will use the more general term "OAuth 2" except when referring to a specific version of the framework specification.

The previous sections provided a brief history of different solutions for managing identities and authenticating users. We'll close with a few words on the benefits of standard protocols.

Standard Protocols

The next several chapters will describe three commonly used industry standard identity protocols and how they work. But first, why use an industry standard protocol? First, as open standards, these protocols have been scrutinized for flaws by many people, so they are less likely to have vulnerabilities than something you'd invent yourself. Second, these protocols are widely used, providing interoperability between your application and service providers which support the protocols. Third, if you wish to access user profile data from services such as Google, you will have to use the standard protocols as implemented by these services. Similarly, if your application will be used by enterprises, the enterprise may expect your application to use one of these protocols. Fourth, the protocols designed for authentication support single sign-on which represents convenience for your users. Finally, using an existing protocol can save you time as many programming languages offer SDKs that support them. So, there you have five good reasons to use industry standard identity protocols!

If you are new to the identity space, it may at first seem a little daunting to learn these protocols and possibly tempting to invent a simpler authentication scheme of your own. We have two words for that: "Just Don't!" We hope this book will make it easier for you to understand how to use these protocols. We hate to discourage innovation, but innovation in the authentication space should be done with care. Your innovative energies would be better spent on the core value proposition of your application.

Summary

We've reviewed several approaches to identity management, authentication, and authorization. The advantages and disadvantages of each are helpful to keep in mind when evaluating the benefits of new designs. Before deciding upon the protocol(s) you need, however, it's helpful to consider where the information on your users will come from and reside. This is part of identity provisioning which we'll cover next.

Key Points

- Identity management, authentication, and authorization approaches have evolved over time.

- Early approaches often involved application-specific identities and credentials.

- Centralization of identity data with directory services enabled a single identity and credential, but this had to be entered by a user into each application (in the absence of other complementary technology).

- Single sign-on servers provided session management so users could log in once and access multiple applications, within the same domain, with one authentication.

- SAML 2 and WS-Fed provide single sign-on and federated identity across domains.

- OAuth 2 provides a solution for authorizing applications to call APIs.

- OIDC provides a layer on top of OAuth 2 for authenticating users and returning information to applications in a standard format about the authenticated user.

- OAuth 2.1, currently in draft form, consolidates several OAuth 2–related specifications and best practice documents released after the publication of the original OAuth 2.0 authorization framework specification.

Notes

i.   http://saml.xml.org/saml-specifications

ii. http://docs.oasis-open.org/wsfed/federation/v1.2/os/ws-federation-1.2-spec-os.html

iii. http://docs.oasis-open.org/wsfed/federation/v1.2/os/ws-federation-1.2-spec-os.html

iv. https://openid.net/specs/openid-authentication-1_1.html

v.   https://tools.ietf.org/html/rfc6749

vi. https://openid.net/specs/openid-connect-core-1_0.html

vii. https://oauth.net/2.1/

CHAPTER 4

Identity Provisioning

The more identities a man has, the more they express the person they conceal.

—John le Carré, from *Tinker, Tailor, Soldier, Spy* (1974)

The first step in the life of an identity is its creation. If Descartes had lived in the time of Internet identity, he might have quipped, "Ego signati sursum, ergo sum" (I signed up, therefore I am). Provisioning is the act of establishing identities and accounts for your application. As defined in Chapter 2, an identity includes at least one identifier and various additional user profile attributes. An online account is associated with an identity and can be used to access protected online resources. The objective of the provisioning phase is the creation or selection of a repository of user accounts and identity information that will be used in the authentication and authorization of users as they access protected resources.

Provisioning Options

For an application developer, the identity provisioning phase involves getting users and creating accounts and identity profiles for them. One obvious approach for this is to have users sign up for a local application account, but that isn't the only possibility. A list of approaches to consider includes

- A user creates a new identity by filling out a self-registration form.

- A special case of self-registration is sending select users an invitation to sign up.

© Yvonne Wilson, Abhishek Hingnikar 2023
Y. Wilson and A. Hingnikar, *Solving Identity Management in Modern Applications*,
https://doi.org/10.1007/978-1-4842-8261-8_4

- User identities are transferred from a previously existing user repository.

- An identity service with an existing repository of user identities is leveraged.

- An administrator or automated process creates identities.

These approaches are not mutually exclusive; in some cases, a combination of approaches might work best. We'll describe each in more detail along with some advantages and disadvantages for each.

Self-Registration

One option is to have users create a new account for your application and specify their identity information via self-service sign-up. This requires enticing users to your site, having them fill out a registration form and then storing the collected information. This is a common approach for consumer-facing sites and requires you to design and create the sign-up form(s). The sign-up form and process must be capable of scaling to the expected volume of user sign-ups especially for a big, widely announced launch. Self-registration also necessitates privacy notices about the information you are collecting and obtaining the user's consent for the planned use of the information collected. You should keep the information requested to a minimum as users may abandon the registration process if too much data is required.

With a self-registration form, you control the user sign-up experience. You can customize the information you collect and ask the user directly for information that may not be available from other sources. Self-registration is more scalable, at least compared to having administrators manually create accounts. On the flip side, there is work to implement and maintain a registration form, along with procedures for obtaining user consent for the data collection and processing. In addition, having to fill out a registration form may deter some users from signing up. Table 4-1 summarizes some of the advantages and disadvantages of using a registration form.

Table 4-1. *Self-Registration*

Advantages	Disadvantages
• Ability to collect user attributes that don't exist elsewhere.	• May deter some prospective new users from signing up.
• Control over user registration experience.	• Liability associated with storing login credentials.
• Scalability through self-service.	

Progressive Profiling

You can reduce the information a user has to enter upon sign-up by using progressive profiling, the practice of building up user profile attributes for an identity over time, instead of requesting them all at once. With progressive profiling, a user is asked to provide minimal attributes when they sign up. If the user later performs a transaction that requires more information, it is collected at that time. Alternatively, additional information can be gathered after a certain amount of time has passed or a set number of logins. Progressive profiling reduces the sign-up friction that a lengthy initial sign-up form would present. It is often used in conjunction with self-registration sign-up, but can be used with other provisioning options.

Invite-Only Registration

A variant of the self-service registration approach is the invite-only registration flow. In this scenario, specific users are invited to sign up. The invitation may be triggered by another user. Some social networking sites use this approach to have users invite their friends to join the site. The invited user gets a link which takes them to a sign-up form where they can register. The invited user should create the password for their account when they register, rather than having it included in the invitation, so that only the user knows the password.

An invitation may also be triggered by an administrator of a site. This case may involve a registration form for the user, or, if the administrator has already provided all account data needed, it might only involve email address validation and/or a password reset. This technique might be useful to invite specific users to test an early access (alpha) version of an application or release.

With an invite-only sign-up, access to the registration form is restricted to a select group of users who receive an invitation. The invitation can be delivered via channels such as email or text message and contains a link that allows the user to register. The registration page can lock the email address or phone number to that used in the invitation so it cannot be changed at the time of registration. This prevents an uninvited person from stealing someone else's invitation and signing up as themselves. The link in the invitation can also have an expiration associated with it, if necessary, and each invitation is usually tracked so it can only be used once.

An invite-only flow can also be used for situations where you need to create an account in order to assign privileges to it before sending the invitation. This approach could be used to establish employee accounts for new hires or customer accounts for access to early access (alpha) application environments. An administrator or automated process can create the account, assign it privileges, and then trigger the sending of the invitation link to the new user. The user clicks the link and provides additional information in a registration form if needed. The information entered by the user can be associated with the previously created account. The account is then ready for the person to use and has the privileges previously assigned to the account by the administrator.

The invite-only flow has similar considerations to the self-registration option described previously. It can additionally protect against registrations by hackers and bots, unless, of course, they find a way to finagle an invitation. An invite-only registration flow obviously requires extra work to implement the invitation mechanism as well as access control to limit access to the invitation distribution. It may require work by an administrator to issue the invitations or to create an automated process to do this. As with open self-registration, the invite-only registration process should be capable of supporting the expected volume of invited sign-ups. Some advantages and disadvantages of the invite-only sign-up approach are shown in Table 4-2.

Table 4-2. *Invite-Only Registration*

Advantages	Disadvantages
• Ability to collect user attributes not available from other sources.	• The work to implement the invitation mechanism and control access to it.
• Control over user registration experience.	• The work to issue invitations.
• Some protection against registration by hackers and bots.	• May deter some prospective new users from signing up.
• Scalability through self-service if users invite others.	• Liability associated with storing login credentials.

Identity Migration

If identities already exist elsewhere, they can be moved from one repository, such as a legacy database, to another repository that can be used by the new application. The advantage is that users don't have to provide information they already entered elsewhere, and the new repository can be quickly populated with users from the legacy repository.

While most user profile attributes can be extracted and moved, passwords represent a challenge. Passwords are typically stored in a hashed format. Hashing converts them to a string of random characters, and this cannot be reversed to get the original "cleartext" value. Each time the user logs in and enters their password, it is hashed and the hashed value is compared to the password that was hashed and stored when the user registered or last reset their password. Storing passwords in hashed format allows validation of entered passwords but prevents administrators with access to password repositories from seeing cleartext passwords and makes it difficult to use the passwords if the storage repository is compromised or stolen.

There are different algorithms for hashing passwords and different inputs passed to the hashing algorithms such as salts and iteration counts. As a result, a password hashed in one system cannot necessarily be imported and used by another system. If two different systems use different hashing algorithms or different inputs to the same algorithm, it is not possible to move a hashed password from one system to the other and have it be usable by the new system. In such circumstances, there are a few solutions to consider for migrating identities to a new system.

Support Legacy Hashing Algorithm

One solution is to move the hashed passwords to the new system and update the new system to support the hashing algorithm(s) used by the legacy system. This requires implementing in the new system the legacy system's hashing algorithm(s) and a means of determining which hashing algorithm to use with each account. This will enable moving all identity data and hashed passwords from the legacy system to the new system without requiring the users to reset a password. Table 4-3 summarizes some advantages and disadvantages of supporting legacy hashing algorithms.

Table 4-3. *Supporting Legacy Hashing Algorithms*

Advantages	Disadvantages
• Avoids need for password reset. • Transfers all accounts in a usable state.	• Work to implement legacy hashing algorithm(s). • Liability associated with storing login credentials. • Inherits any weakness associated with legacy hashing algorithms.

Bulk Identity Migration

If it is not possible for the new system to support the legacy hashed passwords, it may be possible to extract the users' identity data, minus the hashed passwords, from the legacy system and import it into the new system. The new system would then need to send each user a unique password reset link to establish a new password for their account in the new system. This requires the identity information in the legacy system to include a validated email address, and that a password reset link sent via email is deemed adequately secure for the sensitivity of the information handled by the new system. If other forms of communication besides email are used, the same validation and security requirements apply. This solution may also be useful if the passwords in the legacy system were not stored in a hashed form and the new system requires newly reset, hashed passwords for improved security. Users should be notified in advance about the migration, so they will know to expect the password reset message and not view it as an attempted phishing attack.

When forcing users to reset their passwords is acceptable, a bulk transfer can be done all at once, making it possible to retire the legacy system soon after the transfer. Table 4-4 summarizes some advantages and disadvantages of a bulk transfer of users.

Table 4-4. *Bulk Migration of Users*

Advantages	Disadvantages
• Transfers all users at once. • Enables immediate shutdown of legacy user repository. • No latency added at login time to check a legacy system for a user account. • Code to transfer identities can be independent of application code.	• Transfers all accounts, even inactive accounts, unless they are filtered out during the transfer. • Requires all users to set new password via account recovery, unless the new system can support the legacy hashed passwords. • Migrating all users at once may cause an outage or delay the migration if things go wrong with the migration and there is no backout plan. • If multiple applications use the legacy repository, they must migrate at the same time if the legacy repository is to be shut off after migration. • Liability associated with storing login credentials.

Gradual Migration of Users

Identities can also be transferred gradually as users log in. This requires a login mechanism that prompts users for credentials, validates the credentials against the legacy repository, and, if validated, retrieves identity information from the legacy repository and stores it along with the entered credentials in the new repository. The password entered by the user, after validation against the legacy system, is hashed by the new system using its hashing algorithm and stored in the user's account in the new system. This option will only migrate users who log in and requires the new authentication system to have direct access to the legacy system to validate the entered password and retrieve user profile information. This is convenient for users because no password reset is required, but it means the legacy system must remain operational until the identities have been migrated. This solution will not transfer inactive accounts (users who don't log in).

With the gradual migration approach, a subset of users may not log in and therefore not have their identity information migrated. You can set a cutoff date for the migration and decide what to do about any identities that have not been migrated by that date. One possibility is to declare the unmigrated accounts inactive and abandon them. A common approach is to use the bulk move option described previously on the inactive accounts so you can decommission the old system. You may want to migrate only a subset of identities that you have reason to believe will be active again in the future. If you do not migrate all remaining identities, you should consider reserving the account identifiers of unmigrated identities to prevent them from being used by new accounts in the future. Chapter 15 explains why.

Of course, a user whose identity has not yet been migrated might forget their password. The user could use the new system to enter their email and get a password reset token or link. The user would confirm receipt of the email and be prompted to enter a new password. The new system would create an account for the user in the new system, with information retrieved from the legacy system for an account with matching email address. This scheme is only appropriate if there is no possibility that an email address used in the old system could have been recycled and assigned to a different user.

The gradual migration of active identities, combined with bulk migration of remaining identities and credential reset, provides a nice user experience for active users while not abandoning infrequent users. If using this approach, care should be taken to minimize exposure of login credentials, ideally by using an identity provider service that implements such a migration. In this case, the credentials are only exposed to the identity provider service that will handle authentication with those credentials going forward.

A final consideration with the gradual migration option is that it may be confusing for users if other applications are using the legacy identity store and the user resets their password in the new application to which their account has been migrated. If the new password is not synchronized back to the legacy identity store, the user may have one password for the applications that continue to use the legacy identity store and a different password for the new application. Performing synchronization back to the legacy system would depend on technical feasibility, cost, and the security of the legacy system. Alternatively, clear differentiation of the legacy and new login screens could reduce confusion to some extent.

Table 4-5 summarizes some advantages and disadvantages of a gradual migration.

Table 4-5. *Gradual Migration of Users*

Advantages	Disadvantages
• Inactive accounts can be weeded out. • No password reset required (for users who log in during migration). • Spreads out risk of outages by migrating identities gradually (no big bang risk). • Can support continued use of previous sign-up mechanisms or applications that use the legacy identity repository during the gradual migration.	• Requires that legacy identity store is accessible from new application's authentication mechanism. • Legacy identity store must remain accessible until enough identities are transferred. • Transfer mechanism must be maintained throughout the gradual migration. • A user's first login after migration starts may have some latency as identity data is transferred from the legacy system. • Potential for user confusion after password reset if other applications continue to use the legacy data store. • Potential for user confusion if users can make user profile updates in both legacy and new systems after migration. • Implementation work cannot be easily decoupled from the application team. • Liability associated with storing login credentials.

Any time identity data is moved from one system to another, it is important to consider any changes that might occur during the transition. The easiest approach is to prohibit users from making changes to either the old or new system during the transition, but this may not be feasible in some cases. If users are allowed to make changes to their identity information in the old system during an identity data migration, a plan is needed for how to identify and transfer such interim changes from the old system to the new system. In the case of a gradual identity migration, the user's account in the old system can be disabled when the user's account is migrated, preventing further changes in the old system. This assumes there are no other applications which will continue to use the old system. Requirements for each environment can be unique, so creating a plan that takes into account all applications in an environment, the migration timing, and potential for user changes during the migration is essential.

Administrative Account Creation

Yet another solution to consider for creating accounts and identities is to have an administrator or automated process create them. The best approach for a situation should take into account

- The size of an organization

- The frequency with which new users need to be added

- Whether provisioning needs to be done across domains

The following sections provide a few variants of this solution to consider.

Manual Account Creation

Having an administrator manually create accounts for new identities will only be practical for very small organizations (low tens of users) with an infrequent need to add new users and few applications. For very small organizations, the work to implement account provisioning automation may not be justified. In the absence of automation, written procedures and checklists can be used to ensure necessary account provisioning steps are consistently followed. If passwords are used as credentials, the account provisioning procedures should ensure that administrators do not know the user's password. This can be done by sending a password reset link to the user and/or requiring a password reset upon initial login. If the organization grows or starts to need more than a handful of applications, some form of automation will be beneficial for consistency, accuracy, security, and trackability.

Automated Account Creation

This approach is often used for employee identities. When a new employee joins a company, the company can automatically create an account for the employee using identity information from a Human Resources (HR) system. If large volumes of accounts need to be created on an ongoing basis, workflow software or specialized account provisioning software can be used to automate account creation and provide identity attributes for accounts.

Cross-Domain Account Creation

In several situations, account provisioning may need to occur across domains. This can occur when

- Maintaining employee accounts in external SaaS (Software-as-a-Service) applications

- Maintaining partner accounts in corporate identity repositories or applications

- Maintaining business customer user accounts in business-facing applications

- Maintaining guest professor or student accounts in collaborating universities' systems

- Maintaining guest user accounts in collaborating government agencies' systems

Ideally, modern authentication protocols would convey user profile attributes to applications in authentication tokens at the time of login, but provisioning or synchronizing identity information across domains may still be needed if

- Applications are not designed to extract identity information from authentication tokens.

- The identity profile information is too large to convey in authentication tokens.

- User logins are not frequent enough to keep profile information sufficiently up to date.

When needed, the provisioning of accounts and identity information across domains is still commonly done using proprietary solutions, but an industry standard protocol, SCIM 2.0 (System for Cross-domain Identity Management),[i] was defined in 2015 to provide a more standard approach to sending and updating identity information from one domain to another. SCIM 2.0 provides a standard REST API for one system to send requests to another system for adding, modifying, or deleting user and group records. This can be used to keep identity data synchronized between different systems. A common use case is for a centralized identity repository to send user account and profile updates, as well as account deactivation requests, to other service provider systems. SCIM 2.0 also provides an optional common user schema, though user profile attributes vary widely across systems so mapping user profile attributes between systems is usually required.

Table 4-6 shows some advantages and disadvantages of administrative account provisioning.

Table 4-6. *Administrative Account Creation*

Advantages	Disadvantages
• User doesn't fill out registration form.	• Time-consuming if not automated.
• Administrator can assign customized privileges for the account.	• Requires care to ensure that only the user knows the password for the account created.
• Can incorporate manual identity validation step if required by the organization creating account.	• Liability associated with storing login credentials if stored locally.
• Can be automated via workflow or identity provisioning software.	

Leverage Existing Identity Service

It's also possible to leverage an identity that already exists for a user in an identity provider service. This allows users to employ an account they already have such as at a social provider like Facebook or Google, a corporate identity provider service operated by their employer, or a government identity service. With this option, your application delegates responsibility for authenticating users to an identity provider and receives back a security token with information about the user's authenticated session and, optionally, attributes about the user.

Leveraging accounts in an existing identity provider service may mean less work for users if it reduces the data they have to enter into a registration form. It also usually means users don't need to set up another password. This may translate to less development work if you don't have to implement a login form or account recovery mechanism because all users authenticate via an identity provider service. It may also reduce your risk somewhat if user passwords are not stored in your infrastructure. If an identity provider service does not contain all the attributes your application needs about the user, you can always collect additional data later. Of course, it's a good idea to vet an external identity service before trusting it, and the use of an identity provider service requires collaborative troubleshooting as described in Chapter 16. Table 4-7 summarizes some advantages and disadvantages of using an external identity service.

Table 4-7. *Leveraging an Existing Identity Service*

Advantages	Disadvantages
• Better user experience if it reduces the data required to sign up. • Easier for user to remember password if identity provider account is used frequently. • You may not have to implement a login form or account recovery mechanism if all users authenticate via the identity provider service. • Less risk if you do not store user passwords.	• You may have to collect additional profile information not available from the identity provider service. • You need to evaluate the service and availability levels of the external identity service to ensure it meets your needs. • May require additional development or configuration work for each identity provider service to be used. • May require configuration work at each identity provider service for each application you have, unless you use an authentication broker service (described in Chapter 7). • May require collaborative troubleshooting with another organization when issues occur.

In addition to existing identity provider services, you can of course set up your own, new identity provider service for use by your application. If you choose that route, many cloud services are available to facilitate the task, and any of the previous provisioning options could be used to populate the new identity provider service with users.

Selecting an External Identity Service

If you choose to leverage an external identity service, it's important to consider the strength of the identity issued by a service as well as the suitability and availability of a provider for a particular environment. The strength of an identity is one factor in determining how much trust can be placed in the identity, and several factors influence the strength of an identity:

- The validation of the information used to establish the identity

- The identity's implementation that prevents it from being forged or used by others

- Recognition of certain issuers of identities as authoritative for a particular domain

Table 4-8 provides a comparison of characteristics of strong vs. weak identities.

Table 4-8. *Characteristics of Strong vs. Weak Identities*

Strong Identities	Weak Identities
• Linked to a real person, who can be held accountable for actions taken with the identity and associated accounts.	• Anonymous, cannot be linked to a real person.
• Identity attributes are validated during account issuance process.	• Little validation of identity attributes.
• Issued by entity recognized as authoritative for a particular context.	• Issued by an entity with little recognized authority.
• Contains mechanisms to protect against forgery or unauthorized use.	• Few protections against forgery or unauthorized use.

The strength of an identity is based on the trustworthiness of the issuer, the validation of identity data, the practices behind the issuing and distribution of the identity, and, in some cases, agreements, either implicit or explicit, between the issuer and any entities trusting identity information from the issuer. The next sections provide examples.

Self-Registered Identities

A self-registered identity, such as a basic Gmail or Yahoo email account, is an example of a weak identity. You can sign up for these accounts using any identifier that has not already been taken, such as frodo_baggins@gmail.com or santa.claus@yahoo.com. You do not have to supply true information in the sign-up form, and the service provider does not validate most of the identity data. Several social providers have added security features to protect against unauthorized use of accounts, but self-registered accounts are typically not considered authoritative for identity information due to the lack of validation. Identity providers with self-registered accounts and little validation of attributes are most suitable for consumer-facing applications that do not require strongly validated identity data and would otherwise rely on self-registered information. Allowing users to authenticate via such providers gives users convenience and the ability to reuse a common profile.

Organization Identities

Many organizations, such as companies or universities, will issue an online identity for their members, such as employees or students, respectively. These identities meet some of the criteria for a strong identity. For example, in the United States, one must show government-issued identity when starting a new job. This enables validation of the identity attributes used to establish an online account within the company and ties the account to a real person. Most companies implement measures in their identity service such as minimum password length and possibly stronger forms of authentication, to protect an account against unauthorized use. The corporate identity service is authoritative for user login, at least within the domain of the issuing company. However, a user typically cannot log in via their corporate identity service and access services outside the organization and its contracted SaaS services. A user could not, for example, expect to log in via their corporate identity service and access a government site to buy stamps as the government site would not have any basis to trust the corporate identity service. Organization identity services are primarily suitable for use by applications selected by the organization to provide services to organization members.

Government Identities

A government-issued online identity, such as those issued by the United Kingdom's EasyID,[ii] Belgian eID,[iii] or Estonian e-identity,[iv] is an example of a stronger identity. These require supplying information that is checked by a validation process. Some require applying in person at a government office, and some can be done online. Required documentation includes government-issued identity documents and photos that clearly show one's face and may include fingerprints and financial questions. The resulting identity contains validated information and employs several security mechanisms to prevent unauthorized use.

The EasyID service, for example, can be used within the United Kingdom to prove identity and access various services conducted via the Post Office. The Belgian eID program issues an electronic identity that can be used for identification, digitally signing documents, and logging in to public services. Estonia issues a mandatory, secure, national digital identity and card which Estonians use to travel within the EU, as well as access e-services such as voting and logging in to bank accounts, access medical records, file taxes, and sign documents with a digital signature. Government-issued identities provide more strongly validated identities, but may be limited to users from one country and may be limited to use at the issuing government's services. Wider use would need international standards similar to those for passports as well as a model for funding the incremental service operation costs.

Industry Consortium Identities

The Belgian Mobile ID[v] project is a consortium of financial institutions and mobile network operators to provide a strongly validated identity for anyone with a Belgian-issued eID and a mobile phone. It's used to register at services, digitally sign documents, and securely log in as well as confirm transactions. The service includes a mobile application, "itsme," which is used to authenticate without the need for passwords. The service is used to access Belgian government services such as social security and tax services as well as telecom and ebanking applications.

Identity Provider Selection

If you are creating a consumer-facing application that does not require validated identity information, allowing users to authenticate via an existing self-registered identity, such as a social provider account, offers users convenience over signing up with the same self-registered information at multiple sites.

If you are creating an employee-facing application, however, relying on social identity provider accounts to access company applications can be problematic because the user owns their identity and account at these providers. The credential standards of the provider may not meet company needs, and when an employee leaves the company, you could not delete their account to terminate their access. If, on the other hand, a social provider account is linked to a local application account, to enable logging in to the application via the social provider identity, the link can be removed and the local account disabled if an employee leaves. In the absence of such account linking, access would often need to be removed within individual applications, and one or more applications might be missed. For employee-facing applications, therefore, it's best to use an identity service where the employing organization owns the accounts. The same logic applies to other organizations, such as educational institutions.

An organization-controlled identity service provides a single place at which the organization can provision accounts as well as shut off accounts if an employee or member leaves the organization. It also gives a single point at which to enforce credential strength/policy and deploy multi-factor authentication as well as log authentication activity. There are several cloud vendors that offer an identity service on a subscription basis. Cloud services such as Google Apps, Azure AD, Auth0,[1] Amazon Cognito, and Okta offer cloud-based identity services. Organizations can provision employees or members into these services and have complete control over the accounts including the ability to quickly terminate or disable the accounts of anyone who leaves the organization.

If you are creating an application where your customers are businesses, you will likely need to support a variety of different identity providers because each business may have its own preferred identity provider service and want their users to sign in to your application via their chosen identity provider. Your business-to-business (B2B) customers may ask you to support authentication against cloud identity providers, such as those mentioned in the previous sections, or private identity providers that they operate themselves on their corporate network. It is best to do this via standard identity protocols such as OIDC or SAML 2. Implementing authentication directly against a customer's internally hosted database or directory service would involve custom work for each customer and may expose your staff to passwords or administrative access which significantly increases your potential liability. Table 4-9 summarizes the types of identity providers that are most common for different scenarios.

---

[1] Full disclosure: At the time of writing this book, the authors worked for Auth0.

Table 4-9. *Identity Providers for Different Customer Types*

Scenario	Common Type(s) of Identity Provider
B2C: Business to consumer	Social Identity Providers[2] Identity services such as Azure AD or Auth0 Application-specific repository
B2E: Business to employee	Identity services such as Google Apps, Azure AD, Auth0 Any OIDC or SAML 2–compliant identity provider
B2B: Business to business	Identity services such as Google Apps, Azure AD, Auth0 Any OIDC or SAML 2–compliant provider controlled by the business customer

To recap, you should consider the target audience and strength of identity needed by your application. If a strong identity is required, it must be issued by a process which validates the information used to establish the identity and includes protections, such as strong password requirements or multi-factor authentication, to prevent unauthorized use of the identity. It must also be issued by an entity recognized as authoritative for the application's domain.

Identity Proofing

The need for validated identity has been increasing. One important driver is the need to combat fraud, identity theft, and money laundering, especially in industries such as the financial sector. In the United States, the USA Patriot Act[vi] requires financial institutions to validate the identity of account holders, maintain records of the information used in such validation, and check if an account holder is on a list of known or suspected terrorists or traffickers. These measures are designed to reduce funding for organizations involved in terrorism, narcotics, and human trafficking. Similar requirements have been enacted by governments around the world, and they are sometimes called Know Your Customer (KYC) and Anti-Money Laundering (AML) requirements.

---

[2] Social Identity Providers are identity services such as are offered by Facebook, Twitter, Google, GitHub, or LinkedIn.

There are additional drivers for identity validation. In the United States, the Immigration Reform and Control Act (IRCA) of 1986 requires employers to validate the identity and employment eligibility of new employees. Businesses with sensitive intellectual property may validate the identity of new employees to reduce the risk of espionage. Applications targeted for a specific group, such as members of a trade union, may need to validate identity as part of eligibility requirements. Background checks can validate that an identity meets certain requirements, but at some point, the person applying must prove that they are the person represented by the submitted identity information. In the past, identity validation often took place via in-person presentation of identity documents. When an online service has no storefront at which in-person identity verification can take place, or when businesses hire remote employees, previous validation approaches may no longer be feasible. Many businesses may need to validate the identity of online users, and this process is known as identity proofing. The National Institute of Standards and Technology (NIST) in the United States has published a document on Digital Identity Guidelines[vii] that outlines different identity assurance levels and the type of identity validation required for each.

A variety of digital services have sprung up to assist with this need. Some services validate an identity by having an applicant answer a series of multiple-choice questions that only the legitimate owner of an identity is likely to know, such as questions about past financial transactions. Other services will have a user record a selfie video to prove liveness, match the face on the video with a government-issued identity document, validate the identity document is legitimate, and retrieve validated identity attributes about the person from the identity document. Some providers can additionally check an identity against government lists of people and organizations on global sanctions and watchlists.

At the time of writing, providers such as ID.me, Sumsub, Socure, and Trulioo are a few examples of vendors offering solutions to help validate the identities of self-registered users. They can help businesses automate the process of identity verification to comply with government regulations, combat money laundering, or validate a user is a member of a particular class such as a military veteran or credentialed teacher. If validated identity is a requirement for your project, using such services can help validate user identity and profile attributes, freeing up application developers to focus on differentiating innovation for your application. It is important to note, however, that online identity validation services may not yet meet requirements for certain cases, such as identity verification for employment in the United States with the I-9 form required by the IRCA.

Choosing and Validating Identity Attributes

A common question that arises during the design of provisioning processes is how to identify a user. Email addresses have been widely adopted as identifiers. Using an email address as an identifier has the advantage that it includes a domain name and thus provides built-in uniqueness across domains. This eliminates the need for a user to find a name on each site that hasn't been taken already. An email address is probably easier for a user to remember because it is used frequently, and it can double as a communication attribute. Email address identifiers, however, create several issues. Users may need to change their email address for any number of reasons and still retain access to their account as well as transactions performed using the previous email address. In addition, an email provider may reassign a previously used email address to a new owner. For business-facing applications, some businesses do not provide their employees with email accounts which can be an issue if an application assumes the availability of an email address. Similarly, applications marketed to children should recognize that some children may not have an email address.

Using a user-selected username also has advantages and disadvantages. A username may make it easier for a person to set up multiple accounts if needed and is typically shorter and therefore easier to type on mobile devices. A user must choose a unique username, however, and if their favorite username is already taken on a site, they have to choose another. It may be hard for users to remember which username was used at each site, which may create a need for a forgotten username feature. When one company acquires another, it often requires the merging of user repositories which may involve eliminating duplicate usernames. Table 4-10 lists some common advantages and disadvantages of different identifiers.

Table 4-10. *Advantages and Disadvantages of Account Identifiers*

Advantages	Disadvantages
Email: Globally unique.	**Email:**
No need to hunt for a name that isn't taken already.	May need to be changed by a user.
May be easier to remember than a username.	May be reassigned by an email provider to a new user.
Can double as a communication attribute, such as for password resets.	May be reassigned by a corporate provider to a new user.
	Terminated by the employer if a user leaves.
	Not all companies issue email addresses.
	Children may not have email addresses.
	Family members may share an email address.
	May expose personal information (user's name).
	Exposure as display name may result in spam email.
Username:	**Username:**
Easier to set up multiple accounts at a site.	Only unique within an application domain.
May be shorter to type on mobile devices.	Merging user repositories problematic after acquisitions.
Can be used in searches, allowing other attributes with personal data to be encrypted.	May be harder for a user to remember which username was used at each site.
	A user may want to change a username over time.
	May expose personal information if used for display and it contains personal information.

(continued)

Table 4-10. (*continued*)

Advantages	Disadvantages
Phone number:	**Phone number:**
Globally unique (with country code).	Exposure as display name may cause spam calls.
No need to hunt for a free identifier. Can double as a communication attribute, such as for password resets.	Might be reassigned to a new user over time.
	May involve a charge to obtain a phone number.
May be easier for a user to remember than a username.	More difficult for a person to set up multiple accounts at the same site.
	May be changed by a user for various reasons. May be terminated by a phone provider.

Attribute Usage

Some of the disadvantages listed earlier stem from using the same attribute for multiple purposes. They can be avoided by decoupling and using a different attribute for each of the following purposes:

- Identifier for logging in

- Display name

- Notification/communication/account recovery

- Internal account implementation such as for

    - Linking an identity/account to application records

    - Capturing user activity in log files

    - Consistent identifier for a user over time for audit purposes

The last three in the list are used for internal account implementation and should use a unique, internal account identifier that is not impacted by a user's need to change profile attributes such as their email address, phone number, or their legal name. In addition, the following suggestions can avoid some of the other disadvantages outlined in Table 4-9:

- Avoid exposing identifiers that may contain personal data.

  - Use an internal account identifier in log files to avoid directly exposing personal data in logs.

  - Use an internal account identifier in application records.

  - Allow users to specify a display name for use on screens/printouts to protect privacy.

- Identifiers/attributes for logging in, display, and notification should be distinct and easily changeable by the user.

- Allow setting multiple attributes for notification purposes, such as a primary and secondary email, in case one becomes inoperable.

- Allowing usernames that are long, contain special characters, and that can be changed by users enables flexibility. Users can use an email address as their username if that is easier for them to remember, while other users can use other values. A separate profile attribute besides the username should be used for display purposes and another for notification/contact information to decouple these different usages.

If your application will leverage an identity provider, and users will access multiple applications through that identity provider, the use of Pairwise Pseudonymous Identifiers (PPIDs) reduces the ability for someone to correlate the user's activity across different applications. For each user, a unique identifier is used between the identity provider and each application. A given user might be identified with "a8h3" for one application site and "c37j" for another. (In practice, the identifiers would be long, opaque, unguessable strings.) Support for PPIDs may vary by identity provider.

Validating Critical Attributes

In addition to using different profile attributes for different functions, it is important to validate email addresses and other profile attributes if used in activities that impact security and privacy. This includes attributes used for

- Authorization decisions

- Account recovery

- Delivery of sensitive information to the user

For example, if a user profile includes an email address, and the email address attribute is used in authorization decisions, you should implement email address validation. Similarly, email address attributes used for notification in account recovery or delivery of sensitive information should be validated. The same holds true if a phone number is used for such purposes. If you import identities from elsewhere, you should ensure email addresses or other critical attributes used for the listed functions have been validated before accepting them so that you can rely on the profile attributes.

Security and privacy-related issues can arise with unvalidated attributes. If users can sign up using a fictitious, unvalidated email address and this attribute is used for authorization, their fictitious email address may match authorization rules that grant access to resources they are not really entitled to access. Validating email addresses also prevents accidental entry of an incorrect address. Incorrect email addresses could enable account takeover via account recovery mechanisms or result in the delivery of sensitive information to the wrong recipient. For these reasons, it is critical to decouple attributes for different purposes and validate any email addresses or other profile attributes that are used in authorization decisions, account recovery mechanisms, or to deliver sensitive information to users.

Consent Management

A less obvious requirement that must usually be addressed as part of provisioning processes is obtaining any necessary user consent for the collection, processing, and use of their personal data as well as notifying users about their rights related to such collection, processing, and use. Privacy legislation varies by jurisdiction but typically requires that a site provide privacy-related notification to users and have a legal basis for collecting and using data about individuals. Such legal bases include obtaining user consent, fulfilling a contract, satisfying a legal obligation, or performing a task that is vital to a data subject, in the public interest, or for a legitimate business purpose.

It is beyond the scope of this book to cover privacy requirements in detail, but we will provide some considerations of technical features related to consent management that may be useful for the account provisioning process. A need to obtain user consent is primarily driven by privacy legislation, but, if done well, can facilitate user trust, which in turn may make users more willing to engage with your site by sharing information, responding to surveys, and consenting to practices such as personalization. Consent management encompasses the processes and mechanisms for providing privacy-related notification to users, obtaining their consent when required, allowing users to set privacy-related preferences, and securely storing consent records to support compliance with relevant privacy legislation.

Consent management includes displaying privacy notice(s) that describes data collection and processing practices, including the use of cookies and tracking technologies. Rather than a single opt-in vs. opt-out, best practices have evolved to provide more granular choices that enable users to opt in to the use of various cookies and tracking technologies, as well as the use of their data for functions such as marketing, ongoing communications, and analytics. Progressive consent gathering can be used to reduce consent fatigue on the part of users, but consent must be obtained prior to collection and use of data about users unless another legal basis applies. Consent must also be obtained in a way that complies with applicable privacy legislation. For example, in some jurisdictions, a user's ability to access content on your site cannot require the user to agree to the use of their data for purposes such as analytics, personalization, or cross-marketing.

You will need to keep a record of consent obtained from users. Consent records should include information such as

- Who gave consent, in the form of an identifier, such as email address or other account identifier, or in more anonymous cases, a cookie or device ID

- When the consent was given, in the form of a timestamp

- The site for which consent was given

- The purposes of processing for which the user has consented

- The version of privacy/consent notice used at the time of consent

- Any subsequent changes or withdrawal of consent

The data about users' consent choices may be used in several ways, so the decision about how and where to store it should consider such needs. It should be possible for users to view and update their consent choices over time. User consent data may need to be accessible by applications to trigger the execution of code which gathers data on user behavior, for feedback and learning about users. Marketing applications may also need consent data to govern communications sent to users. Lastly, auditors may need to review records that show that user consent has been obtained. To support these requirements, user consent data should be centralized and accessible by different business functions and systems.

A site may collect different types of data about users, including what is known as zero-party data, first-party data, and third-party data. Zero-party data is a term coined by Forrester Research and refers to data that users provide themselves, such as preferences, survey responses, or sharing information about themselves. First-party data is data collected by an application about a user. It can include observations of user behavior on a site and transactions the user submits. Third-party data is that collected or purchased from third parties, to augment data collected by an application. The data you hold about users may be subject to Data Subject Access Requests (DSARs).

Privacy legislation typically gives users, also known as data subjects in this context, the right to access data held about them. Companies must respond to DSAR requests in a timely manner, with the exact time varying by jurisdiction. The data collected about a user during the provisioning process and beyond may be subject to such requests. Applications must support a user's right of access, right to rectification, right to erasure, right to restrict processing, right to data portability, and right to object to processing. Users must be able to see data held about them, rectify it if needed, and erase data, as well as revoke or adjust any consent given earlier. You will need to implement processes and/or online mechanisms to support these rights.

Summary

We've covered several approaches that can be used to establish accounts for the users of your application, including self-registration, progressive profiling, transferring users from elsewhere, administrative processes, and leveraging identity provider services. In selecting a provisioning approach, you will want to consider the strength and suitability of the identity offered by each option against the sensitivity and target audience of your application. You may need to design consent management processes to provide notification and obtain user consent for the collection and processing of personal data, and you may additionally need to utilize identity proofing services to validate the identities of your users. Once you have an idea how your users will be created, you can start implementing authentication and access control. Modern applications are often designed starting with APIs, so we'll start off in the next chapter with OAuth 2, which is designed for protecting APIs.

Key Points

- Provisioning is the process of creating an account and associated identity information.

- Applications can create new accounts for users or leverage identities in existing identity provider services.

- Progressive profiling can be used to build up user profiles over time.

- Email addresses and other attributes used for notifications to users must be validated.

- Identities can be classified as weak or strong depending on a provider's practices.

- Weak identities are created with unvalidated information.

- Strong identities are based on validated information and mechanisms to prevent forgery and unauthorized use. They must be issued via secure distribution mechanisms by authoritative providers.

- In choosing identity providers, a service should match the strength of the identity offered by the provider with the identity validation and strength requirements of an application.

- A variety of services are available to perform online identity verification which can help prevent fraud and meet legislative requirements for knowing your customer and combatting money laundering.

- Application designers should decouple and designate appropriate user profile attributes for each of several purposes, including login, display, notification, and internal tracking.

- To comply with privacy regulations, provisioning processes should include consent management to provide privacy notifications to users and obtain and securely store user consent for the collection and processing of their personal data.

Notes

i. https://tools.ietf.org/html/rfc7644

ii. https://www.postoffice.co.uk/identity/easyid

iii. https://eid.belgium.be/en/what-eid

iv. https://e-estonia.com/solutions/e-identity/

v. https://www.itsme-id.com/why-itsme

vi. www.fincen.gov/resources/statutes-regulations/usa-patriot-act

vii. https://nvlpubs.nist.gov/nistpubs/SpecialPublications/NIST.SP.800-63a.pdf

CHAPTER 5

OAuth 2 and API Authorization

The possession of great power necessarily implies great responsibility.

—William Lamb, British Member of Parliament, Home Secretary, and Prime Minister. From a speech in the House of Commons, 1817

Modern applications are often designed around APIs. APIs enable applications to reuse logic and take advantage of innovative services. APIs provide access to valuable data or services, so they typically need to restrict API access to authorized parties. Applications therefore need authorization to call APIs. If an application wants to call an API on a user's behalf to access resources owned by the user, it needs the user's consent. In the past, a user often had to share their credentials with the application to enable such an API call on their behalf. This gave the application an unnecessary amount of access, not to mention the responsibility of safeguarding the credential. In this chapter, we will cover how the OAuth 2 Authorization Framework provides a better solution for authorizing applications to call APIs.

In this chapter, we will provide an overview of the OAuth 2 Authorization Framework aligned with the draft OAuth 2.1 version (draft 6) of the specification.[i] OAuth 2.1 is a consolidation of the earlier OAuth 2.0 Authorization Framework,[ii] several subsequent specifications, and security best practice documents. We will also point out key elements of the framework which changed or were removed between OAuth 2.0 and OAuth 2.1. At the time of writing, OAuth 2.1 is still in draft status, so there may be further revisions in the future. Application owners and developers should check for ongoing changes and best practice guidance.

© Yvonne Wilson, Abhishek Hingnikar 2023
Y. Wilson and A. Hingnikar, *Solving Identity Management in Modern Applications*,
https://doi.org/10.1007/978-1-4842-8261-8_5

For the remainder of this chapter, we will use the term OAuth 2 when describing benefits or impacts of the OAuth Authorization Framework in general. We will use the term OAuth 2.1 when specifically referring to the OAuth 2.1 Authorization Framework specification and OAuth 2.0 when specifically referring to the OAuth 2.0 Authorization Framework specification.

API Authorization

An application may need to call an API on behalf of a user, to access content owned by the user, or on its own behalf if the application owns the desired content. Figure 5-1 illustrates these two cases using a sample scenario.

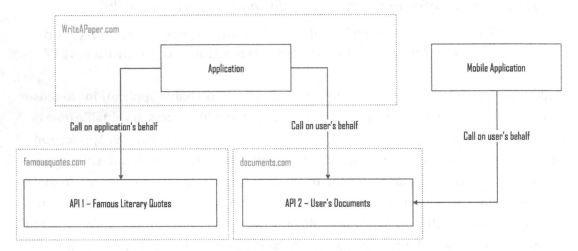

Figure 5-1. *API Authorization: User-Based vs. Client-Based Flow*

In this scenario, the application, WriteAPaper.com, is a specialized editor that helps users write and edit research papers. It calls two APIs, both of which are owned by different organizations. The first is famousquotes.com which provides validated quotes for use in papers. The second API is at documents.com and provides a document storage service. There is a second, mobile application that calls the documents.com API to provide access to documents from a user's mobile device.

When the WriteAPaper application calls the API at famousquotes.com, it does so on its own behalf. The quotes content is not owned by the user, so the user's consent isn't needed for this access. The application only needs to be a registered client authorized to call the quotes API. When the application calls the API at documents.com, however, to obtain a user's documents, the request must be made on behalf of the user. In this case, the content accessed belongs to the user, and the application must obtain the user's consent to retrieve the user's documents. The client application has no right by itself to access the user's data at another site.

The mobile application provides read-only access to a user's documents and doesn't offer access to the quotes service. It requires authorization from a user to call the documents API and retrieve the user's documents. We've included the mobile application in the example because we'll show in the following sections how OAuth 2 could be used to enforce different privileges for the two applications.

OAuth 2

The OAuth 2 Authorization Framework, originally published as OAuth 2.0 in 2012 and revised starting in 2020, and continuing through 2022 to create OAuth 2.1, was designed to enable an application to obtain authorization to call third-party APIs. With OAuth 2, an application can obtain a user's consent to call an API on their behalf, without needing the user's credentials for the API site. An application can also obtain authorization to call an API on its own behalf if it owns the content to be accessed.

The primary use case involves a user, called a resource owner, who wishes to allow an application to access a protected resource, owned by the resource owner, at a logically separate site, known as the resource server. Using our example from Figure 5-1, the resource owner (the user) has stored documents at a resource server (documents.com). The resource owner is using the WriteAPaper application to write a paper based on content they've uploaded to documents.com. The resource owner wants to grant the WriteAPaper application access to their content at documents.com so it can retrieve the content for use in their research paper.

Before OAuth 2, the usual solution involved some risks. The user had to give the WriteAPaper application their documents.com credentials so WriteAPaper could retrieve their documents at documents.com. Once it had the user's credentials, however, WriteAPaper could retrieve anything from the user's account and even modify or delete documents as the user. There was no way for the user to restrict what the WriteAPaper application could do. Furthermore, WriteAPaper might need to retain the password in a decryptable form, or worse, in cleartext form, to access documents.com later.

If WriteAPaper were compromised, and the password decryption key or cleartext passwords stolen, the user's data at documents.com would be at risk. The user also had no way of revoking WriteAPaper's access to documents.com except by changing their credentials. Unfortunately, changing credentials to revoke one application's access would effectively revoke access for any other applications using the credentials to access documents.com on their behalf. The scenario prior to OAuth 2 is depicted in Figure 5-2.

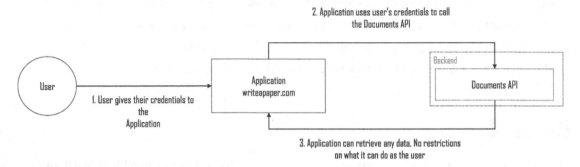

Figure 5-2. *Access Requests Prior to OAuth 2*

OAuth 2 provides a better solution. OAuth 2 enables a user to explicitly authorize an application to call an API on the user's behalf, without giving their credentials for the API site to the application and in a way that limits what the application can do. With OAuth 2, when an application needs to call an API on behalf of a user, it sends an authorization request to an authorization server for the API. An authorization server handles access requests for an API and returns a security token that can be used by the application to access the API. In the authorization request, the application gives an indication of what it wants to request from the API. The authorization server evaluates the request and, if authorized, returns a token to the application.

If the application asks for content owned by the user, the API's authorization server authenticates the user and then asks the user to give their consent for the application to access the requested data. The authentication step ensures the user providing the consent is the owner of the resource being accessed. The authorization server uses details in the application's authorization request to prompt the user for their consent. If the user consents to the requested access, the application receives a token to call the API on the user's behalf. The token is called an access token, and it enables the application to make API requests within the scope of what the user authorized when they gave their consent for the request. This solution eliminates the need for the user to share credentials with the application and gives the user more control over what the application can access. (Note: The exact process by which the application gets the access token is described here in a simplified form but will be explained more accurately in subsequent sections.) Figure 5-3 shows the solution with OAuth 2 in the picture.

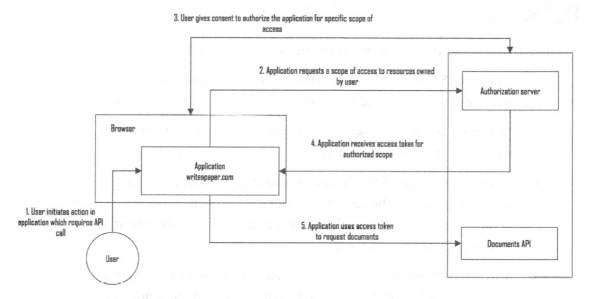

Figure 5-3. *Access Requests with OAuth 2*

To recap, the OAuth 2 protocol provides an authorization solution, not an authentication solution. It enables an application to call an API on its own behalf or a user's behalf, with the call constrained to the scope of an authorized request. The authentication step in OAuth 2 validates the user is entitled to give consent to authorize an access request for a particular resource. The OAuth 2 access token is only intended for API access and not to convey information about the authentication event or the user. The use of OAuth 2 is therefore appropriate for authorizing API calls but not as an authentication solution (at least in the absence of any proprietary additions to the base protocol, which some providers have implemented). OIDC, described in the next chapter, can be used to authenticate a user to an application, but this chapter focuses on describing how OAuth 2 works for the purpose of API authorization.

Terminology

To describe OAuth 2 in more detail, we need to describe a few terms.

Roles

OAuth 2 defines four roles involved in an authorization request:

- **Resource Server** – A service (with an API) storing protected resources to be accessed by an application.

- **Resource Owner** – A user or other entity that owns protected resources at the resource server.

- **Client** – An application which needs to access resources at the resource server, on the resource owner's behalf or on its own behalf. We'll generally use the term application instead of client, for consistency across chapters.

- **Authorization Server** – A service trusted by the resource server to authorize applications to call the resource server. It authenticates the application or resource owner and requests consent from the resource owner if the application will make requests on the resource owner's behalf. With OAuth 2, the resource server (API) is a relying party to the authorization server. The authorization server and resource server may be operated by the same entity.

Confidential and Public Clients

OAuth 2 defines two client types[1]:

- **Confidential Client** – An application that can securely store confidential secrets with which to authenticate itself to an authorization server or use another secure authentication

---

[1] Earlier versions of OAuth 2.1 defined a "Credentialed Client" as an application with no previously established relationship with the authorization server, but able to securely store confidential secrets with which to authenticate itself, such as a dynamically registered mobile client. At the time of writing, this client type has been removed from OAuth 2.1.

mechanism for that purpose. Confidential clients typically execute primarily on a protected server.

- **Public Client** – An application that can neither securely store a secret or credentials to authenticate itself to an authorization server nor use another secure authentication mechanism for that purpose. Public clients typically execute primarily on the user's client device or in the client browser.

Client Profiles

OAuth 2 defines three profiles for client applications based on application topologies:

- **Web Application** – A confidential client with code executing on a protected, back-end server. The server can securely store any secrets needed for the client to authenticate itself as well as any tokens it receives from the authorization server. Such credentials and tokens are not exposed to the resource owner.

- **Browser-Based Application** – Assumed to be a public client with code executing in the user's browser. Example: A JavaScript-based, single-page application running in the browser. Such an application is assumed to be incapable, with current technology (at the time of writing), of adequately securing credentials with which to authenticate itself to an authorization server.

- **Native Application** – Assumed to be a public client that is installed and executed on the user's device, such as a mobile application or desktop application.

In practice, these definitions may overlap because a web application may serve up HTML pages that contain some JavaScript, and single-page applications may have a small back end. For further discussion on this, see the description in Chapter 6 of the OIDC Hybrid Flow.

Tokens and Authorization Code

OAuth 2 defines two security tokens and an intermediary authorization code:

- **Authorization Code** – An intermediary, opaque code returned to an application and used to obtain an access token and optionally a refresh token. Each authorization code is used once.

- **Access Token** – A token used by an application to access an API. It represents the application's authorization to call an API and has an expiration.

- **Refresh Token** – An optional token that can be used by an application to request a new access token when a prior access token has expired.

How It Works

The OAuth 2 Authorization Framework defines different methods by which an application interacts with an authorization server to obtain authorization to call an API. Each method uses a credential to represent the authorization. These credentials are known as authorization grants and are used by an application to obtain an access token with which to call an API. The type of authorization grant to use depends on the use case.

The following authorization grant types are defined:

- Authorization code

- Client credentials

- Refresh token

In OAuth 2.0, there were two additional authorization grant types that were removed in OAuth 2.1. We will describe these briefly to explain why they have been removed and should not be used. These obsolete grant types are

- Implicit (*removed*)

- Resource owner password credentials (*removed*)

An additional authorization grant type has been designed for devices which have limited capabilities for user interaction. This grant type is not part of the core OAuth 2.1 specification (at the time of writing) but is useful to include as it is designed for scenarios involving devices that make up the Internet of Things (IoT). This grant type is

- Client device

The following sections will describe how each of these authorization grant types work, as well as why the obsolete authorization grant types were removed.

Authorization Code Grant

The authorization code grant type uses two requests from the application to the authorization server to obtain an access token. In the first request, the user's browser is redirected to the authorization endpoint at the authorization server with a request to authorize an API call to be made on the user's behalf. The browser redirect enables the authorization server to interact with the user to authenticate them and obtain their consent for the authorization request. After obtaining the user's consent, the authorization server redirects the user's browser back to the application with an authorization code. The application uses the authorization code to send a second, back-channel request to the authorization server's token endpoint to obtain an access token. The authorization server responds with an access token issued to the application which it can use to call the API. Figure 5-4 shows the sequence of steps.

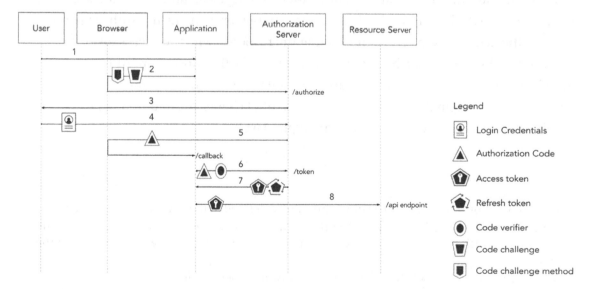

Figure 5-4. *Authorization Code Grant Type + PKCE*

1. The user (resource owner) accesses the application.

2. The application redirects the browser to the authorization server's authorize endpoint[2] with an authorization request.

3. The authorization server prompts the user for authentication and consent.[3]

4. The user authenticates and provides consent for the request.

5. The authorization server redirects the user's browser back to the application's callback URL[4] with an authorization code.

6. The application calls the authorization server's token endpoint,[5] passing the authorization code.

7. The authorization server responds with an access token (and optionally a refresh token).

8. The application calls the resource server (API), using the access token.

The authorization code grant type was originally optimized for confidential clients. The first (authorization) request redirects the user to the authorization server so it can interact with the user. The second request could be made by the application's back end directly to the authorization server's token endpoint. This enables an application back end, which is assumed to be capable of securely managing an authentication secret, to authenticate itself to the authorization server when exchanging the authorization code for the access token. It also means that the response with the access token can be delivered to the application back end, which will make the subsequent API calls. An added side benefit is that the tokens are returned via secure back-channel response. However, while originally optimized for confidential clients, the addition of PKCE enables other client types to use this grant type as well.

---

[2] The authorization server's authorization endpoint is defined in the OAuth 2 specification.

[3] The mechanism by which a user is authenticated to provide consent is outside the scope of the OAuth 2 specifications. It is shown in the diagram (steps 3 and 4) to show where it occurs in the sequence.

[4] The application's callback URL is defined in the OAuth 2 specification.

[5] The authorization server's token endpoint is defined in the OAuth 2 specification.

Authorization Code Grant Type + PKCE

The authorization code grant type diagram shows the use of Proof Key for Code Exchange (PKCE).[iii] PKCE is a mechanism that can be used with authorization and token requests to prevent a malicious process, especially on mobile devices and with public clients, from intercepting an authorization code and using it to get an access token. PKCE does not authenticate clients. Rather, it ensures that the application that requested an authorization code is the same application that uses the authorization code to obtain an access token. PKCE was defined after OAuth 2.0, but has been incorporated into the core OAuth 2.1 specification for use with the authorization code grant type.

To use PKCE, the application creates a cryptographically random string, called a code verifier, that is long enough to provide sufficient protection against guessing. The application then computes a derived value, called a code challenge, from the code verifier. This derived value is typically a hash of the code verifier. It should not be possible to compute the code verifier from the derived value in a time period that would enable compromising the transaction. When the application sends an authorization request in step 2 in the diagram, it includes the code challenge, along with the method used to derive it.

When the application sends the authorization code to the authorization server's token endpoint to get the access token in step 6, it includes the code verifier. The authorization server transforms the code verifier value using the transformation method received in the authorization request and checks that the result matches the code challenge sent with the authorization request. This enables an authorization server to detect if a malicious application is trying to use a stolen authorization code. Only the legitimate application will know the code verifier to pass in Figure 5-4's step 6 that will match the code challenge passed in step 2.

The PKCE specification lists two transform methods that can be used to derive the code challenge from the code verifier, namely, "plain" and "S256." With the "plain" method, the code challenge and verifier are identical, so there is no protection against the code challenge being compromised. Applications using the authorization code grant with PKCE should use the S256 transform method which uses a base64 URL encoded SHA256 hash of the code verifier to protect it.

The Authorization Request

Here is a sample application's API authorization request with PKCE. It would be directed to an authorization server's authorization endpoint.[6]

```
GET /authorize?
response_type=code
& client_id=<client_id>
& state=<state>
& scope=<scope>
& redirect_uri=<callback uri>
& resource=<API identifier>
& code_challenge=<PKCE code_challenge>
& code_challenge_method=S256 HTTP/1.1
Host: authorizationserver.com
```

Table 5-1 shows common parameters for the authorization request.

---

[6] The parameters for all of the examples may vary somewhat for your specific provider. See the documentation for your provider and the OAuth 2.1 specification for additional optional parameters.

Table 5-1. *Authorization Request Parameters*

Parameter	Meaning
response_type	Indicates the OAuth 2 grant type. "code" is used for the authorization code grant type.
client_id	Identifier for the application, assigned when it registered with the authorization server.
state	A nonguessable string, unique for each call, opaque to the authorization server, and used by the client to track state between a corresponding request and response to mitigate the risk of CSRF attacks. It should contain a value that associates the request with the user's session. This could be done by including a hash of the session cookie or other session identifier concatenated with an additional unique-per-request component. When a response is received, the client should ensure the state parameter in the response matches the state parameter for a request it sent from the same browser. This parameter should not include any sensitive information in plain text.
scope	Indicates the scope of access privileges for which authorization is requested. For example. "get.documents". This parameter should not include any sensitive information in plain text.
redirect_uri	The authorization server sends its response with the authorization code to this callback URL at the application. The specified URI must exactly match the callback URI previously registered at the authorization server for the client application. For example: https%3A%2F%2Fclient%2Eapplication%2Ecom%2 Fcallback. (An exception to the exact match requirement is noted for the port number in local host redirect URLs in native applications.)
resource	Identifier for a specific API registered at the authorization server for which the access token is requested. Some implementations may use other names, such as "audience." Primarily used in deployments with custom APIs. This parameter isn't needed unless there are multiple possible APIs.
code_challenge	PKCE code challenge derived from the PKCE code verifier using the code challenge method specified in the code_challenge_method parameter, as described in Section 4.2 of the PKCE specification.[iv]
code_challenge_ method	"S256" or "plain." Applications capable of using S256 must use it.

The scope parameter is used by an application to request a scope of access privileges. Using our WriteAPaper application example from the beginning of the chapter, the primary, single-page application would request a scope of "get:documents update:documents," whereas if the mobile client only needed read access to documents, it would only request "get:documents." There are additional parameters available which applications can use to express richer, more detailed authorization requests. These will be discussed in Chapter 8.

The redirect_uri parameter must exactly match a redirect URI specified at the time the client application was registered with the authorization server. While OAuth 2.0 allowed the URI registered with the authorization server to contain wildcards, OAuth 2.1 now disallows the use of wildcards in the redirect URI registered for a client application. This change reduces the possibility of open redirect attacks.

The resource parameter was not in the original OAuth 2.0 specification. Since that time, authorization servers have been written to handle requests for multiple APIs and, in such cases, may support an additional parameter to indicate a specific API for an authorization request. This parameter is defined in the Resource Indicators for OAuth 2.0 extension.[v] This parameter may be called the "resource" or "audience" depending on the authorization server implementation.

Response

The authorization server sends a response like the following to the application's callback, specified in the redirect_uri parameter of the authorization request:

```
HTTP/1.1 302 Found
Location: https://clientapplication.com/callback?
code=<authorization code>
& state=<state>
```

Table 5-2 shows the response parameters.

Table 5-2. *Authorization Response Parameters*

Parameter	Meaning
code	The authorization code to be used by the application to request an access token.
state	The state value, unmodified, sent in the authorization request. The application must validate that the state value in the response matches the state value sent with the initial request.

Calling the Token Endpoint

After receiving an authorization code, the application uses it in a second request to the authorization server's token endpoint to obtain the access token.

```
POST /token HTTP/1.1
Host: authorizationserver.com
Authorization: Basic <encoded application credentials>

Content-Type: application/x-www-form-urlencoded
grant_type=authorization_code
& code=<authorization_code>
& client_id=<client id>
& code_verifier=<code verifier>
& redirect_uri=<callback URI>
```

The parameters for this example request to the authorization server's token endpoint are shown in Table 5-3.

Table 5-3. *Token Request Parameters*

Parameter	Meaning
grant_type	Must be "authorization_code" for the authorization code grant.
code	The authorization code received in response to the authorization call.
client_id	Identifier for the application, assigned when it registered with the authorization server.
code_verifier	The PKCE code verifier value from which the code challenge was derived. It should be an unguessable, cryptographically random string between 43 and 128 characters in length, inclusive, using the characters A–Z, a–z, 0–9, "-", ".", "_", and "~" and formed as described in Section 4.1 of the PKCE specification.[vi]
redirect_uri	The callback URI for the authorization server's response. Should match the redirect_uri value passed in the authorization request to the authorize endpoint.

The response from the token endpoint will be similar to the following:

```
HTTP/1.1 200 OK
Content-Type: application/json;charset=UTF-8
Cache-Control: no-store
Pragma: no-cache
    {
       "access_token":"<access_token_for_API>",
       "token_type":"Bearer",
       "expires_in":<token expiration>,
       "refresh_token":"<refresh_token>"
    }
```

The parameters for the response are shown in Table 5-4.

Table 5-4. *Token Endpoint Response Parameters*

Parameter	Meaning
access_ token	The access token to use in calling the API. Different authorization servers may use different formats for access tokens.
token_type	Type of token issued. "Bearer," for example.
expires_in	How long the token will be valid.
refresh_ token	A refresh token is optional. It is up to an authorization server's discretion whether to return a refresh token or not. See the "Refresh Tokens" section later in this chapter for further information.

An authorization server may include an additional parameter "scope" to indicate the actual scope of access granted with the issued access token. This is necessary when an authorization server issues an access token for a more restrictive scope than requested by the client.

There are different types of access tokens in use. Some authorization servers issue an opaque access token in the form of an encoded string. A resource server receiving such an access token can call a token introspection endpoint at the issuing authorization server to obtain information about the token, such as the client that requested the token, the intended audience (resource server) for the token, the token expiration, whether the token has been revoked, and the scopes included in the token. The OAuth 2.0 Token Introspection specification[vii] defines the token introspection endpoint and how resource servers can use it to obtain information about opaque tokens issued by authorization servers.

Another common format for access tokens is a JSON Web Token (JWT). This is a structured format that is cryptographically signed and contains various claims about the token such as the client that requested the token, the intended audience (resource server), when the token expires, and the scopes authorized for the token. With self-contained tokens, a resource server can obtain the claims directly from the token without having to call a token endpoint at an authorization server. The JSON Web Token (JWT) Profile for OAuth 2.0 Access Tokens[viii] defines this type of token along with a set of mandatory and optional claims. The documentation for your authorization server should indicate the type of access token it issues and the steps a resource server should take to validate the token and obtain the claims represented by the token.

Client Credentials Grant

The client credentials grant type is used when an application calls an API to access resources the application owns. An example is shown in Figure 5-1 with the call to the quotes service. A quote is not owned by the individual user who needs the quote, so the call can be made on the application's behalf. The application uses the client credentials grant type and authenticates to the authorization server with its own credentials to obtain an access token. The use of this grant type requires that the application have the ability to maintain confidential secrets (or use another secure mechanism) to authenticate itself. The sequence diagram for this grant type is shown in Figure 5-5.

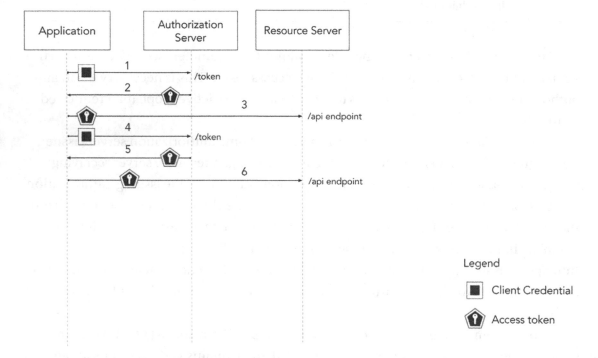

Figure 5-5. *Client Credentials Grant Type*

1. The application sends an authorization request including the application's credentials to the authorization server.

2. The authorization server validates the credentials and responds with an access token.

3. The application calls the resource server (API) using the
    access token.

4. The steps repeat if the access token has expired by the next time
    the application calls the API.

No end-user interaction with the authorization server is required for this flow. The application credentials serve as the authorization for the application and are used to request an access token from the token endpoint. Our sample uses a client ID and client secret obtained when the application registered with the authorization server.

The Authorization Request

A sample token request for the client credentials grant type follows, with parameter definitions the same as those for the previous grant type but with the grant_type set to "client_credentials". The application authenticates in this example with a client ID and secret registered at the authorization server, one of several options.

```
POST /token HTTP/1.1
Host: authorizationserver.com
Authorization: Basic <encoded application credentials>
Content-Type: application/x-www-form-urlencoded
grant_type=client_credentials
& scope=<scope>
& resource=<API identifier>
```

A successful client credentials grant request will result in a response from the token endpoint with an access token, similar to the example in the previous section for the authorization code grant.

Implicit Grant (Removed in OAuth 2.1)

Note   The implicit grant type was removed in OAuth 2.1. It is included here to explain its original purpose, why it is no longer needed, and what should be used in its place.

OAuth 2.0 defined an implicit grant type which was optimized for use with public clients such as single-page applications. The use of this grant type returned an access token to an application in one request. It was designed at a time when the CORS (Cross-Origin Resource Sharing) standard[ix] was not widely supported in browsers so that web pages could only "phone home." In other words, they could only make calls to the domain from which the page was loaded which meant they couldn't call an authorization server's token endpoint. To compensate for this limitation, the implicit grant type had the authorization server respond to an authorization request by returning tokens to the application in a redirect with a URL hash fragment. The interaction for the implicit grant type is shown in Figure 5-6.

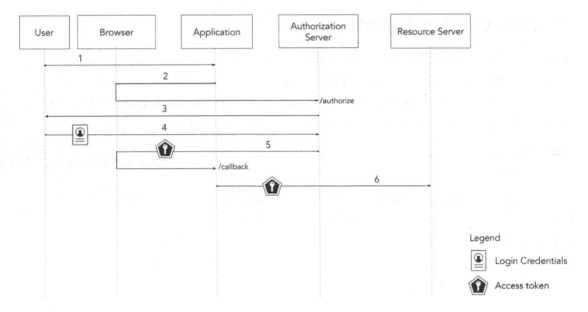

Figure 5-6. *OAuth 2.0 Implicit Grant Type (Removed in OAuth 2.1)*

1. The user (resource owner) accesses the application.

2. The application redirects the browser to the authorization server's authorize endpoint with an authorization request.

3. The authorization server prompts the user to authenticate and provide consent.[7]

---

[7] The mechanism by which a user is authenticated to provide consent is outside the scope of the OAuth 2 specifications. It is shown in the diagram (steps 3 and 4) to show where it occurs in the sequence.

4. The user authenticates and provides consent for the authorization request.

5. The authorization server redirects back to the application's callback URL with an access token.

6. The application uses the access token to call the resource server (API).

Since the OAuth 2.0 specification was originally published, CORS has become supported by most browsers. Consequently, the implicit grant type isn't needed anymore for its original purpose. Furthermore, returning an access token in a URL hash fragment exposes the access token to potential leakage via browser history or referer headers. The OAuth 2.0 implicit grant type has therefore been removed from OAuth 2.1.[x] The authorization code grant type with PKCE should be used instead.

New applications should avoid the use of the implicit grant type. For existing applications, it is possible that existing authorization servers will continue to support the use of the implicit grant for some time. However, given the security concerns associated with this grant type, existing applications should migrate to the authorization code grant type with PKCE to reduce the risk from leaked tokens, avoid a rushed upgrade if an authorization server decides to end support for the implicit grant, and align with OAuth 2.1.

Resource Owner Password Credentials Grant (Removed from OAuth 2.1)

Note   The resource owner password credentials grant type was removed from OAuth 2.1. It is included here to explain its initial purpose and why it should not be used.

With the OAuth 2.0 resource owner password credentials grant type, the application collected the user's credentials directly instead of redirecting the user to the authorization server. The application passed the collected credentials to the authorization server for validation as part of its request to get an access token. This grant type was intended to support situations where an application was trusted to handle end-user credentials and no other grant type was possible.

The interaction for resource owner password grant type is shown in Figure 5-7.

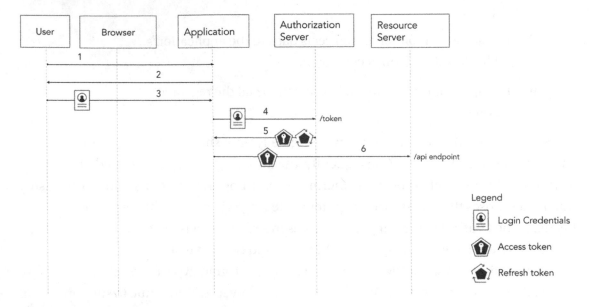

Figure 5-7. *Resource Owner Password Credentials Grant Type (Removed from OAuth 2.1)*

1. The user (resource owner) accesses the application.

2. The application prompts the user for their credentials.[8]

3. The user provides their credentials to the application.

4. The application sends a token request to the authorization server's token endpoint, with the user's credentials.

5. The authorization server responds with an access token (and optionally a refresh token).

6. The application calls the resource server (API), using the access token.

---

[8] The mechanism by which the application obtains the user credentials is outside the OAuth 2 specification. It is shown in the diagram (steps 2 and 3) to provide a more complete picture of the solution.

The use of this grant type was not actively encouraged for several reasons. First, it exposed the user's credentials to the application. A vulnerability in the application could compromise the user's credentials. There was also no specification for how to extend this grant to provide multi-factor authentication, so applications might have added multi-factor authentication capabilities in custom ways that might not have received adequate security review. In addition, this grant type did not involve a user consent step, so an application could request any access it wished using the user's credentials. The user had no way to prevent abuse of their credentials.

This grant type has been used for mobile apps, legacy embedded login pages, and user migration scenarios. Some mobile applications used this grant type when calling first-party APIs. This was often done because login flows that redirected via browsers on mobile devices were originally perceived as cumbersome. This has since improved, and OAuth 2.1 has incorporated the guidance of RFC 8252, OAuth 2.0 for Native Apps,[xi] to use the authorization code grant, combined with PKCE, for native applications using the system browser.

This grant type was also used when login fields were embedded within an application page. This was often done to conform to corporate user interface standards or simply a desire to have an embedded login screen rather than the disruption of a browser redirect. For the reasons stated earlier, this grant type has been removed from OAuth 2.1. Applications should redirect users to the authorization server using the authorization code grant type with PKCE, rather than collect user credentials themselves.

Another scenario for this grant type was user migration use cases. When users needed to be migrated from one identity repository to another with incompatible password hashes, the new system could prompt a user for their credentials, use the resource owner password grant to validate them against the old system, and, if valid, retrieve the user profile from the old system and store it and the credentials in the new system. This avoided the necessity for large-scale forced password resets when migrating identity information. However, if passwords in the old system were compromised, either directly or via password reuse, this scheme would add vulnerable accounts to the new system, unless password checks were implemented as part of the transfer.

To mitigate some of the risk associated with this grant type, the client was supposed to throw away the user credentials as soon as it had obtained the access token, to reduce the possibility of compromised credentials. This guidance, however, only addresses one aspect of the risk associated with this grant type. With other risks remaining, the resource owner password credentials grant type has been removed from OAuth 2.1.[xii]

New applications should avoid the use of this grant type. For existing applications, it is possible that existing authorization servers will continue to support this grant type for some time. However, given the security and liability concerns associated with this grant type, existing applications should migrate to the authorization code grant type with PKCE to reduce the risk from credentials exposed to client applications, facilitate use of multi-factor authentication, and avoid a rushed upgrade if an authorization server decides to end support for this grant type. While legacy applications that cannot be upgraded will probably continue to use this grant type for some time, application owners should understand that applications that continue to use the resource owner password credentials grant type will have the responsibility and liability associated with reviewing the security of their approach. They also risk being forced to upgrade if their identity provider ends support for this grant type.

Device Authorization Grant

Since the publication of OAuth 2, there has been a proliferation of Internet-connected devices often called the Internet of Things (IoT). As with applications, the functionality of IoT devices can be greatly enhanced by calling APIs. A classic example is a digital picture frame. Rather than manually uploading photos to a digital picture frame, it would be nice if you could simply authorize the frame to retrieve photos you have already uploaded to a social media site. This requires you as the owner of the pictures to authenticate to the social media site and provide your consent for the frame to retrieve photos from your account.

The OAuth 2 authorization code grant requires user interaction on the client device for authentication and authorization, yet a digital picture frame and many IoT devices have very limited facilities for user interaction. While a digital frame might be able to implement a touch screen and some limited browser capability to support the redirects and input required, that would increase the complexity and cost of the device which may not be feasible for such devices from a technical or business perspective.

The OAuth 2.0 Device Authorization Grant[xiii] provides a mechanism for the user interaction to occur on another device. With this grant, the user triggers an action on the primary device (an IoT device) that requires an API call. This action could be anything from turning on a device like a TV or making a specific request such as retrieving pictures from a specific social media account. In response to the action, the primary device initiates an authorization request to the authorization server for the API. The authorization server responds with a URL and code that the primary device displays to the user, along with instructions.

The user follows the instructions and accesses the URL on a secondary device, such as a mobile phone. The user interacts with the authorization server on the secondary device to authenticate, input their code, and provide their authorization for the requested action. While the user is doing this, the primary device polls the authorization server. Once the user has completed the interaction on the secondary device, the primary device's next polling request will result in a successful response with an access token and, optionally, a refresh token. The primary device can then use the access token to make an API call on the user's behalf.

Figure 5-8 shows the sequence of steps for the Device Authorization Grant.

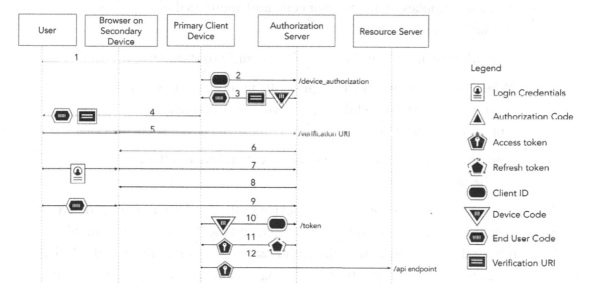

Figure 5-8. *Device Authorization Grant*

1.   The user (resource owner) accesses the primary device.

2.   The primary device sends an authorization request to the authorization server for the API. This request includes the device's client ID.

3.   The authorization server responds with a device code, end-user code, and a user verification URI.

4. The primary device displays or communicates to the user the URI and end-user code.

5. The user accesses the verification URI on a secondary device such as a phone.

6. The authorization server interacts with the user on the secondary device to authenticate them.

7. The user supplies their login credentials to the authorization server.

8. The authorization server prompts the user for their user code and for authorization of the API call.

9. The user supplies their end-user code and approves the authorization request.

10. The primary device continually polls the authorization server.

11. When the user approves the request, the authorization server responds to the next polling request with an access token and optionally a refresh token.

12. The primary device can then use the access token to call the API on the user's behalf.

There are several requirements for this Device Authorization Grant to work. The primary device must be connected to the Internet, and the device must be capable of making outbound HTTPS requests to the authorization server for the desired API. The primary device must also be capable of displaying or communicating to the user the user verification URI, an end-user code, and instructions for how to proceed. This grant also requires the user to have a secondary device capable of supporting the user interaction to authenticate and authorize the API requests.

The following sections show the steps for the Device Authorization Grant in more detail.

The Authorization Request

An example of a primary device's authorization request is shown here. It would be directed via HTTP-POST to an authorization server's device_authorization endpoint.

```
POST /device_authorization HTTP/1.1
Host: authorizationserver.com
Content-Type: application/x-www-form-urlencoded
client_id=<client id>
& resource=<API identifier>
& scope=<scope>
```

Table 5-5 shows common parameters for the authorization request.

Table 5-5. *Authorization Request Parameters*

Parameter	Meaning
client_id	Identifier for the primary device, assigned when it registered with the authorization server.
scope	The scope of access privileges for which authorization is requested. For example: "get:photos".
resource	Identifier for a specific API registered at the authorization server and for which the access token is requested. Some implementations may use other names, such as "audience." Primarily used in deployments with custom APIs. This parameter isn't needed unless there are multiple possible APIs.

The scope parameter is used by the primary device to request a scope of access privileges. Using our digital photo frame example, the digital frame would request a scope of "get:photos" as it needs to retrieve photos for display in the frame. There are additional parameters which can be used to express richer authorization requests and which will be discussed in Chapter 8.

An authorization server may support a parameter to indicate a specific API for an authorization request as defined in the Resource Indicators for OAuth 2.0 extension.[xiv] This parameter may be called the "resource" or "audience."

Authorization Response

The authorization server responds to the primary device's authorization request with a device code, a user code, and a verification URI, as well as an expiration and polling interval. A sample HTTP response body with these parameters follows:

```
HTTP/1.1 200 OK
Content-Type: application/json;charset=UTF-8
Cache-Control: no-store
Pragma: no-cache

{
        "device_code": <code issued for device>,
        "user_code": <code issued for end user>,
        "verification_uri": "https://authorizationserver.com/device",
        "expires_in": 600,
        "interval": 5
    }
```

Table 5-6 shows the authorization response parameters.

Table 5-6. *Authorization Response Parameters*

Parameter	Meaning
device_code	A code generated by the authorization server for the primary device, to be used by the device when it makes the subsequent token request.
user_code	A code generated by the authorization server for a particular end user's device authorization session, to be used when the user subsequently interacts with the authorization server on a secondary device to authorize the primary device's request.
verification_uri	A URI to be displayed or communicated to the user by the primary device, along with instructions for the user to access that URI from a secondary device to consent to the authorization request.
expires_in	Validity period for the device_code and user_code. Specified in seconds.
interval	Minimum time, specified in seconds, that the primary device should wait between polling requests.

The primary device receives an authorization response with a user verification URI, a device code, and a user code. The primary device communicates the verification URI and user code to the user in any format suitable for the device and which facilitates the user's interaction. For example, the primary device could display a text URL or a QR code. The primary device also provides instructions for the user to navigate to the verification URI on a secondary device, such as a smartphone, and enter the user code when prompted. The secondary device needs to have a user agent, such as a browser, that can support redirects to the authorization server. It also must allow the user to interact with the authorization server for authentication and consent.

When the user navigates to the verification URI, the authorization server will prompt the user to log in, enter the user code, and consent to the authorization request. The exact sequence and process for this interaction may vary by authorization server.

While the user is interacting with the authorization server on the secondary device, the primary device periodically polls the authorization server.

Polling the Authorization Server

The primary device polls the authorization server by repeatedly posting an access token request to the authorization server's token endpoint. The precise mechanism by which the primary device authenticates itself for the request may vary by authorization server and configuration settings chosen when the primary device registers at the authorization server. The interval between polling requests should be governed by the "interval" parameter returned by the authorization server, as described in Table 5-6. The following shows a sample primary device's token request, specifying the "device_code" grant type, the device code, and the client ID:

```
POST /token HTTP/1.1
Host: authorizationserver.com
Content-Type: application/x-www-form-urlencoded
grant_type=urn%3Aietf%3Aparams%3Aoauth%3Agrant-type%3Adevice_code
& device_code=<device code>
& client_id=<client id>
```

Table 5-7 shows common parameters for the token request.

Table 5-7. Token Request Parameters

Parameter	Meaning
grant_type	Indicates the type of grant requested. For this scenario, it must be set to "urn:ietf:params:oauth:grant-type:device_code".
device_code	A code generated by the authorization server for the primary device and used by the device when it makes the token request.
client_id	Identifier for the primary device, assigned when it registered with the authorization server.

The client ID and device code are used by the authorization server to associate the polling request with the primary device's initial authorization request. The primary device should make polling requests no more frequently than the number of seconds specified in the interval parameter from the authorization server response. The device code and interval parameter are shown in Table 5-6. The primary device continues polling while the user interacts with the authorization server.

If the user has not yet completed the interaction, the client device will receive either an "authorization_pending" status or a "slow_down" status. The slow_down status indicates the client device should send subsequent polling requests less frequently. If the user does not approve the request, a status of "access_denied" will be returned, and if too much time passes, a status of "expired_token" may be returned, indicating the device code is no longer valid. These error codes are in addition to the general OAuth 2 error responses for conditions such as invalid requests, client IDs, grants, grant_types, and scopes or unauthorized requests.

When the user successfully completes the interaction on the secondary device to authenticate and authorize the access request, the primary device's next polling request will result in a success response with an access token and, optionally, a refresh token as described in Table 5-4. The primary device can then use the access token to make an API call on the user's behalf, as described in the following section.

Calling an API

Once an application receives an access token via one of the grant types described in the previous sections, it can call the resource server, sending the access token with its request. OAuth 2.1 specifies that an access token must be sent in either the HTTP Authorization request header or HTTP request payload. OAuth 2.1 specifically prohibits the access token from being sent in a URI query parameter.

A common approach has been to send the access token as a bearer token, using the HTTP "Authorization" request header field with an authentication token type of "Bearer" followed by the access token as shown in the following snippet:

```
GET /api-endpoint HTTP/1.1
Host: api-server.com
Authorization: Bearer <access_token>
```

A drawback with a bearer token is that it can be used by anyone that possesses the token. If an access token is stolen, an unauthorized party could use it to make a request to the API for which the token was issued. OAuth 2.1 recommends several measures, including short-lived access tokens, to mitigate the risk of access tokens being captured and used in an unauthorized manner. These are discussed in the "Token Usage Guidance" section later in this chapter.

Refresh Tokens

As mentioned previously, access tokens have an expiration. When an access token expires, an application could make a new authorization request, but with short-lived access tokens, this could result in frequent consent requests for users which would be cumbersome. OAuth 2 defines an alternative approach that involves another type of token called a refresh token. Authorization servers may, at their discretion, return a refresh token along with an access token. If an application receives a refresh token from an authorization server, it can use it to obtain a new access token when a previous access token expires. The use of a refresh token to obtain a new access token does not require user interaction, so an application can use a refresh token to obtain a new access token when the user is offline, which facilitates ongoing API access from native mobile applications.

OAuth 2 does not include a mechanism for applications to request refresh tokens, leaving the issuance up to authorization servers. The handling of refresh tokens may therefore vary across individual authorization servers. Some issue refresh tokens automatically, and others expect an application to explicitly request a refresh token via a proprietary mechanism. (The OIDC specification, covered in the next chapter, includes a mechanism for an application to request a refresh token for one specific use case.) The documentation for your chosen authorization server should explain the implementation-specific details for refresh tokens.

A sample call with a refresh token to an authorization server's token endpoint to request a new access token is shown in the following sample. The client must authenticate itself for the request.

```
POST /token HTTP/1.1
Host: authorizationserver.com
Authorization: Basic <encoded application credentials>
Content-Type: application/x-www-form-urlencoded
grant_type=refresh_token
& refresh_token=<refresh_token>
```

The access token will be returned in a response similar to that described in previous sections. The scope parameter is optional and, if used, must be equal to, or lesser than, the scope in the original authorization request, and the client credentials passed must be those of the application which made the original authorization request.

The use of refresh tokens applies primarily to authorization flows where a user is the resource owner. There is no need for a refresh token with the client credentials grant because an application can simply request an access token programmatically at any time, without a need for user interaction.

In addition to the basic mechanics of using access tokens and refresh tokens, there are several usage guidelines which we'll cover in the next section.

Token Usage Guidance
Access Tokens

An access token is intended to be consumed by a resource server API. An application should not depend on using data in the access token (in the absence of proprietary extensions). Depending on the authorization server implementation, the format of an access token may be an opaque token or a JSON Web Token (JWT) as defined by the JSON Web Token (JWT) Profile for OAuth 2.0 Access Tokens.[xv] In the case of an opaque token, a resource server calls the authorization server's token introspection endpoint to obtain the relevant information associated with the token. In the case of a JWT, the token is self-contained and a resource server can view the JWT attributes in the token. In either case, a resource server that receives an access token must validate it before processing the request it accompanies. The process for validating a token may vary by authorization server implementation.

Access tokens have an expiration time, and in general, it is recommended that access token duration be short-lived and a new access token obtained only when needed, if the previous access token has expired. It may be tempting to automatically refresh an access token as soon as it expires, but in keeping with the principle of least privilege, it is better to only refresh an access token when it is needed, rather than always keeping a current access token on hand. The access token expiration should be determined based on the sensitivity of the resources to be accessed.

Though access tokens have an expiration, they are not one-time-use tokens. Access tokens can be cached, for a period of time less than or equal to their expiration, as a performance optimization. Caching access tokens can also reduce the risk of hitting rate limits via excessive calls to an authorization server.

An access token must have been granted the appropriate scope of privileges for an application's API calls. This should not, however, encourage the use of overly broad scopes, such as "do:anything" to avoid the work of designing an appropriate set of scopes. Applications should follow the security principle of "least privilege" to request access tokens with the minimum scope needed for a particular scenario. For example, a document viewer application that doesn't provide editing features should only request a scope such as "get:documents" rather than scopes that would allow modifying or deleting documents.

Scopes should typically be used to model the coarse-grained privileges that an application can request of an API on a user's behalf, such as "get:documents" rather than granular privileges involving specific resources. Baking specific resources into scopes can cause the number of scopes to become unwieldy to administer as the number of resources grows. In an enterprise scenario, baking user profile attributes or organization attributes used for access control into scopes will result in rework when the inevitable reorganizations occur. In addition, when the scope parameter is sent via URL, it can hit a length limitation. Additional options for authorization and access enforcement will be discussed further in Chapter 8.

Where possible, applications should request access tokens restricted to a particular resource server via a "resource" or "audience" parameter. This can prevent an access token issued for one resource server from being used at another resource server. Narrowing down the scope and intended recipient of the token can reduce the possibility of an access token being abused.

Refresh Tokens

Refresh tokens provide a convenient way for applications to obtain new access tokens. This facilitates the use of access tokens with a short duration, which minimizes risk if an access token is compromised. However, the use of refresh tokens introduces a different risk, namely, the risk of a stolen refresh token. Refresh tokens are sensitive credentials because they can be used to obtain access tokens. Applications must therefore protect and securely store both access tokens and refresh tokens. Applications should utilize the secure storage options available with their underlying platform when storing such tokens. At the time of writing, secure storage for single-page applications executing in browsers is limited. This means that use of static, long-lived refresh tokens is problematic, especially for public clients that lack mechanisms for securely storing sensitive tokens.

There are solutions to reduce the risk of compromised refresh tokens. The OAuth 2.0 Threat Model and Security Considerations[xvi] document proposed the notion of refresh token rotation to detect if a refresh token has been stolen and is being used by two or more clients. This scheme has the authorization server return a new, single-use refresh token with each access token renewal request. If a refresh token is stolen and used twice, once by the legitimate client and again by a second, malicious client, the authorization server is supposed to detect it as an anomalous situation and invalidate the refresh token.

Another approach is the use of sender-constrained tokens, which can be used with both access tokens and refresh tokens. With this approach, the authorization server binds a token it issues to the authorized client application which requested it. If an unauthorized client application steals a token and attempts to use it, the authorization server or API will detect that the client attempting to use the token is not the client to which the token was issued. Several approaches for sender-constrained tokens have been defined. We will describe two methods. At the time of writing, it is not yet clear which approach(es) will become widely adopted.

One approach for sender-constrained tokens leverages Mutual-TLS. For this scheme, a client application authenticates to an authorization server using Mutual-TLS authentication, so that the authorization server can bind an access or refresh token to the client certificate used in the Mutual-TLS authentication. When the client wants to use the token, it must authenticate to the resource server, again using Mutual-TLS, proving that it possesses the private key associated with the certificate bound with the token. This scheme is defined in the OAuth 2.0 Mutual-TLS Client Authentication and Certificate-Bound Access Tokens specification.[xvii] This specification has moved out of draft status but may result in a confusing user experience in some cases, if users are prompted to select an appropriate certificate to use.

Another scheme for sender-constrained tokens is defined in the draft (at the time of writing) OAuth 2.0 Demonstrating Proof-of-Possession at the Application Layer (DPoP) specification.[xviii] With DPoP, when a client application sends an authorization grant or refresh token to get an access token, it creates and cryptographically signs a JSON Web Token (JWT). This token, called a DPoP proof JWT, includes the public key that corresponds to the private key used to sign the JWT. The client application includes the DPoP proof JWT in its request to the authorization server. The authorization server responds with an access token that includes a hash of the public key from the request. This binds the token to the public key. When the client application makes a request to the resource server, it sends the token, bound to the public key, and also sends another DPoP proof JWT demonstrating that it has possession of the original signing material. DPoP is currently being actively developed and we expect it will be adopted in the future.

OAuth 2.1 specifies that authorization servers must use either refresh token rotation or sender-constrained refresh tokens (bound to a particular client) with public clients to mitigate the risk of compromised refresh tokens. At the time of writing, it is not yet clear which of these solutions will become widely adopted and how long it will take. Check the documentation for your OAuth 2 provider for details on support for refresh token rotation and/or sender-constrained tokens.

Confidentiality and Integrity

The protocol interactions we have described in this chapter assume the use of a suitably up-to-date version of Transport Layer Security (TLS) between the application and the OAuth 2 authorization server, between the application and the resource server, and for interaction between the resource server and authorization server, if any. The OAuth 2 specifications state that authorization servers must require the use of TLS for requests to the authorization and token endpoints and that applications should enforce the use of TLS for the application callback. Further security implementation guidance can be found in the Security Considerations section of the OAuth 2.1 Authorization Framework document.[xix]

Applications must take suitable measures to ensure the security of access tokens and refresh tokens. Applications must perform all token validation checks recommended by their authorization server as well as a TLS certificate check when calling the resource server to ensure a request is sent to the correct resource server. Applications must use secure storage when storing sensitive tokens and take care to prevent leakage of such tokens. In addition, secure coding practices must be used, including implementing measures against attacks such as Cross-Site Scripting (XSS) and Cross-Site Request Forgery (CSRF), as applicable for the type of application.

Token Revocation

Applications should revoke refresh tokens and access tokens if possible, when they are no longer needed. The OAuth 2.0 Token Revocation[xx] specification defines a mechanism for clients to request the revocation of access tokens and refresh tokens. The ability to revoke access tokens, however, is not a mandatory feature, so some authorization servers may not support it. You'll need to check the documentation for your OAuth 2 provider to determine support for revoking tokens. Additional discussion of token revocation with respect to logout is discussed in Chapter 13.

Further Learning

The preceding sections covered an introduction to how an application requests API authorization via OAuth 2. We realize it may seem like a lot to learn. An SDK may abstract and simplify the OAuth 2 interaction for you, and we recommend checking for the availability of SDKs for your platform. We should also note that it is beyond the scope of this chapter to cover every application implementation requirement mentioned in the specifications as they vary by application scenario. Application implementers should review the specifications for the latest version of implementation requirements for their type of application as well as guidance from any SDKs used.

Advanced Use Cases

There are additional, more complex use cases for which additional parameters and extensions to the core protocol have been advanced, such as the "OAuth 2.0 Token Exchange" specification.[xxi] It is beyond the scope of this book to provide sufficient guidance for how to implement such use cases securely, so we will only mention that there is a lot more to explore and learn about. We hope that this introduction to OAuth 2 prepares and encourages you to explore additional use cases and extensions in the future.

Summary

The OAuth 2 protocol enables an application to obtain authorization to call an API on either a user's behalf or on its own behalf. This eliminates the requirement for users to share their credentials with the application. It also provides the user greater control over what the application can do and a limit on the duration of API access. The user can revoke API access for an individual application without impacting the ability of other applications to call the API on their behalf. Once you have an application authorized to call an API, you'll want to authenticate users to that application, which is covered in the next chapter.

Key Points

- OAuth 2 enables applications to request authorization and obtain an access token to call resource server APIs.

- With OAuth 2, a user has control over API authorizations for applications.

- Scopes can be used to control the access an application has when calling an API.

- The original OAuth 2.0 specification defined four authorization grant types but two of these were removed in OAuth 2.1.

- The OAuth 2.1 specification removes the implicit authorization grant type as it is no longer needed and can expose an access token to potential compromise. The authorization code grant type with PKCE should be used instead.

- The OAuth 2.1 specification removes the resource owner password credentials authorization grant type as it exposes user credentials to client applications.

- The authorization code grant type with PKCE can be used by traditional web applications, public applications, as well as native applications.

- The client credentials grant type is for API calls where the application owns the requested resource.

- The Device Authorization Grant type is an extension defined to enable flows involving client devices that lack the capability needed for user interaction to authenticate and authorize requests.

- A refresh token is used to obtain a new access token when a previous access token has expired.

- Refresh tokens should be sender-constrained or employ a refresh token rotation scheme.

- Applications must take measures to secure access tokens and refresh tokens.

- Applications must use a suitably up-to-date version of Transport Layer Security (TLS) for communications with an OAuth 2 authorization server.

Notes

i. https://datatracker.ietf.org/doc/html/draft-ietf-oauth-v2-1-06

ii. https://tools.ietf.org/html/rfc6749

iii. https://www.rfc-editor.org/rfc/rfc7636

iv. https://www.rfc-editor.org/rfc/rfc7636#section-4.2

v. https://datatracker.ietf.org/doc/html/rfc8707

vi. https://www.rfc-editor.org/rfc/rfc7636

vii. https://datatracker.ietf.org/doc/html/rfc7662

viii. https://datatracker.ietf.org/doc/html/rfc9068

ix. https://www.w3.org/wiki/CORS

x. https://datatracker.ietf.org/doc/html/draft-ietf-oauth-security-topics-21#section-2.1.2

xi. https://tools.ietf.org/html/rfc8252

xii. https://datatracker.ietf.org/doc/html/draft-ietf-oauth-security-topics-21#section-2.4

xiii. https://datatracker.ietf.org/doc/html/rfc8628

xiv. https://datatracker.ietf.org/doc/html/rfc8707

xv. https://datatracker.ietf.org/doc/html/rfc9068

xvi. https://datatracker.ietf.org/doc/html/rfc6819

xvii. https://datatracker.ietf.org/doc/html/rfc8705

xviii. https://datatracker.ietf.org/doc/html/draft-ietf-oauth-dpop

xix. https://datatracker.ietf.org/doc/html/draft-ietf-oauth-v2-1-06#section-7

xx. https://datatracker.ietf.org/doc/html/rfc7009

xxi. https://datatracker.ietf.org/doc/html/rfc8693

CHAPTER 6

OpenID Connect

In the social jungle of human existence, there is no feeling of being alive without a sense of identity.

—Erik Erikson, German-American developmental psychologist and psychoanalyst who coined the phrase "Identity crisis," from *Identities: Youth and Crisis* (1968)

As described in the previous chapter, OAuth 2 provides a framework for authorizing applications to call APIs, but isn't designed for authenticating users to applications. The OpenID Connect (OIDC)[1] protocol provides an identity service layer on top of OAuth 2, designed to allow authorization servers to authenticate users for applications and return the results in a standard way. Some implementations of OAuth 2 added proprietary additions to do this, but a standard solution was needed. In this chapter, we'll describe the problem OIDC solves in more detail and how an application can use OIDC to authenticate a user.

Problem to Solve

The scenario OIDC is designed to solve involves a user who needs to be authenticated in order to access an application. OIDC enables an application to delegate user authentication to an OAuth 2 authorization server and have it return to the application a set of claims about the authenticated user and authentication event in a standard format. Figure 6-1 provides an illustration of how this works.

© Yvonne Wilson, Abhishek Hingnikar 2023
Y. Wilson and A. Hingnikar, *Solving Identity Management in Modern Applications*,
https://doi.org/10.1007/978-1-4842-8261-8_6

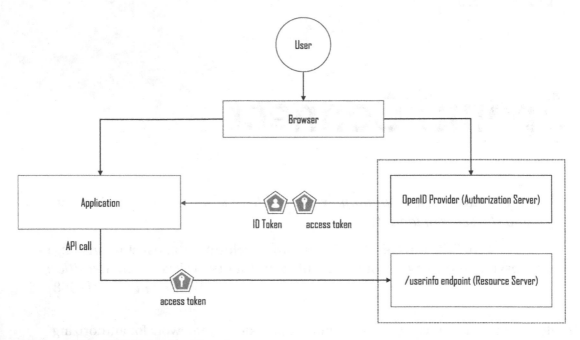

Figure 6-1. *OIDC Authentication*

When a user accesses an application, it redirects the user's browser (or similar user agent for native/mobile apps) to an authorization server that implements OIDC. OIDC calls such an authorization server an OpenID Provider, so we'll use that term in this chapter. The OpenID Provider interacts with the user to authenticate them (assuming they haven't logged in already). After authentication, the user's browser is redirected back to the application. The application can request that claims about the authenticated user be returned in a security token called an ID Token. Alternatively, it can request an OAuth 2 access token and use it to call the OpenID Provider's UserInfo endpoint to obtain the claims. Because OIDC is a layer on top of OAuth 2, an application can use an OpenID Provider for both user authentication and authorization to call the OpenID Provider's API. We've glossed over a few details in this first description just to convey the basic concept. The next section will define some additional terms so we can provide further details and a more accurate description.

Terminology

OIDC defines the following terms.

Roles

There are three different roles involved in the OIDC solution:

- **End User** – The end user is a subject to be authenticated. (We will use the term "user" for simplicity and consistency across chapters.)

- **OpenID Provider (OP)** – The OpenID Provider is an OAuth 2 authorization server that implements OIDC and can authenticate a user and return claims about the authenticated user and the authentication event to a relying party (application).

- **Relying Party (RP)** – An OAuth 2 client which delegates user authentication to an OpenID Provider and requests claims about the user from the OpenID Provider. We will generally use the term "application" for the relying party for consistency across chapters, but a relying party could be another identity provider in more advanced use cases.

Client Types

The OIDC specification references the public and confidential application types as described in the previous chapter as well as native applications, defined in the "OAuth 2.0 for Native Apps"[ii] best current practice document as applications installed on, and run natively on, a user's device.

Tokens and Authorization Code

OIDC uses the authorization code, access token, and refresh token as described in the previous chapter for OAuth 2 and defines a new token called an ID Token.

- **ID Token** – A token used to convey claims about an authentication event and an authenticated user to a relying party (application).

Endpoints

OIDC utilizes the authorization and token endpoints described in the previous chapter for OAuth 2 and adds the UserInfo endpoint.

- **UserInfo Endpoint** – Returns claims about an authenticated user. Calling the endpoint requires an access token, and the claims returned are governed by the access token.

ID Token

An ID Token is a security token used by an OpenID Provider to convey claims to an application about an authentication event and authenticated user. ID Tokens are encoded in JSON Web Token (JWT)[iii] format. Figure 6-2 shows a sample ID Token.

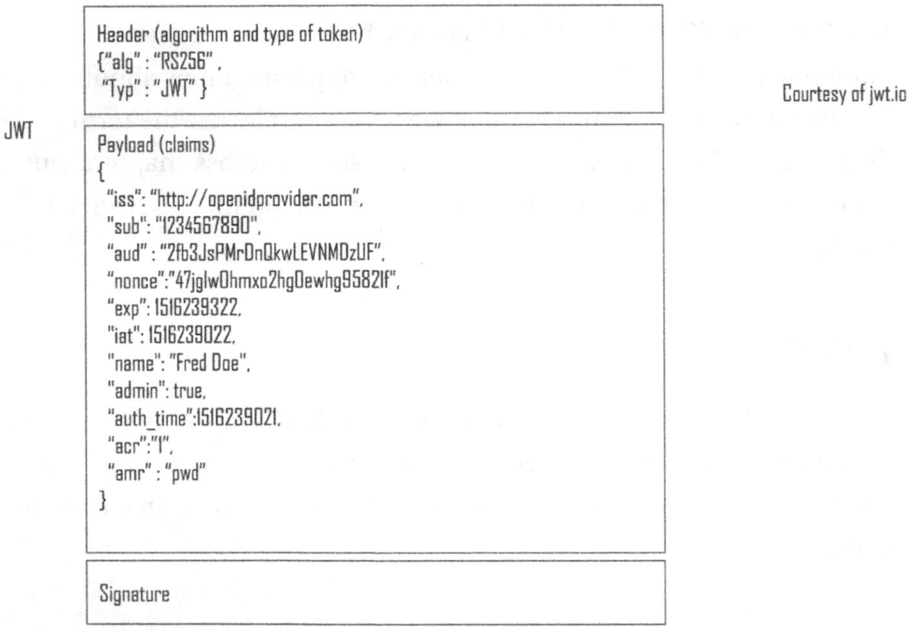

Figure 6-2. Sample ID Token

The JWT format is designed to convey claims between two parties. As a JWT, an ID Token consists of a header, a payload, and a signature. The header section of the ID Token contains information on the type of object (JWT) and the specific signature algorithm used to protect the integrity of the claims in the payload. Common signature algorithms are HS256 (HMAC with SHA256) or RS256 (RSA Signature with SHA256).

The payload section contains the claims about a user and the authentication event. The signature section contains a digital signature based on the payload section of the ID Token and a secret key known to the OpenID Provider.

The OpenID Provider signs the JWT in accordance with the JSON Web Signature (JWS) specification.[iv] A relying party application can validate the signature on the ID Token to check the integrity of the claims in it. For confidentiality, the OpenID Provider can optionally encrypt the JWT using JSON Web Encryption (JWE)[v] after it is signed. If this is done, it produces a nested JWT.

The name:value pairs in the payload section of the ID Token JWT are the claims about an authenticated user and authentication event. The OIDC specification (Section 2) defines a set of claims for ID Tokens applicable to all types of OIDC authentication requests,[vi] shown in Table 6-1.

Table 6-1. *OIDC Claims in ID Tokens for All OIDC Flows*

Claim	Meaning
iss	Issuer of the ID Token, identified in URL format. The issuer is typically the OpenID Provider. The "iss" claim should not include URL query or fragment components.
sub	Unique (within the OpenID Provider), case-sensitive string identifier for the authenticated user or subject entity, no more than 255 ASCII characters long. The identifier in the subclaim should never be reassigned to a new user or entity.
aud	Client ID of the relying party (application) for which the ID Token is intended. May be a single, case-sensitive string or an array of the same if there are multiple audiences.
exp	Expiration time for the ID Token, specified as the number of seconds since January 1, 1970, 00:00:00 UTC to the time of token expiration. Applications must consider an ID Token invalid after this time, with a few minutes of tolerance allowed for clock skew.
iat	Time at which the ID Token was issued, specified as the number of seconds since January 1, 1970, 00:00:00 UTC to the time of ID Token issuance.
auth_ time	Time at which the user was authenticated, specified as the number of seconds since January 1, 1970, 00:00:00 UTC to the time of authentication.

(continued)

Table 6-1. (*continued*)

Claim	Meaning
nonce	Unguessable, case-sensitive string value passed in authentication request from the relying party and added by an OpenID Provider to an ID Token to link the ID Token to a relying party application session and to facilitate detection of replayed ID Tokens.
amr	String containing an authentication method reference – used to indicate the method(s) of authentication used to authenticate the subject of the ID Token. The Authentication Method Reference Values specification[vii] defines a set of initial standard values for this claim.
acr	String containing an authentication context class reference – used to indicate authentication context class for the authentication mechanism used to authenticate the subject of the ID Token. Values may be decided by OpenID Provider or agreed upon between relying party and OpenID Provider and might use standards such as the draft OpenID Connect Extended Authentication Profile ACR values.[viii]
azp	Client ID of the authorized party to which the ID_Token is issued. Typically not used unless the ID Token only has a single audience in the "aud" claim and that audience is different from the authorized party, though it can be used even if the audience and authorized party are the same.

An ID Token can contain additional claims beyond those listed in Table 6-1. Examples of additional standard claims[ix] which may be added are the user's name, given_name, family_name, email, email_verified, locale, and picture. A list of additional standard claims can be found in Section 5.1 of the OIDC core specification.[x] Specific types of OIDC requests (flows) may involve additional claims. Custom claims can also be defined and added by an OpenID Provider.

How It Works

OIDC defines three different flows by which an application can interact with an OpenID Provider to make an authentication request.

OIDC Flows

The OIDC flows are designed around the constraints of different types of applications and bear some similarity to the grant types defined in OAuth 2. The original OIDC core specification defines the following flows:

- Authorization Code Flow

- Implicit Flow

- Hybrid Flow

The following sections cover each of these flows in more detail.

OIDC Authorization Code Flow

The OIDC Authorization Code Flow is similar to the OAuth 2 authorization code grant in relying upon two requests and an intermediary authorization code. To authenticate a user, an application redirects the user's browser to an OpenID Provider. The OpenID Provider authenticates the user and redirects the user's browser back to the application with an authorization code. The application uses the authorization code to obtain an ID Token, access token, and optionally a refresh token, from the OpenID Provider's token endpoint. Figure 6-3 depicts this flow, assuming the application requested all three security tokens and the user had no existing login session. This diagram also shows the use of PKCE, as explained in Chapter 5.

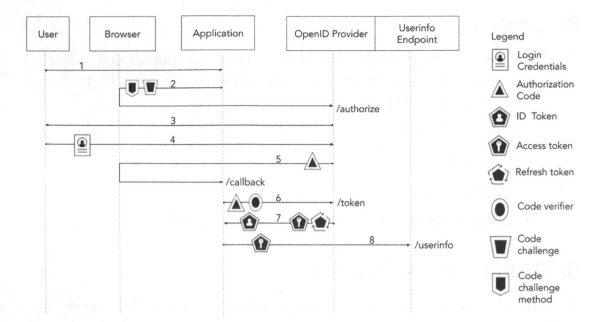

Figure 6-3. *OIDC Authorization Code Flow*

1. The user accesses the application (relying party).

2. The user's browser redirected to the OpenID Provider with an authentication request.

3. The OpenID Provider interacts with the user for authentication and to obtain consent for the scope of user info request.

4. The user authenticates and gives consent, and the OpenID Provider creates or updates an authentication session for the user.

5. The user's browser redirected back to the application with authorization code.

6. The application sends a token request to the OpenID Provider, with the authorization code.

7. The OpenID Provider responds with an ID Token, access token, and optionally a refresh token.

8. The application can use the access token at the OpenID Provider's UserInfo endpoint, described later in this chapter.

The second call to the token endpoint to obtain the security tokens assumes the application has the ability to authenticate itself to the OpenID Provider. Public client applications that cannot securely maintain a secret for such authentication can use Proof Key for Code Exchange (PKCE) as described in the previous chapter. The use of PKCE is designed to mitigate the risk of an authorization code being intercepted by an unauthorized party. The following sample requests assume the use of PKCE.

Authentication Request

An application redirects the user's browser with an authentication request to the OpenID Provider's authorization endpoint such as

```
GET /authorize?
response_type=code
& client_id=<client_id>
& state=<state_value>
& nonce=<nonce_value>
& scope=<scope>
& redirect_uri=<callback_url>
& code_challenge=<code_challenge>
& code_challenge_method=<code_challenge_method> HTTP/1.1
Host: authorizationserver.com
```

The parameters used in the example are described in Table 6-2, but may vary by individual OpenID Provider.

Table 6-2. *OIDC Authentication Request Parameters*

Parameter	Meaning
response_type	The response type indicates which OIDC flow to use. "code" indicates that the Authorization Code Flow should be used.
response_mode	An optional parameter used to request a nondefault mechanism to be used by the authorization server to deliver response parameters to the client application.
client_id	The client ID for the relying party application, obtained when it registered with the OpenID Provider (authorization server).
state	An unguessable value passed to the OpenID Provider in the request. The OpenID Provider is supposed to return the exact same state parameter and value in a success response. Used by the relying party application to validate the response corresponds to a request it sent previously. This helps protect against token injection and CSRF (Cross-Site Request Forgery).
nonce	An unguessable value passed to the OpenID Provider in the request and returned unmodified as a claim in the ID Token if an ID Token is requested. Used to protect against token replay.
scope	A string specifying the claims requested about the authenticated user. Example scope: "openid%20profile%20email".
redirect_uri	URI where the OpenID Provider directs the response upon completion of the authentication request. For example: "https%3A%2F%2Fclient%2Eexample%2Ecom%2Fcallback".
code_challenge	PKCE code challenge derived from the PKCE code verifier using the code challenge method specified in the code_challenge_method parameter, as described in Section 4.2 of the PKCE specification.[xi]
code_challenge_method	"S256" or "plain." Applications capable of using S256 (SHA256 hash) must use it.

The response_type parameter in the authentication request is used to indicate the desired OIDC flow. For the Authorization Code Flow, the response_type should be "code," appropriately named as it returns an authorization code to the application. This OIDC flow is similar to the authorization code grant described in the previous chapter.

The optional response_mode parameter governs the method by which the response parameters are returned to the application. With the "query" response mode, the response from the OpenID Provider is returned in a query string appended to the redirect URI specified in the request. This mode is the default when the "code" response type is used. With the "fragment" response mode, the response from the OpenID Provider is included in a fragment appended to the redirect URI. This is the default response mode for the "token" response type, discussed later in this chapter. These two response modes are defined in the "OAuth 2.0 Multiple Response Type Encoding Practices" specification.[xii] Unless otherwise noted, the examples in this chapter do not include response_mode as they assume the use of the default response mode for each flow.

The scope parameter in OAuth 2 is used to request API privileges to be represented via an access token. With OIDC authentication requests, the scope is used to indicate the use of OIDC and request particular claims about the authenticated user. OIDC authentication requests must include the "openid" scope value. The string "openid profile email" is a sample scope value. Adding "profile" to the scope value requests a set of default user profile claims such as name, family name, and given name. Adding "email" requests the user's email address and whether that address has been validated. When the response_type results in the issuance of an access token, the scope applies to the claims returned by the OpenID Provider's UserInfo endpoint. If an access token is not issued, the requested claims will be included in the ID Token. Additional details on requesting claims can be found in Sections 5.4 and 5.5 of the OpenID Connect Core specification.[xiii]

Another optional parameter, called "nonce," is important to mention. The nonce value should be included if an ID Token is requested. When an application makes an authentication request to an OpenID Provider, it should specify a unique, nonguessable nonce value that is tied to the session an application has started for the user. One option is to generate a random value, store it securely in the user session, and use its hash as the nonce. When the application receives an ID Token, it must check that the token contains the exact nonce value specified in the authentication request and that the nonce matches the hash of the value previously stored in the session. This links an ID Token with a user's application session and mitigates the risk of ID Tokens being replayed.

There are several additional, optional parameters which may be passed in an authentication request to govern how and whether an OpenID Provider prompts a user to authenticate and provide consent, to specify preferred language(s), to pass hints about a user's session or identifier, or to request specific user claims. See Section 3.1.2.1 of the OpenID Core specification[xiv] for further information.

Authentication Response

The OpenID Provider returns a response to the redirect URI specified in the authentication request and which must be registered with the OpenID Provider. For the Authorization Code Flow, the default response mode returns the authorization code using a query parameter to the redirect URI (callback) specified in the authentication request. It also returns the exact state value that was passed in the authentication request.

```
HTTP/1.1 302 Found
Location: https://clientapplication.com/callback?
code=<authorization_code>
& state=<state_value>
```

The application should check to see if the response contains any error codes and if the state value returned with a response matches the state value it sent in its authentication request. It can then use the authorization code to make a token request. An application should take care to only use each authorization code once as the server is obligated to respond with an error if an authorization code has already been used.

Token Request

The authorization code returned by an OpenID Provider is used by an application in a token request to the OpenID Provider's token endpoint. The following sample request assumes a confidential client application that was registered at the OpenID Provider to authenticate with a client secret and HTTP Basic authentication.

```
POST /token HTTP/1.1
Host: authorizationserver.com
Content-Type: application/x-www-form-urlencoded
Authorization: Basic <encoded client credentials>
 grant_type=authorization_code
& code=<authorization_code>
& redirect_uri=<redirect_uri>
& code_verifier=<code_verifier>
```

The registration for an application at an OpenID Provider may specify one of several authentication methods to be used with token requests. Further information on the defined authentication methods can be found in Section 9 of the OIDC Core specification.[xv] The parameters for the sample token request are shown in Table 6-3.

Table 6-3. *OIDC Parameters for Sample Token Request*

Parameter	Meaning
grant_type	"authorization_code" is used when exchanging an authorization code for tokens.
code	The authorization code received in response to the authentication request.
redirect_ uri	Callback location at the application for the OpenID Provider's response from this call.
code_ verifier	The PKCE code verifier value from which the code challenge in the authentication request was derived. It should be an unguessable, cryptographically random string between 43 and 128 characters in length, inclusive, using the characters A–Z, a–z, 0–9, "-", ".", "_", and "~" and formed as described in Section 4.1 of the PKCE specification.[xvi]

The OpenID Provider will respond with the requested tokens in JSON format. The following shows a sample response:

```
HTTP/ 1.1 200 OK
Content-Type: application/json;charset=UTF-8
    Cache-Control: no-store
    Pragma: no-cache
{
    "id_token" : <id_token>,
    "access_token" : <access_token value>,
    "refresh_token" : <refresh_token value>,
    "token_type" : "Bearer",
    "expires_in" : <token lifetime>
}
```

The sample response elements are described in Table 6-4.

Table 6-4. *Response Elements for Token Requests*

Parameter	Meaning
id_token	The ID Token with user claims.
access_token	The access token for the OpenID Provider's UserInfo endpoint.
refresh_token	A refresh token, if a refresh token was requested or is returned by default.
token type	Bearer is typically used unless an OpenID Provider has documented another type.
expires_in	The lifetime of the access token, in seconds.

Before relying on claims in an ID Token, an application should validate the ID Token following guidance provided by the issuing OpenID Provider and the validation steps in the JWT specification.[xvii] The application can obtain claims about the authenticated user from the ID Token or by using the access token to call the OpenID Provider's UserInfo endpoint.

OIDC Implicit Flow

The Implicit Flow in OIDC is similar to the OAuth 2 grant type of the same name. As explained in Chapter 5, the use of the OAuth 2 implicit grant to obtain an access token, at least with default response mode, is no longer recommended and has been removed from the OAuth 2.1 version of the specification. However, that guidance is based on the risk of exposing an access token in a URL fragment which can be leaked via the browser history or referer header. An application that only needs to authenticate users and can obtain user information via an ID Token does not need an access token. In this case, the OIDC Implicit Flow may be acceptable. Figure 6-4 shows this flow with the application receiving only an ID Token.

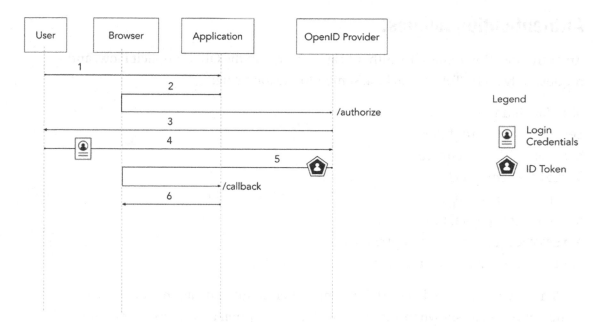

Figure 6-4. *OIDC Implicit Flow*

1. The user accesses the application (relying party).

2. The user's browser redirected to the OpenID Provider with an authentication request.

3. The OpenID Provider interacts with the user for authentication and to obtain consent for the scope of user info request.

4. The user provides login credentials and consent, and the OpenID Provider creates or updates an authentication session for the user.

5. The user's browser redirected back to the application with an ID Token.

6. The application obtains user claims from the ID Token and displays suitable application content to the user.

Authentication Request

An authentication request to authenticate a user with the OIDC Implicit Flow, and request only an ID Token, will look similar to the following:

```
GET /authorize?
response_type=id_token
& client_id=<client_id>
& state=<state_value>
& nonce=<nonce_value>
& scope=<scope_value>
& redirect_uri=<callback_url> HTTP/1.1
Host: authorizationserver.com
```

The parameters used in the OIDC Implicit Flow authentication request have the same definition as shown in Table 6-2, with the exception of response_type values. For the Implicit Flow, the allowed response_type values are

- "id_token" – Response contains only an ID Token.

- "id_token token" – Response contains an ID Token and access token.

By default, the OIDC Implicit Flow returns all tokens via front-channel browser interaction to the redirect URI, using a URL fragment. The use of "id_token token" response_type is not recommended with the default response mode as it would expose an access token to potential compromise through a referer header or the browser's history.[xviii] Using the OIDC Implicit Flow with the default response mode and "id_token" response_type to return only an ID Token avoids this risk, assuming the ID Token does not contain sensitive data.

Another option is to use a nondefault response mode. The OAuth 2.0 Form Post Response Mode specification[xix] defines a response mode, "form_post," which results in the response from the authorization server being encoded in an HTML form sent via HTTP-POST to the application. This response mode could be considered for applications needing only an ID Token. This avoids exposing the ID Token and data in it via a URL fragment, but this response mode may not be feasible for some application types. Public clients needing an access token and/or ID Token with sensitive elements should use the Authorization Code Flow with PKCE instead.

It is unclear if authorization servers and OpenID Providers will terminate support for the Implicit Flow. New applications should use the Authorization Code Flow with PKCE instead of Implicit Flow. Existing applications that use the Implicit Flow should consider replacing it to reduce the risk of access token exposure as well as a potential end-of-life announcement from their OpenID Provider.

Authentication Response

The following shows a sample response to an Implicit Flow authentication request that used an "id_token" response type to request only an ID Token. This approach can be used if the claims in the ID Token do not contain sensitive data.

```
HTTP/1.1 302 Found
Location: https://clientapplication.com/callback#
 id_token=<id_token>
& state = <state>
```

OIDC Hybrid Flow

The OIDC Hybrid Flow includes elements of both the OIDC Authorization Code Flow and OIDC Implicit Flow. It is designed for applications with both a secure back end and a front end with client-side JavaScript executing in a browser. The OIDC Hybrid Flow enables models such as returning an ID Token and authorization code in a front-channel response to the application front end, leaving the application back end to obtain an access token (and optional refresh token) from the token endpoint using the authorization code. This flow is shown in Figure 6-5.

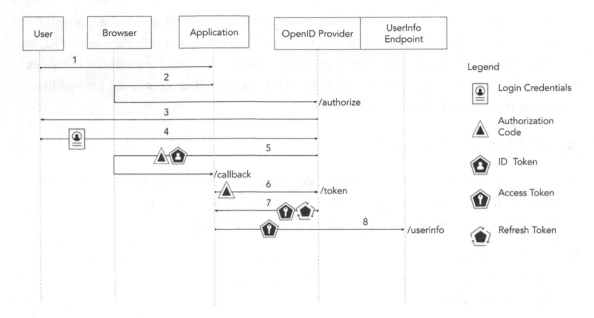

Figure 6-5. *OIDC Hybrid Flow*

1. The user accesses the application (relying party).

2. The user's browser redirected to the OpenID Provider with an authentication request.

3. The OpenID Provider interacts with the user for authentication and to obtain consent for the scope of user info request.

4. The user authenticates and provides consent, and the OpenID Provider creates or updates an authentication session for the user.

5. The user's browser redirected back to the application front end with an authorization code and ID Token.

6. The client application validates the ID Token, and, if valid, the back end calls the token endpoint with authorization code to get additional tokens.

7. The OpenID Provider token endpoint returns requested tokens.

8. The client application can call the OpenID Provider's UserInfo endpoint with an access token.

Authentication Request

The parameters for the authentication request are as defined in Table 6-2 with the exception that the response_type for the OIDC Hybrid Flow uses three different values to govern which tokens are returned in the response from the OpenID Provider's authorization endpoint. Additional tokens can be requested via the subsequent token request to the token endpoint. Table 6-5 summarizes the possible values for response_type.

Table 6-5. *OIDC Hybrid Flow Response Types*

response_type	Returned from Authorization Endpoint
"code id_token"	Authorization code, id_token
"code token"	Authorization code, access token – NOT recommended with default response_ mode
"code id_token token"	Authorization code, id_token, access token – NOT recommended with default response_mode

The response_types which return an access token via front-channel response from the authorization endpoint, namely, "code token" and "code id_token token," are not recommended for use with the default response mode as the access token would be exposed as a URL fragment in the browser and possibly leaked via referer headers or browser history.[xx] If the default response mode is used, the "code id_token" response_ type should be used to return only the ID Token and authorization code using a front-channel response to the browser. An access token, and optional refresh token, can then be obtained from the OpenID Provider's token endpoint via secure back-channel interaction from the application's back end. In practice, the Hybrid Flow is not widely used. Using this flow requires an application implementation that will provide both the front-end and back-end with information, such as nonce and state, with which to validate any responses and security tokens they receive as well as prevent attacks such as CSRF or token injection. Applications should consider using the Authorization Code Flow with PKCE unless they have a specific use case that requires the OIDC Hybrid Flow.

A sample authentication request using the OIDC Hybrid Flow and "code id_token" response type and default response mode is shown in the following example, with parameter definitions similar to previous examples:

```
GET /authorize?
response_type=code%20id_token
&client_id=<client_identifier>
&redirect_uri=<callback_url>
&scope=<scope_value>
&state=<state_value>
&nonce=<nonce_value> HTTP/1.1
Host: authorizationserver.com
```

Authentication Response

When the application receives the response, the application back end can use the authorization code at the OpenID Provider's token endpoint as described in the previous section for OIDC Authorization Code Flow.

UserInfo Endpoint

An application can retrieve claims about a user from the OpenID Provider's UserInfo endpoint. The UserInfo endpoint is an OAuth 2 API endpoint, and to call it requires an access token issued by the OpenID Provider. When requesting the access token, an application uses the scope parameter to indicate the desired claims about the user. The OpenID Provider authenticates the user and obtains their consent for the requested claims and then issues the access token with the authorized scope for the claims to the application. The application then uses the access token to request the claims from the UserInfo endpoint. A sample application request to the UserInfo endpoint looks like the following:

```
GET /userinfo HTTP/1.1
Host: authorizationserver.com
Authorization: Bearer <access_token>
```

The OpenID Provider's UserInfo endpoint response returns claims with a JSON object (unless signed or encrypted responses are used). The following sample response assumes the requested scope was "openid profile email":

```
HTTP/1.1 200 OK
Content-Type: application/json
{
    "sub": "1234567",
    "name": "Fred Smith",
    "given_name": "Fred",
    "family_name": "Smith",
    "preferred_username": "fred.smith",
    "email": "fred.smith@example.com",
    "email_verified": true,
    "picture":"https://example.com/fred.smith/fred.smith.jpg",
}
```

An application should perform any validation on responses recommended by its specific OpenID Provider.

The UserInfo endpoint is primarily useful if the desired user profile claims are too large for an ID Token returned via a URL fragment or if the claims contain sensitive information.

Further Learning

The three OIDC flows described earlier all assume that the end user initiates an action in an application on their device, which triggers the need for authentication, which in turn redirects the user to an OpenID Provider. In other words, the application that initiates the authentication request is assumed to be running on the same device where the user will authenticate. There are some common scenarios, however, where a different flow is needed. The OIDC Client-Initiated Backchannel Authentication Flow (CIBA) defines a flow where an application used by a third party, such as a bank teller, a support agent, or even a self-service point-of-sale terminal, can initiate an authentication request to an OpenID Provider to have it authenticate and provide claims about a particular user. The OpenID Provider then initiates an interaction with the user on a device, such as a cellphone, to authenticate them. The key difference with this flow is that the application that needs to authenticate the user is not running on the user's device. Covering this flow in detail is beyond the scope of this introductory book, but it is mentioned here for awareness and a more detailed description can be found in the OpenID Connect Client-Initiated Backchannel Authentication Flow specification.[xxi]

Summary

In this chapter, we've discussed a mechanism for authenticating a user and how an application can obtain information from an OIDC Provider about the authenticated user. The OpenID Connect protocol provides an identity layer on top of OAuth 2 that supports authenticating users to applications and enables single sign-on. Adding to OAuth 2, OIDC adds an ID Token and a UserInfo endpoint, which return claims about an authentication event and the authenticated user to the application. Using OIDC allows applications to delegate user authentication to an OpenID Provider, and using OIDC and OAuth 2 together solves both authentication and API authorization. In later chapters, we'll cover additional application tasks, such as the need to maintain a session for a user, single sign-on, and logout, including awareness of when a user's session at the OIDC Provider has terminated. Before we leave the topic of authentication, however, in case you encounter customers that ask you to support the older authentication protocol known as SAML 2, we'll cover an overview of that in the next chapter.

Key Points

- OIDC provides an identity layer on top of OAuth 2 to authenticate users.

- OIDC enables single sign-on.

- OIDC provides an ID Token and UserInfo endpoint to obtain user profile info.

- OIDC defines a set of standard claims that can be obtained about a user.

- OIDC allows for the use of additional, custom claims.

- OIDC defines three grant flows for different client profiles.

- OIDC provides several options for returning an authorization code and/or security tokens via front-channel or back-channel response.

- Returning access tokens or refresh tokens via front-channel responses should be avoided by using a back-channel response or alternate response mode.

- Returning sensitive information in ID Tokens via front-channel responses should be avoided by using a back-channel response or the UserInfo endpoint or encrypting the ID Token if encryption is supported.

- The OIDC CIBA flow allows an application used by a third party to send a request to an OpenID Provider to authenticate a user via a device in the user's possession such as their cellphone.

Notes

i. https://openid.net/connect/

ii. https://tools.ietf.org/html/rfc8252

iii. https://tools.ietf.org/html/rfc7519

iv. https://tools.ietf.org/html/rfc7515

v. https://tools.ietf.org/html/rfc7516

vi. https://openid.net/specs/openid-connect-core-1_0. html#IDToken

vii. https://datatracker.ietf.org/doc/html/rfc8176

viii. https://openid.net/specs/openid-connect-eap-acr-values-1_0.html

ix. https://openid.net/specs/openid-connect-core-1_0. html#StandardClaims

x. https://openid.net/specs/openid-connect-core-1_0. html#StandardClaims

xi. https://tools.ietf.org/html/rfc7636

xii.   https://openid.net/specs/oauth-v2-multiple-response-types-1_0.html

xiii. https://openid.net/specs/openid-connect-core-1_0.html#ScopeClaims

xiv.   https://openid.net/specs/openid-connect-core-1_0.html#AuthRequest

xv.   https://openid.net/specs/openid-connect-core-1_0.html#ClientAuthentication

xvi.   https://tools.ietf.org/html/rfc7636

xvii. https://tools.ietf.org/html/rfc7519#section-7.2

xviii. https://datatracker.ietf.org/doc/html/draft-ietf-oauth-security-topics-21#section-2.1.2

xix.   https://openid.net/specs/oauth-v2-form-post-response-mode-1_0.html

xx.   https://datatracker.ietf.org/doc/html/draft-ietf-oauth-security-topics-21#section-2.1.2

xxi.   https://openid.net/specs/openid-client-initiated-backchannel-authentication-core-1_0-final.html

CHAPTER 7

SAML 2

To be trusted is a greater compliment than to be loved.

—George MacDonald, from *The Marquis of Lossie* (1877)

The Security Assertion Markup Language (SAML) 2[i] is known for providing two important features, cross-domain single sign-on (SSO) and identity federation. SAML 2 has been adopted in many enterprise environments because it enabled the enterprise to have applications used by employees, customers, and partners delegate user authentication to a centralized enterprise identity provider. This gave the enterprise a central place to manage and control identities. If you are writing an application for large enterprise customers, they may expect you to support authentication using SAML 2.

In this chapter, we'll provide an overview of SAML 2, the problem it is designed to solve, and the cross-domain single sign-on and identity federation features in SAML 2. We'll also provide a suggestion for how to leverage newer protocols like OIDC in your application and still efficiently implement support for SAML.[1]

Problem to Solve

The most common use case for which SAML is used in our experience is cross-domain single sign-on. In this scenario, a user needs to access multiple applications which reside in different domains, such as application1.com and application2.com. Without cross-domain single sign-on, a user might have to establish an account in each application and log in to each application individually. This means potentially many different usernames and passwords for a user to remember. If the user is a corporate employee and the

---

[1] All unqualified uses of the term "SAML" refer to SAML 2.0.

© Yvonne Wilson, Abhishek Hingnikar 2023
Y. Wilson and A. Hingnikar, *Solving Identity Management in Modern Applications*,
https://doi.org/10.1007/978-1-4842-8261-8_7

applications are SaaS applications, it would be difficult for the enterprise to manage all the SaaS application accounts their employees create.

SAML was designed as an "eXtensible Markup Language (XML)–based framework for describing and exchanging security information between online business partners."[ii] SAML enables applications to delegate user authentication to a remote entity known as an identity provider. The identity provider authenticates the user and returns to the application an assertion with information about the authenticated user and authentication event. If the user accesses a second application shortly afterward, which delegates authentication to the same identity provider, the user will be able to access the second application without being prompted again to log in. This capability is single sign-on.

SAML also provides a mechanism for an application and identity provider to use a common shared identifier for a user in order to exchange information about the user. This is known as federated identity. The federated identity can use the same identifier across systems, or it can use an opaque, internal identifier which is mapped to the identifier for the user in each system. We'll see more about how these features work in the following sections, but, first, we need to explain some terms we'll use.

Terminology

The SAML specifications define the following terms:

- **Subject** – An entity about which security information will be exchanged. A subject usually refers to a person, but can be any entity capable of authentication, including a software program. For the use cases we'll discuss, the subject is a user of an application.

- **SAML Assertion** – An XML-based message that contains security information about a subject.

- **SAML Profile** – A specification that defines how to use SAML messages for a business use case such as cross-domain single sign-on.

- **Identity Provider** – A role defined for the SAML cross-domain single sign-on profile. An identity provider is a server which issues SAML assertions about an authenticated subject, in the context of cross-domain single sign-on.

- **Service Provider** – Another role defined for the SAML cross-domain single sign-on profile. A service provider delegates authentication to an identity provider and relies on information about an authenticated subject in a SAML assertion issued by an identity provider in the context of cross-domain single sign-on.

- **Trust Relationship** – An agreement between a SAML service provider and a SAML identity provider whereby the service provider trusts assertions issued by the identity provider.

- **SAML Protocol Binding** – A description of how SAML message elements are mapped onto standard communication protocols, such as HTTP, for transmission between service providers and identity providers. In practice, SAML request and response messages are typically sent over HTTPS using either HTTP-Redirect or HTTP-POST, using the HTTP-Redirect and HTTP-POST bindings, respectively.

How It Works

The most common SAML scenario is cross-domain web single sign-on. In this scenario, the subject is a user that wishes to use an application. The application acts as a SAML service provider. The application delegates user authentication to a SAML identity provider that may be in a different security domain. The identity provider authenticates a user and returns a security token, known as a SAML assertion, to the application. A SAML assertion provides information about the authentication event and the authenticated user, known as the subject. We will use the term application along with service provider for consistency across chapters, but should note that an entity acting as an identity provider can also act as a service provider by further delegating authentication to another identity provider.

To establish the ability to do cross-domain web single sign-on, the organizations owning the service provider (application) and identity provider exchange information, known as metadata. The metadata contains information such as URL endpoints and digital certificates. This data enables the two parties to exchange messages that are digitally signed and optionally encrypted. The metadata is used to configure and set up a trust relationship between the service provider and the identity provider and must be done before the identity provider can authenticate users for the service provider (application).

Once mutual configuration of providers is in place, when a user accesses the service provider (application), it redirects the user's browser over to the identity provider with a SAML authentication request message. The identity provider authenticates the user and issues a redirect back to the application with a SAML authentication response message. The response contains a SAML assertion with information about the user and authentication event, or an error, if an error condition occurred. The identity provider can tailor the identity claims in the assertion as needed for each service provider. Please see Appendix C for sample SAML authentication request and response messages and a description of commonly used elements within each.

SP-Initiated SSO

The simplest form of cross-domain single sign-on is illustrated in Figure 7-1. In this example, the user starts at the service provider (SP) (application) so it is known as the "SP-initiated" flow. (The diagram and accompanying description of steps depict a scenario where the user does not have an existing authentication session at the identity provider and therefore has to authenticate.)

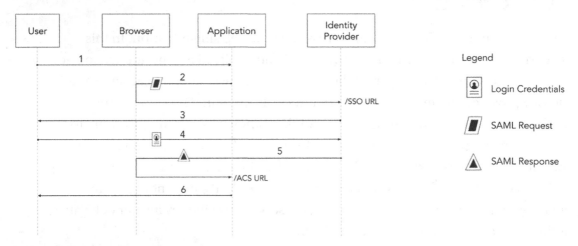

Figure 7-1. *SAML SP-Initiated Single Sign-On*

1. The user visits a service provider (application).

2. The service provider redirects the user's browser to the identity provider with a SAML authentication request.

3. The identity provider interacts with the user for authentication.

4. The user authenticates. The identity provider validates credentials.

5. The identity provider redirects the user's browser back to the service provider with a SAML response containing a SAML authentication assertion. The response is sent to the service provider's Assertion Consumer Service (ACS) URL.

6. The service provider consumes and validates the SAML response and responds to the user's original request (assuming the user was successfully authenticated and has sufficient privileges for the request).

Single Sign-On

Figure 7-1 shows the user accessing a single application. Multiple service providers can choose to delegate user authentication to the same identity provider. When this occurs, a user can access a first application and be redirected to authenticate to the identity provider to establish an authentication session there, as shown in Figure 7-1. The user can then use the same browser to access a second application which relies on the same identity provider. When the user is redirected by the second application to the identity provider, the identity provider will recognize the user already has a session and won't ask them to authenticate again. The identity provider will simply redirect the user's browser back to the second application with a successful SAML authentication response. This is called single sign-on (SSO), and it will be covered in more detail in Chapter 11.

To keep things simple, the example in this chapter assumes that both applications require the same strength of authentication mechanism, namely, password authentication. In Chapter 12, we will discuss stronger forms of authentication and how this impacts single sign-on.

IdP-Initiated Flow

Figure 7-1 showed an interaction sequence with the user starting at the service provider (application). This is called "SP-initiated" because the user initiates the interaction at the service provider (SP). SAML also defined another flow, known as "IdP-initiated," where the user starts at the identity provider (IdP), and which is shown in Figure 7-2. In this case, the identity provider redirects the user's browser to the service provider with a SAML response message without the service provider having sent any authentication request. This flow is found in some enterprise environments where a user accesses applications via a corporate portal.

When the user initially accesses the corporate portal, they are redirected to the corporate identity provider to log in. After logging in, the user is returned to the portal and sees a menu of application links on the portal. Clicking one of these links redirects the user to the identity provider, with the application URL as a parameter. The identity provider detects the user already has an authenticated session and redirects the user's browser to the application, with a SAML response message as in the SP-initiated case. The IdP-initiated flow does not require a portal, but we've chosen to show it as it is a common way this flow is used.

The IdP-initiated flow with a portal has been used in enterprises because it provides single sign-on and ensures users go to the correct URL for each application which reduces the risk of users being phished. The IdP-initiated flow is shown in Figure 7-2. (This diagram assumes the user does not have an existing authentication session.)

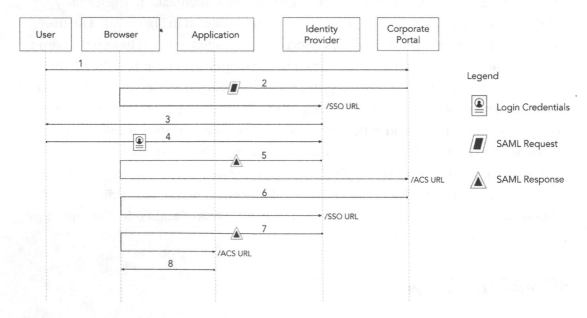

Figure 7-2. *SAML IdP-Initiated Single Sign-On*

1. The user visits a corporate portal.

2. The portal redirects the user's browser to the identity provider with a SAML authentication request.

3. The identity provider interacts with the user for authentication.

4. The user authenticates. The identity provider validates credentials.

5. The identity provider redirects the user's browser back to the portal with a SAML response for the portal (response #1) containing an authentication assertion. The user is logged in to the portal which displays content to the user, including a list of applications.

6. The user clicks a link in the portal for an application. The link directs the user's browser to the identity provider with a parameter indicating the desired service provider application. The IdP checks the user's session. This diagram assumes the user's session is still valid.

7. The identity provider redirects the user's browser to the service provider's Assertion Consumer Service (ACS) URL, with a new SAML response (response #2) for that service provider (the application).

8. The service provider (application) consumes the SAML response and authentication assertion and renders an appropriate page for the user, assuming their identity and privileges are sufficient for their request.

For more detailed information on the contents of SAML authentication requests and responses, as well as some application validation steps, see Appendix C. In general, with IdP-initiated flows, there are fewer checkpoints with which to validate incoming SAML responses, which may make applications more vulnerable to certain types of replay or injection attacks, especially if IdP-initiated flows can initiate actions within an application. We recommend using a flow that initiates from a Service Provider rather than one that initiates from an Identity Provider.

Identity Federation

With SAML, identity federation establishes an agreed-upon identifier that is used between a service provider (application) and an identity provider to refer to a subject (user). This enables a service provider to delegate authentication of the user to an identity provider and receive back an authentication assertion with identity claims that include an identifier for the authenticated subject that will be recognizable by the service provider.

Figure 7-3 illustrates an example. A user named Ann Smith has an account in two applications, application1 hosted at app1.com and application2 hosted at app2.com. In application1, her account identifier is ann@corp.com, and in application2, her account identifier is "ann." Ann also has an account at a corporate identity provider where her account identifier is ann@corp.com.

The administrators for application1 and the identity provider exchange metadata about their environments and use it to set up federation information between application1 and the identity provider. The same is done by the administrators of application2 and the identity provider. In practice, the administrators of an identity provider configure it to send assertions to each service provider that contain appropriate identifiers and attributes for the service provider (application).

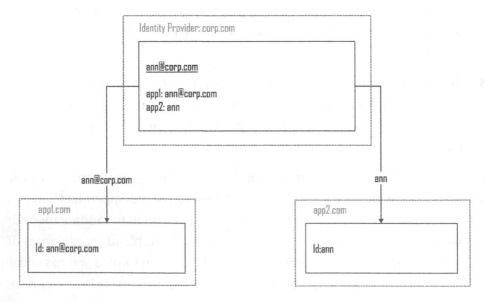

Figure 7-3. *Identity Federation*

When Ann accesses application1, it redirects her browser to her employer's identity provider at "corp.com". The identity provider authenticates Ann and redirects her browser back to application1 with an authentication assertion containing a naming attribute identifying her as ann@corp.com. Application1 uses the same identifier for Ann, so it recognizes her based on that identity.

When Ann accesses application2, it redirects her browser to the identity provider which recognizes that she already has a session. If the identity provider returns an authentication assertion identifying her as ann@corp.com, however, application2 will not recognize her as a valid user by that name. The identity provider needs to return an appropriate identifier for each service provider. In this case, when the identity provider delivers the authentication assertion to application2, it needs to identify the subject of the assertion with a naming attribute using "ann."

The logical link between the identity for a person at a service provider and at an identity provider can be set up in different ways. In practice, a user's email address is often used as the identifier for a user at both the service provider and identity provider. This can be problematic, however, as a user may need to change their email address, and it can conflict with privacy requirements. The use of a specific identifier attribute can be requested dynamically in a request, or an identity provider can be configured to send a particular identifier to a service provider. It is also possible for an identity provider and service provider to exchange information using an opaque, internal identifier for a user that is mapped on each entity's side to the user's profile within that entity. The use of a unique identifier for each federation is privacy-friendly and prevents correlation of user activity across providers, but this has not been widely done in practice. The approach to use is set up when the owners of the service provider and identity provider exchange metadata and configure their servers to establish the trust relationship (often called a federation) between the service provider and identity provider.

Authentication Brokers

Authentication brokers can be used by applications to easily enable support for multiple authentication protocols and mechanisms. If you are building a new application and plan to use OIDC for authentication, you may receive requests to support SAML from business customers who want their users authenticated at their corporate SAML identity provider. SAML is a complex protocol, which would require significant work to implement and support across many customers because each customer's SAML Identity Provider may be configured differently, resulting in minor differences in the assertions.

Rather than implement SAML directly in your application yourself, you can use an authentication broker to simplify the task of supporting SAML.[2] An authentication broker allows your application to use a newer identity protocol like OIDC and rely on the authentication broker to communicate via different protocols to a variety of identity providers. Figure 7-4 depicts an application implemented to use OIDC and OAuth 2 with an authentication broker which communicates in turn with several identity providers, each of which uses a different protocol. The use of an authentication broker allows an application team to implement newer identity protocols in their application and focus on the core features of their application instead of spending time to directly implement and support older identity protocols requested by customers.

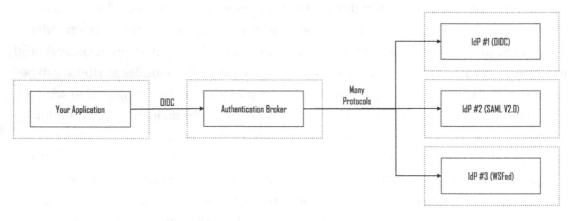

Figure 7-4. *Benefits of an Authentication Broker*

If you elect not to use an authentication broker, we recommend at least using a SAML library rather than attempting to implement SAML yourself. SAML assertions are lengthy, with many XML elements to parse and validate, making it a complex protocol to implement. Using a SAML library will allow you to spend more time on your application's core features instead of fiddling around with a lot of XML.

---

[2] Full disclosure: At the time of writing, the authors of this book worked for Auth0, a vendor of an authentication broker service.

Configuration

Whether you use an authentication broker or a library, Tables 7-1 and 7-2 show the elements that typically need to be configured at the service provider (application) and identity provider and their meaning. The owners of the service provider and identity provider need to exchange the information in these tables to enable the configuration of the federation.

In practice, the information is often available via a discovery URL. The owner of the service provider can consult the discovery URL at the identity provider to obtain the information to enter into the service provider's configuration for the federation, and vice versa for the owner of the identity provider. The identity provider must furthermore be configured to send an assertion that contains an identifier for the user that will be recognized by the service provider application. The assertion must also contain any additional attributes needed by the application. These attributes might include user profile attributes used to customize the user experience or information about roles or groups that are needed for the application's access control enforcement.

Table 7-1. *Common Service Provider Configuration*

Element	Description
SSO URL	Single sign-on URL of the identity provider. This is where the service provider will send its authentication requests.
Certificate	Certificate(s) from the identity provider. Used to validate signatures on SAML responses/assertions from the identity provider. Also used if a service provider sends encrypted requests. Some providers allow different certificates for the two uses.
Protocol binding	Protocol binding to use when sending requests. HTTP-Redirect for simple requests or HTTP-POST if requests are signed, which is recommended.
Request signing	Whether to digitally sign SAML authentication requests and, if so, via which signature algorithm. Signing is recommended. It can protect request elements from modification and make DOS attacks more costly to perform.
Request encryption	Whether to digitally encrypt a SAML authentication request.

Table 7-2. *Common Identity Provider Configuration*

Element	Description
ACS URL	AssertionConsumerService URL of the service provider. This is where it will receive SAML authentication responses from the identity provider.
Certificate	Certificate(s) from the service provider. Used to validate signatures on SAML requests. Also needed if responses are to be encrypted. Some providers allow different certificates for the two uses.
Protocol binding	Protocol binding to use when sending a response. HTTP-POST is typically required to accommodate signed messages.
Response signing	Whether to digitally sign the SAML authentication response, the assertion, or both and, if so, via which signature algorithm. Signing is mandatory.
Response encryption	Whether to digitally encrypt a SAML response.

The configuration elements listed in Table 7-1 are set up at the Service Provider for each Identity Provider it will rely upon. Similarly, the configuration elements in Table 7-2 are configured at the Identity Provider for each Service Provider that will rely upon the Identity Provider. The correct configuration of the federation at the Service Provider and Identity Provider is necessary for the Service Provider to redirect users to a trusted Identity Provider and to receive and trust the SAML responses from the Identity Provider.

You'll need to consult the documentation for the authentication broker or SAML library you've chosen for the specific details of where and how to configure the preceding elements. Once both providers are configured and you have attempted a trial authentication, it's common for authentication to fail the first time. You can debug issues by attempting an authentication, capturing a trace of the SAML request and response message, and examining them. We've provided guidance for how to troubleshoot in Chapter 16 and details on what to look for in the SAML request and response messages in Appendix C.

As time passes, the information used to establish the federation may change. The most common change is for the digital certificates or cryptographic keys to expire. These are exchanged during the setup of a federation relationship between providers and used to validate digital signatures on SAML messages and optionally to decrypt encrypted SAML messages. If a certificate or key expires, the identity provider may not be able to consume a SAML request from the service provider, or the service provider will not be able to consume and validate the SAML assertion from the identity provider, and authentication requests will fail. The owners of service providers and identity providers need to notify the other party for each federation when a change is coming and work out an appropriate procedure to make updates without disrupting service. Some providers may facilitate such changes by either dynamically checking for updates at a provider's discovery URL or allowing the configuration of two values. The latter option requires the provider to try one value, and if it fails, try the second value. These capabilities can save a lot of administrator time and minimize risk of downtime from changes, especially in scenarios where an application must support a lot of different identity providers or an identity provider is used by many service providers.

Another operational requirement is to ensure providers have accurate time. SAML assertions have an expiration, which is often just long enough for the assertion to be transmitted to the recipient and consumed. If the servers for the service provider or identity provider are not synchronized with an accurate time source, their internal clock may slowly drift. This can cause a service provider to receive an assertion that is already expired. Therefore, in addition to the configuration in Tables 7-1 and 7-2, it is imperative for the service provider and identity provider to synchronize their time with an accurate time service such as the Network Time Protocol (NTP).[iii]

Summary

SAML 2 provides an industry standard solution for web single sign-on and identity federation. These key features enabled enterprises to use cloud applications and still maintain centralized control of identities. The use of SAML eliminates exposure of static password credentials to applications and provides users the convenience of single sign-on. Many enterprises have implemented SAML identity providers and expect SaaS application vendors to support it.

At this point, however, SAML is an older protocol compared to OIDC. Now that OIDC and OAuth 2 exist, modern applications designed around APIs will benefit from implementing these newer protocols, as they provide support for both authentication and API authorization, respectively, and identity providers that support them exist for both consumer- and corporate-facing scenarios.

If you need to support SAML, rather than implementing it in a new application yourself, it is more efficient to use an authentication broker service that can take care of the SAML implementation complexity for you.[3] This will enable you to implement your application with newer protocols and still support customers who require a variety of older protocols such as SAML and WS-Fed. Alternatively, you can use a library for your chosen platform to implement such protocols. Once authentication is solved, authorization and policy enforcement are needed to govern what a user can do, and that's coming up in the very next chapter.

Key Points

- SAML is an XML-based framework for exchanging security information between business partners.

- SAML provided two features which became widely used: cross-domain single sign-on and identity federation.

- A SAML service provider delegates user authentication to an identity provider.

- A SAML identity provider authenticates a user and returns the results of a user authentication event in an XML message called an authentication response.

- An authentication response contains an authentication assertion with claims about the authentication event and authenticated user.

- Identity federation establishes a common identifier for a user between an identity provider and a service provider.

- Business customers of applications often want to use their corporate identity providers to authenticate their users to applications. Many of these still use SAML and WS-Fed.

- New applications should consider using an authentication broker service to simplify the task of supporting SAML and WS-Fed.

---

[3] Disclosure: At the time of writing, the authors of this book worked for Auth0, a vendor of an authentication broker service.

- Owners of SAML service providers and identity providers need to coordinate when making configuration changes that will impact the other.

- SAML service providers and identity providers need to be synchronized with an accurate time source.

Notes

i. https://wiki.oasis-open.org/security/FrontPage

ii. www.oasis-open.org/committees/download.php/27819/sstc-saml-tech-overview-2.0-cd-02.pdf (Section 2)

iii. www.ntp.org/

CHAPTER 8

Authorization and Policy Enforcement

A people that values its privileges above its principles soon loses both.

—Dwight D. Eisenhower, 34th president of the United States,
from first inaugural address

The previous chapters covered the mechanics of authorizing an API call and authenticating a user. This chapter will discuss authorization vs. the enforcement of access policy and how identity protocols can be used to help implement them.

Authorization vs. Policy Enforcement

In governing what a user or application can do, there are two distinct functions. We use the term authorization for the granting of privileges. In contrast, access policy enforcement is defined as the act of checking that a person or application has been granted the necessary privilege before responding to a request for a protected resource. For example, if you buy a theater ticket, the ticket constitutes your authorization to attend the performance. On the night of the performance, the ticket taker at the door enforces policy by checking to ensure that only authorized patrons (with tickets) enter the theater.

Authorization may be granted well in advance of a resource being requested or at the time of requesting access. It may be done using an interface provided by the entity containing the requested resource or by a trusted third party with the authorization information conveyed securely to the policy enforcement point. Access policy enforcement is done at the time a resource request is made and ideally at an

Y. Wilson and A. Hingnikar, *Solving Identity Management in Modern Applications*,
https://doi.org/10.1007/978-1-4842-8261-8_8

enforcement point within or close to the protected resource to reduce the possibility of the enforcement being bypassed. If a policy enforcement point is separate from the resources it protects, the environment must be designed to ensure the only route to the protected resource involves going through the policy enforcement point, to prevent bypass.

Levels of Authorization and Access Policy Enforcement

There are different levels at which authorization and access policy enforcement may be specified and applied, respectively:

- **Level 1** – Whether an entity can access an application or API at all

- **Level 2** – What functions an entity can use in an application or API

- **Level 3** – What data an entity can access or operate on

Level 1 – Application or API Access

At the highest level, authorization and access policy enforcement can control whether an entity has permission to access an application or API at all. This use case is often found in corporate settings. For example, an employee in a marketing team probably has no business accessing the corporate accounting system. This level of policy enforcement may be handled within an application or by an entity in front of the application as shown in Figure 8-1. The enforcement can be done external to an application by components such as an authentication broker or a reverse proxy that works with an identity and access management (IAM) system. Such systems can act as a high-level enforcement point to deflect users who are not authorized to access an application at all. A similar approach can be used with API Gateways protecting APIs and in both cases is useful to reduce policy enforcement workload on target systems.

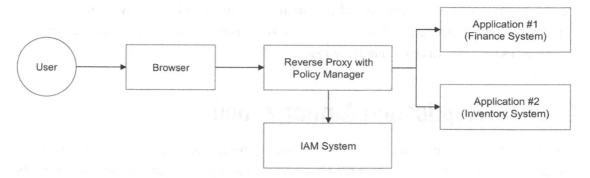

Figure 8-1. *Application-Level Access Policy Enforcement*

Level 2 – Functional Access

Functional-level authorization and access policy enforcement govern the functions or tasks an entity can do within an application or API. For example, a junior accounting clerk in the finance department might be able to access the corporate accounting system and enter individual journal entries but not perform a month-end close, which would typically be done by a more senior, experienced employee. A mobile app for library patrons might be able to call a "place hold" API endpoint, but not an endpoint to modify the description of a library book. This level of authorization and access policy enforcement is sometimes called "coarse-grained" and tends to be application specific. It may leverage information about a user stored in the application or elsewhere, such as roles or groups in a directory service, but is often enforced within an application or API in order to enforce application-specific policy logic.

Level 3 – Data Access

A third level of authorization and access policy enforcement governs access to particular subsets of data or resources. This is sometimes called the fine-grained or granular level of access control. If functional-level access policy enforcement defines the functions or tasks an entity can do, data-level or fine-grained access policy further restricts access to specific data or resources. For example, in a sales order entry application, a user with the role "regional sales manager" may be authorized at a functional level to view sales orders, but data-level access policy restricts them to only view sales orders for their specific region. The user's region would be specified as an attribute in their user profile.

Data-level access is often enforced within an application or API, but may leverage capabilities within an underlying storage layer, such as the ability to restrict access to tablespaces or views in an Oracle Database.

User vs. Application Authorization

We will cover two situations that require authorization and access policy enforcement. The first governs what a user (or entity) can do in an application, and the second controls what an application can request from an API.

A *user* needs authorization to perform various functions within an application. The application may render the application's user interface based on a user's authorized privileges so it doesn't display features a user cannot use. In addition, when a user makes a request, the application back end or API must enforce policy by checking that the user has the necessary authorization for the request before executing it.

An *application* requires authorization to call a protected API. If the content at a third-party API is owned by the user of the application, the application's access is on the user's behalf and requires the user's authorization. This scenario is often found in consumer-facing applications. A common example of this scenario is a user of a photo printing application that wants the application to retrieve and print photos from their account at a social media site.

If, on the other hand, the content at the API is owned by the application or accessed by the application on its own behalf, an authorization server can authorize the application based on permissions previously configured by the administrator of the authorization server. There is no need for the user to authorize the request because the application owns the requested resource. Some examples of this scenario are, respectively, an application front end that calls its own back-end API and a travel application that calls a third-party API to retrieve weather data for the user's destination. In the latter case, the weather data retrieved from the remote site is not owned by the user, and the ability of the application to call the weather API is based on the application's relationship with the weather API. The application owner may pay a subscription fee to access the weather API, for example.

In addition to any authorization by a user or authorization server, an API may still need to enforce additional access policy. In other words, an access token issued by an authorization server is not necessarily the final word on whether an access request should be granted. Some access policy decisions, especially for granular, data-level access, may be most efficiently handled by the API designed to manage the data as opposed to a generic authorization server. For example, a bank application may be authorized to call an API to transfer money to pay a bill, and the user may authorize a particular payment, but if the user's account has insufficient funds, the API will probably reject the payment request, per bank policy.

Regardless of the entity being authorized, there are three steps commonly involved in controlling access:

- Authorization and the specification of access policy

- Delivery of authorization information to the enforcement point (if needed)

- Enforcement of the access policy by the enforcement point

We will discuss these three steps first for users and then applications.

User Authorization

The specification of authorization is a complex topic. So many schemes have been invented for this over the years that covering them in detail is outside the scope of this book. We will provide a brief description of a few common models to show how they can be used with identity protocols. We note that many existing applications vary in their choice of authorization policy model as well as the terms used for collections of privileges and users. For the purposes of this chapter, we will rely on the definitions provided in the following paragraphs.

A relatively simple model is an access control list (ACL).[i] In this scheme, authorization policy is often specified as a list of entities granted access for a specific protected resource. Our sample program uses such a scheme. Each individual file has a list of the users or groups of users which have been granted access to the file. When someone requests access to a file, the policy enforcement point needs to check if the authenticated identity of the requestor is in the list of users in the file's ACL. For our sample program, the resource server API is the policy enforcement point, so it needs a claim from the identity provider (an OIDC Provider in the sample) about the identity of the user as well as any groups to which they belong.

In a role-based access control (RBAC)[ii] model, protected resources have various functions which can be performed on them. For example, an order management system may allow users to create, read, update, and delete sales orders. These actions represent privileges which can be granted to users who need to perform such functions. For administrative convenience, it is common to define roles, which are collections of privileges that would typically be assigned together to a user, to facilitate the role they serve in an organization. For example, a small company may need its sales staff to be able to create, read, update, and delete (CRUD) sales orders, quotes, and invoices in a sales management system. Rather than assigning each of these privileges individually to each sales person, a role can be created that lumps them together. Such a role might be called "salesexecution." The role can then be assigned to a salesperson user, giving them all the privileges they need with one administrative action. Another role could be defined that only had read access to those objects, perhaps called "salesanalysis," and that role could be used for analysts who only need to retrieve sales order data for analytical purposes but not update it.

As a further administrative convenience, collections of users, often called groups, can be defined. This would enable the assignment of a role to sets of users at once, rather than individually. For example, a group called "salespeople" could be defined, with all sales people being members of the group. The "salesexecution" role and other roles needed by sales teams could be assigned to the "salespeople" group. Similarly, sales analysts could be members of a group called "salesanalysts" which would be granted the "salesanalysis" role along with any other roles needed by analysts. With an RBAC model, an application or resource server API serving as a policy enforcement point needs claims about the identity of the authenticated user as well as roles they've been assigned and/or groups to which they belong.

In an attribute-based access control (ABAC)[iii] model, authorization is specified via rules that utilize attributes in a user's profile. For example, access to a finance system might be allowed for all users that satisfy the rule "user_profile:team = finance." In other words, a user will get access if their user profile has a value of "finance" in the "team" attribute. In this case, an application or resource server API acting as a policy enforcement point needs claims about the identity of the user and the relevant user profile attributes needed for evaluation of access control rules.

For access enforcement with these models, the component implementing policy enforcement typically requires trusted claims for the authenticated user's identity and any user profile attributes relevant for access control decisions and enforcement. These claims must originate from an authoritative source and be transmitted to the policy enforcement point in a way that precludes tampering. In the rest of this chapter, we will describe how OIDC and SAML 2 can be used to deliver such claims about a user to an application and how OAuth 2 can be used to authorize access to APIs and deliver claims needed for access policy enforcement.

User Profile Attributes

The attributes used to convey authorization for users can vary, but fall into two main categories. A user's identity may be granted authorization based on roles which they've been assigned in a role-based access control (RBAC)[iv] model, membership in a group or access control list (ACL), or individual user profile attributes evaluated by rules as part of an attribute-based access control (ABAC)[v,vi] model. These attributes are relatively static factors that remain the same, regardless of where the user is or what device they are using at the time of accessing a protected resource.

If such authorization information is specified outside an application, such as in a corporate directory service or policy service, but accessible by the identity provider authenticating a user, these attributes can be delivered to the application by the identity provider. If authorization is specified in the application, the identity provider can deliver an identifier for the authenticated user to the application so it can retrieve the necessary authorization information from its own data store.

The authorization step to grant a user privileges is typically done in advance of the user making a request in an application. For example, if a new employee joins a company's finance team, the business may authorize the employee to access its accounting application by assigning the user roles in a corporate identity system on the new hire's first day. For a consumer-facing application, a user may be assigned access-related user profile attributes when they purchase a particular subscription level for the application.

Transactional User Attributes

Authorization may also be based upon factors that are part of the user's physical environment at the time of authentication or accessing a protected resource. Such factors can include the user's geographic location, whether the user is inside or outside a corporate firewall, or whether the user's device is certified as adhering to certain security configuration standards. The day of the week or time of day may be factors as well as the strength of the authentication mechanism used. These factors are captured at the time of authentication rather than being part of the user's profile. Such factors, if captured by an identity provider, can also be provided to applications in the form of claims in a security token.

Delivery

For applications using OIDC, user profile attributes and authorization information can be delivered to applications as claims in an ID Token or in the response from the OIDC Provider's UserInfo endpoint. Applications using SAML 2 can receive the information via attribute statements in a SAML 2 assertion. For resource servers (APIs) using OAuth 2, such information can be delivered via standard and custom claims, such as described for JWT-format access tokens,[vii] provided the issuing authorization server supports such a feature. User profile information such as a user's roles, groups, or a purchased subscription level, and factors such as a user's IP address or strength of authentication method, can be delivered to an application or API in this way. An application can use the information to tailor the application user interface for the user's allowed capabilities, and an application back end or API can use it to perform access policy enforcement. An example showing the delivery of user profile information via an ID Token to support access enforcement is shown in Figure 8-2. In this example, the application is a movie rental application where users can purchase different subscription levels (such as bronze, silver, and gold) to get access to different selections of movies. The ID Token delivers to the application the user's purchased subscription level.

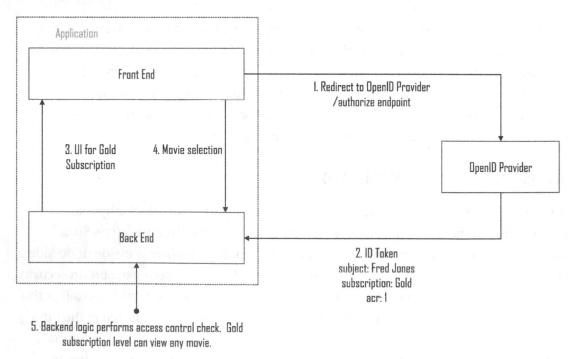

Figure 8-2. Delivering Authorization Attributes to an Application

1. The user redirected to login at the OIDC OpenID Provider.

2. The ID Token includes the user's purchased subscription.

3. Subscription data in the ID Token is used to determine the list of movies displayed.

4. The user selects a movie to view.

5. The application back end checks the user has the required subscription level for their selected movie.

In the example, the information in the ID Token about a user's subscription level is used to display to the user the movies they are entitled to rent. It is also used to perform access policy enforcement. Even though the front end is designed to restrict the list of movies to what the user can view, a malicious user might find a way to get around this, so the access policy enforcement check must be made in the application back end where it cannot be circumvented.

This example uses OIDC, but applications using SAML 2 can follow a similar model, obtaining authorization data from the SAML 2 assertion. This example assumes that the user profile attributes, such as the user's subscription level, are stored in a centralized repository available to the OIDC Provider. Centralizing such information is useful if there are several applications relying on the same user profile attributes.

Alternatively, a stand-alone application may implement features in the application user interface for the administration of authorization and store all authorization information within the application's data store. In this case, the application may only need from the OIDC Provider a claim for the identity of the authenticated user. The application would then use that identity to look up authorization information for the user in its own data store and perform the necessary policy enforcement.

Another possible model involves an API Gateway deployed in front of an application's back-end API or set of APIs. API Gateways can inspect incoming API requests, route them to an appropriate API, and perform load balancing and failover. They can also handle authentication and authorization of requests coming to APIs. As described earlier in this section, application APIs can make use of claims in an access token to perform access enforcement, and API Gateways that support OAuth 2 can be used to perform a similar function.

Enforcement

Before relying on any information in a security token, an application must validate the token. In the case of an ID Token, validation steps include

- Validate the ID Token is a correctly formatted JWT (JSON Web Token)

- Validate the signature on the ID Token

- Check that the token has not expired

- Check the issuer is the correct OpenID Provider

- Check the intended audience for the token is the application

Be sure to check the latest protocol specifications for further guidance, in case of updates, as well as the documentation for your OpenID Provider for the exact validation steps required by their implementation. Similarly, an application receiving a SAML 2 assertion must validate the assertion. This will include steps such as checking that the assertion is signed, validating the signature on the assertion, validating the issuer is a trusted provider, and checking the assertion is within its validity period. Again, check with your SAML provider for the complete list of validation requirements. Once a security token has been validated, the application or API can use relevant claims within the token for access policy enforcement.

Application Authorization

The second case of authorization and policy enforcement is that of applications calling APIs.

Application Attributes

With OAuth 2, application requests to call APIs on a user's behalf are authorized by the user, but requests to call APIs on the application's own behalf are authorized by an authorization server based on configured policy. This policy is typically configured in advance of an application calling an API. If the number of applications or API endpoints is small, the policy specification may be expressed by indicating the specific applications authorized to call specific API endpoints. In scenarios with large numbers of client applications or API endpoints, with widely varying authorization requirements for each, policy specification can become complex. There is no widely adopted standard for such policy administration and specification, so the options available from authorization servers, especially to support complex cases, vary.

Authorization

An application that makes an OAuth 2 request for authorization to call an API can specify its requested scope of access using the scopes parameter to the authorization request. For example, an application requesting an access token for an OpenID Provider's UserInfo endpoint to retrieve user attributes might use "scope = openid profile email". An application calling a third-party API to retrieve a user's documents might request a scope of "get:documents". In these examples, the requested API resources are owned by the user, so the OAuth 2 authorization server will prompt the user, displaying the scopes requested by the application, and ask for the user's consent for the access request before issuing an access token.

There aren't any official rules about how to make use of OAuth 2 scopes, but as a simple string, constrained by URL length limits, scopes may be best suited for simple scenarios like these, where an authorization server requests easily described authorization from a user to allow an application to act on their behalf. For other, more complex access policy scenarios, a richer request mechanism is often needed.

Several newer specifications provide additional capabilities for authorization requests. While still in draft form, the Rich Authorization Request[viii] (RAR) specification defines the ability to submit complex authorization requests to authorization servers in the form of a JSON object. A request can specify information using a set of standardized fields as well as custom-defined fields. Standard fields are defined for request attributes such as the location of resources, the privileges requested, and actions to be performed. A RAR is submitted to an authorization server using the authorization_details parameter, which can be used with requests where the scope parameter can be used. For resources owned by a user, an authorization server can prompt the user to authorize access using information in the RAR. For resources owned by an application, the authorization server can compare the request parameters in the RAR to policy configured in the authorization server to decide whether to issue an access token.

Applications can also encapsulate an authorization request and its parameters in a JWT-secured Authorization Request (JAR)[ix] which enables the application to digitally sign and optionally encrypt the request object. This provides for better authenticity and confidentiality for request parameters. An authorization request can also be pushed by the application directly to an authorization server using a Pushed Authorization Request[x] (PAR). After pushing an authorization request, the application receives a request URI, which it can reference when it makes the authorization call to the authorization server via the browser (or other user agent), further reducing the exposure of authorization request information via browser interaction.

With the client credentials grant, the requested API resources are owned by the application, and no user interaction is required. The privileges granted to each application are specified in the authorization server (or a policy server accessed from it). An authorization server can compare the information in an authorization request with policy configured in the authorization server to decide whether to issue an access token. For scenarios with complex policy, a RAR may be useful to express relevant details of the authorization request.

It is beyond the scope of this book to provide detailed guidance on how to make authorization requests for scenarios with complex access control policy, but a few points are worth considering in designing the authorization requests for an API:

- When access requests are displayed for a user's authorization, it must be easy for a user to understand the access they are granting.

- Users may be unwilling to authorize requests with confusing or overly broad scopes.

- If an application requests many scopes in one authorization request, the request may hit URL length limits.

- If an application has to make many authorization requests, such as when very granular scopes are used, it can generate a lot of traffic to the authorization server.

- Frequently prompting users for authorization may cause users to click "ok" without paying much attention to the request.

- Information needed for access policy decisions can be conveyed in authorization requests by other means than scopes, such as via Rich Authorization Requests (RARs).

- Where supported, custom claims in access tokens can convey additional information useful to APIs for policy enforcement.

- The use of JWT-secured Authorization Requests (JARs) and Pushed Authorization Requests (PARs) enables increased integrity protection and confidentiality for authorization requests and their parameters.

- Access policy decisions and enforcement may be handled by a combination of authorization servers, API Gateways, and APIs.

Delivery

Regardless of whether the protected resource is owned by the user or the application, if the request is authorized, the authorization server will issue an access token to the application for the requested API. An authorization server may allow adding additional custom claims to an access token, such as claims about the user, including user profile attributes and roles they've been assigned. These additional claims may be useful to an API in enforcing access. Support for extensibility via custom claims and attributes about users may vary by individual authorization server implementations.

Enforcement

An API must validate an access token and perform access policy enforcement to make sure the application's request is permitted before responding. The steps to validate and obtain information about an access token will vary depending on the authorization server's implementation for access tokens. You should check the authorization server documentation for details about how to validate any tokens it issues. Once the access token has been validated, the API can use the information in the token, including any custom claims if allowed, to perform its own access policy enforcement before responding to the request.

For example, an application may call an API with a valid access token that contains the scope "get:documents" which allows it to retrieve documents. The API still needs to perform more granular checks, such as whether the specific user, on whose behalf the request is made, is allowed to access the specific documents requested, and whether the authentication mechanism used to authenticate the user met or exceeded the access requirements for the requested documents. Similarly, a banking application client may have an access token that allows it to request a transfer of funds, but the API that receives the request must check, among other things, that the transfer-from account has sufficient funds for the requested transfer. An API may be in a better position than an authorization server to enforce that type of detailed, application-specific enforcement check.

155

Authorization and Enforcement Extensions

Some identity providers have implemented proprietary mechanisms on top of SAML, OIDC, and OAuth in order to provide access enforcement capabilities for applications and resource servers. This enables application administrators to define access policy in the administrative interface for the identity provider using a combination of privileges, roles, groups and rules. When an application makes an authorization request, the identity provider can check the access policies it contains and return an unauthorized status if the requesting user doesn't satisfy the access policies for the request. This relieves the application or resource server from having to implement some policy enforcement logic. There is no standard governing such authorization and enforcement extensions, so check your identity provider's documentation for information regarding any such capabilities.

Leveraging an identity provider for access enforcement may be feasible for applications with simple access control policies. However, applications and APIs often have to take on a significant portion of authorization and access enforcement responsibility for more complex scenarios, as when there is a large number of resources with specific access requirements (such as granular access governing documents in a file system) or when applications must check user profile attributes like "region" that govern tasks such as running a regional month-end close in a financial system. If nothing else, it is challenging to make the administrative interface of access policy understandable when application-specific actions and policies need to be mapped onto a generic identity provider's administrative user interface. It is critical that administrators understand what they have done when they use an interface to specify access policy.

To understand the access requirements for your application, you can inventory the data objects involved in your application. For each item in the inventory, identify the functions that can be performed on it. Be sure to include functions beyond the basic create, read, update, and delete tasks, such as triggering a month-end financial close or certifying a set of audit records. Then consider the policy for who can do each task or operate on each data object and under what conditions. Having a good understanding of your required access policy can help you evaluate if an identity provider's authorization capabilities will be sufficient for your application.

You should also consider how access policy will be administered. Some providers may have an administrative user interface for specifying policy. If the provider only has an API, you may have to develop a custom interface to enable the specification of policy at the identity provider. Creating a custom administrative interface based on a provider's administrative API or using their administrative interface may lock you into using that provider more strongly than simply using a provider's authentication and authorization capabilities. Decisions about where and how to administer policy should be made consciously and strategically rather than solely by convenience.

The specification of access policy can quickly become even more complex if there is a need for delegated administration, where different people administer different portions of the policy. For example, in a large enterprise, managers (rather than centralized administrators) may assign their team members to access control roles or groups because the managers know what each person's job requires. In this case, an interface is needed to specify policy for who can administer each part of the access policy as well as provide a delegated administration interface for managers to assign roles or groups to people. Be sure to consider your requirements for access policy, policy administration, delegated administration, and policy enforcement before deciding upon a solution for access control.

Summary

Authorization involves the granting of privileges, whereas access policy enforcement is a check done at the time a resource is requested, to validate the requestor has been granted the requisite privileges for the request. Authorization and access policy enforcement may be used to govern what a user can do in an application as well as whether an application can make a request to an API.

User authorization may be based on static factors in a user's profile and/or dynamic factors evaluated at the time of authentication, both of which can be delivered to an application in a security token. Application authorization may be based on scopes or more complex parameters and approved by a user or based on configuration in an authorization server and represented by an access token delivered to an application to call an API.

Identity providers may provide custom features that aid access policy enforcement, but applications and APIs often need to implement at least some access policy enforcement themselves. When deciding upon the best option for your application, take into account your access control policy requirements, policy administration requirements, and access policy enforcement requirements as well as which entity in your architecture is best positioned to satisfy each.

In addition to authorizing and enforcing access policy, it is important to consider how frequently to renew access, and this first requires an understanding of sessions, which is the topic of our next chapter.

Key Points

- Authorization is the granting of privileges to access protected resources.

- Access policy enforcement is done when a request is made and checks if a requestor has been granted sufficient authorization for the request.

- Authorization and access policy enforcement apply to users accessing applications as well as applications calling APIs.

- There are many models for specifying access policy, including access control lists, role-based access control, and attribute-based access control.

- Roles and groups are used to facilitate the administration of authorization and access policy.

- Authorization policy for users may be based upon user profile attributes or dynamic factors evaluated at the time a user authenticates or makes a request.

- Authorization for applications to call APIs is granted by users or authorization servers depending on the OAuth 2 grant type used.

- Authorization and access policy enforcement can be specified on multiple levels.

- OAuth 2 scopes are likely best suited for simple authorization scenarios where users authorize easily expressed requests to access APIs on their behalf.

- Applications with complex access policy and enforcement needs should consider the use of JWT-secured Authorization Requests (JARs), Rich Authorization Requests (RARs), and Pushed Authorization Requests (PARs).

- Claims in security tokens can be used as a basis for access policy enforcement decisions in applications and APIs.

- Security tokens must be validated before their claims are used for security decisions.

- Some identity providers have proprietary features that provide simple access policy enforcement.

- Access policy decisions and enforcement may be handled by a combination of authorization servers, API Gateways, and APIs.

- Remember to consider requirements for access policy, policy administration, delegated policy administration, and policy enforcement when designing access control for your application.

Notes

i. https://csrc.nist.gov/glossary/term/access_control_list

ii. https://csrc.nist.gov/Projects/Role-Based-Access-Control

iii. https://csrc.nist.gov/Projects/Attribute-Based-Access-Control

iv. https://csrc.nist.gov/Projects/Role-Based-Access-Control

v. https://nvlpubs.nist.gov/nistpubs/SpecialPublications/NIST.SP.800-162.pdf

vi. https://csrc.nist.gov/Projects/Attribute-Based-Access-Control

vii. https://datatracker.ietf.org/doc/html/rfc9068

viii. https://datatracker.ietf.org/doc/html/draft-ietf-oauth-rar

ix. https://datatracker.ietf.org/doc/html/rfc9101

x. https://datatracker.ietf.org/doc/html/rfc9126

CHAPTER 9

Sessions

Everything measurable passes, everything that can be counted has an end. Only three things are infinite: the sky in its stars, the sea in its drops of water, and the heart in its tears.

—Gustave Flaubert, French novelist, from *The Letters of Gustave Flaubert* (1980)

A user's interaction with an application over a period of time is known as a session. Users expect to navigate through the application and perform various transactions during their session without having to authenticate every time they interact with the application. In order to make this possible, an application needs a way to track that a user has been authenticated. Data about whether, when, and how a user has authenticated may be tracked by an application along with other information it maintains during a user's session. Sessions and session state may be handled differently for web applications, single-page applications, and applications that run natively on a device, such as mobile applications. In this chapter, we'll describe where sessions exist, session expiration, and renewing sessions.

Application Sessions

An application may need to track session information such as the identity of the user, the user's in-flight transactions, or how long the user's session can continue. This is usually accomplished via the creation of a unique session identifier that represents session activity. This identifier can be used to refer to additional details that may be stored in memory, a filesystem, a database, or a shared service like Redis.[i] For web applications, the session identifier and session information is usually stored in a cookie set by the application server, which is then sent by the browser with each request to the application

© Yvonne Wilson, Abhishek Hingnikar 2023
Y. Wilson and A. Hingnikar, *Solving Identity Management in Modern Applications*,
https://doi.org/10.1007/978-1-4842-8261-8_9

server. When a request is received, the server can use the session identifier from the cookie to retrieve the user's session information and process the request. Sometimes, if the session data is small enough, the entire data may be stored in the cookie, eliminating the need for server-side storage. For native applications and single-page web apps, storing data on the client side in memory or local persistent storage is a common strategy. When doing so, special care should be taken so as to not leave sensitive user data on the device.

Traditional web applications often limit the time for which they retain a session. Session information maintained on a server typically consumes server resources. If a user abandons a session by forgetting to log off, or a client loses its connection to a session for some reason, server resources would be wasted. In addition, a session left open and forgotten on a user's computer invites some risk of potentially being taken over by a malicious actor. As a result, traditional web applications often implement a session timeout which effectively limits how long a user's session can last. Session timeout might occur after a period of inactivity or a maximum period of time, with the allowed session duration in either case often based in part on the sensitivity of the application and data involved.

With single-page applications and stateless back-end APIs, server-side sessions for users are no longer required, but the concept of a session timeout persists for other reasons. Applications are still vulnerable to the possibility that a session left open for an extended period might be hijacked. This concern is especially relevant for applications handling sensitive data, many business-facing applications, and applications accessed from shared devices. Having a user reauthenticate when a session times out provides some assurance that the authorized user is still in control of the device and session. As applications increasingly leverage identity providers, a user's reauthentication can renew an identity provider session leveraged by many applications. As a result, a user would not have to actively reauthenticate to every application. Periodic reauthentication to the identity provider is less onerous than having to reauthenticate to every application.

Native applications running on mobile devices have additional considerations. The small form factor and input mechanisms on mobile phones make frequent reauthentication a significant detractor to user experience. Especially for some consumer-facing applications, it is desirable to remove barriers to usage and make it easy for users to stay logged in as long as possible. Native applications often use stateless APIs, resulting in little server-side cost for allowing a user's native application session to continue for an extended period of time. Sensitive applications, such as banking applications, often still implement a session timeout on mobile devices, but less sensitive native mobile applications may allow a session to continue for an extended period, sometimes until a user explicitly logs out. Lengthy sessions on mobile devices rely in part on the fact that mobile devices are often in a user's possession, making session hijacking less likely than with other scenarios, such as shared devices or desktop computers in an open office.

In some cases, in order to improve user experience, mobile applications store a refresh token in the device's native storage system, such as Apple's Keychain, and enforce a check like requiring the user to provide a PIN or Biometric factor to unlock the device. This validation, however, requires the user to have access to the device and have previously enrolled their PIN or Biometric factor to the device.

Identity Provider Sessions

Identity providers also need to maintain a session for a user as a mechanism to remember and recognize an authenticated user across multiple requests. One solution is to create a session object with a session identifier and attributes such as an identifier for the user, the authentication mechanism used, the time of authentication, and when the session will expire. An identity provider can create a cookie in the user's browser that contains all the session information or just a session identifier that maps to a server-side session data store. The browser then sends the identity provider cookie with every request to the identity provider. When a user is redirected to the identity provider, it uses data from the cookie to detect if a user already has an authenticated session.

This scheme helps an identity provider recognize users it has authenticated. After successfully authenticating a user, the identity provider sets or updates in the user's browser a cookie with session information and returns a security token to the application. The application may then create or update its own application session for the user. When the application session expires, the application can check the status of the user's session at the identity provider. It may do this by redirecting the user's browser to the identity provider. Such a request will include any cookies set previously by the identity provider, which contain the user's session information. If the user's session at the identity provider is still valid, the identity provider returns a new security token to the application without forcing the user to authenticate again. Some identity providers may support alternative mechanisms for checking the status of the user's session at the identity provider which can enable an application to avoid a browser redirect when the user's identity provider session is still valid. Of course, if the identity provider session has expired and the user needs to reauthenticate, the user will need to be redirected to the identity provider.

Multiple Sessions

A user may have multiple sessions across different solution components. The user may have a session in one or more applications. If an application delegated authentication to an identity provider, the identity provider may also have a session for the user. If an application delegates authentication to an authentication broker (explained in Chapter 7) that in turn delegates authentication to a remote identity provider, such as a social identity provider or corporate identity provider, there may be three architecture layers at which sessions exist. Figure 9-1 shows three different architectural models and where authentication sessions may exist in each. (Chapter 13 contains further discussion on sessions which may exist and options to detect their status.)

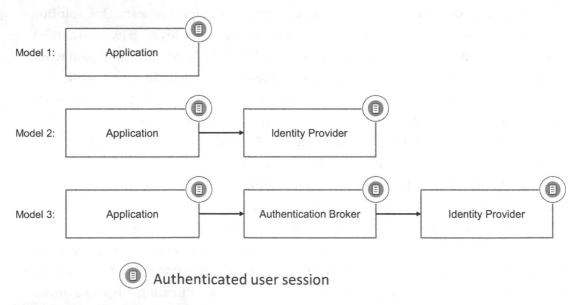

Figure 9-1. *Architectural Layers Where User Sessions May Exist*

Session Duration

Each session established for a user can be terminated at different times and for various reasons. Sessions may time out if they are established with a specific duration. A session may have an idle timeout where the session is invalidated if the user has been inactive for a period of time. A session may also have a maximum session time limit which ends the session after a period of time regardless of the user's activity level.

With an idle session timeout, if a user takes certain types of actions tracked by the application, the idle session timer gets reset, which extends the session. Activity in an application may reset an application session's idle timer, but not be visible to an identity provider and consequently not reset an idle timeout at the identity provider. The identity provider's idle timeout is typically only reset by requests visible to it, such as an authentication request from an application.

If an application enforces an idle session timeout, it can be disruptive to a user to suddenly lose an application session, especially if the user was in the middle of entering a lot of data for a transaction. An application can mitigate the potential for bad user experience by tracking the session duration, providing a warning to users before the session times out, and resetting the idle timeout if the user indicates they wish to continue. Proactively prompting the user when a session timeout approaches and letting them renew their session can avoid bad user experience when enforcing an idle timeout. Alternatively, an application can store the user's progress locally and request the user to reauthenticate when the session times out. Once the user has reauthenticated, the application can retrieve the session data, allow the user to continue working, and submit the user's work to the back end, depending on where the user left off.

The appropriate session duration time for an application will vary based on factors such as the sensitivity of the application or the delivery platform. For an idle timeout, it may help to consider how long you would want to tolerate a user's session remaining open if the user walks away from their desk with the application open. For applications on mobile phones carried around by their owners, it may be less likely for an open application session to be physically accessible by others. For a maximum session timeout, it may help to evaluate how frequently or infrequently the user should reauthenticate to confirm they are still in control of the session as well as how frequently user profile information might need refreshing. It's a balance between protecting the user and data they access and annoying the user by requiring them to authenticate too frequently. The duration may differ for applications run on desktop/laptop computers vs. mobile phones and for consumer-facing applications vs. enterprise applications as well as for applications with data of different sensitivity levels. It can often take some trial and error to get session timeout settings just right.

Sessions may end for reasons other than a timeout. A user may explicitly log out. This is covered in more detail in Chapter 13. An administrator may terminate a user's session at an identity provider for various reasons, such as in response to a report of a compromised credential. A user's session might be terminated if a server is restarted. A user's session might exist at a server, but be irretrievable if the user deleted the cookies in their browser that contain an identifier or other information about their session. The possibilities for session termination should be considered in application designs with appropriate actions defined for each case.

With many ways for sessions to terminate, and multiple sessions in the mix, it is important for application designers to specify or understand the impact on other sessions when any session is terminated. For example, if an application session expires, should the application request the termination of the user's session at an identity provider? If a user's identity provider session is terminated, should that trigger the immediate termination of a session in other applications using the same identity provider? The options to consider may be constrained by identity provider policy when an identity provider is controlled by an external party, but designs should still enumerate what happens for different session termination scenarios.

An application may want to periodically check the status of a user's session at an identity provider. This may be done so the application can terminate its own session when the identity provider's session has ended. This may also be done when an application's session for a user has timed out, with the application checking the state of the user's identity provider session as part of its own session renewal process.

Session Renewal

When an application's session for a user expires, the application may wish to enable the user to renew the session. It can do this by redirecting the user back to the identity provider. The identity provider can authenticate the user if it doesn't have a valid session for them and return new security tokens to the application per the parameters in the application's authentication request. If the user's identity provider session is still valid, the user would not need to reauthenticate, and the application would receive new security tokens based on the user's existing session. The application can then use information in the new security tokens to renew the user's application session.

Applications can use parameters in an authentication request to suppress or force active authentication. It may be desirable, for example, to have reauthentication occur if a certain amount of time has passed since the user last actively authenticated. With OIDC, the optional "prompt" parameter can be added to an authentication request to force or suppress authentication at the OpenID Provider. The optional "max_age" parameter can be used to control how long a user can go without actively reauthenticating. Applications using max_age should still check the auth_time claim in the ID Token to ensure the requested max_age was followed. The use of max_age and auth_time is useful if an OpenID Provider has a relatively long maximum or idle timeout, and a particular application requires more frequent authentication. With SAML 2, applications can use the "ForceAuthn" attribute of the authentication request to force the identity provider to actively authenticate the user. An application can check the "AuthnInstant" element of the SAML response to see when authentication occurred. Such authentication request parameters give applications some measure of control over whether the user is actively reauthenticated when they are redirected to the identity provider. The auth_time claim in an ID Token and the AuthnInstant claim in a SAML response also provide information back to applications that can be used in subsequent security decisions.

Identity providers may support alternative methods for checking the status of a user's session at the identity provider. If a user has a valid session at an identity provider, such methods may enable renewing an application session without requiring a browser redirect. On the other hand, if a user's identity provider session is no longer valid, the user can be redirected to renew the identity provider session.

Token Renewal

In addition to renewing a session, an application may need to periodically renew a security token. The application may have received an ID Token and possibly an access token to call an API. An application may need to periodically request a new ID Token to ensure it has up-to-date claims for an authenticated user. An application may wish to request a new access token because it needs to call an API and the access token it requested previously has expired. It is considered a best practice in many cases, and especially with public clients, to issue access tokens with short expiration times and renew the tokens when needed. As a result, the need for new tokens may occur throughout a session's existence.

During an application session, an application can renew an ID Token or access token using different mechanisms, based on the type of application. Traditional web applications and native applications may be able to obtain a refresh token for use in renewing ID Tokens and/or access tokens, but they are not required to do so. Using a refresh token to renew tokens avoids the need to interrupt the user experience, but back-channel requests with a refresh token may not update the identity provider's session cookie, resulting in a faster idle timeout.

Single-page applications implemented as public clients cannot securely store and handle refresh tokens. They should use an approach that doesn't rely on refresh tokens unless their authorization server implements measures against leaked refresh tokens such as refresh token rotation or sender-constrained refresh tokens.[ii] Applications that do not receive refresh tokens can redirect the user to the OpenID Provider when new tokens are needed. If the user has a valid session, the application will receive new tokens. If the user does not have a valid session, the request will trigger authentication and consent as needed, before new tokens are issued. Even applications with refresh tokens may want to use the redirect approach periodically to update the identity provider's session cookie and idle timeout.

Redirecting the user to the OpenID Provider and back, however, involves challenges as it can interrupt the user experience. With single-page applications, this can result in the loss of a user's work unless the application saves the user's application state and restores it after the return from the OpenID Provider. One alternative has been to do the redirect using a hidden iframe in the application and setting the "prompt" parameter to "none" to avoid interrupting the user experience. If the user had a valid session, the application would receive new tokens. If not, the application would receive an error response and could redirect the user again without the "prompt=none" option to trigger authentication. However, technology changes such as Apple's Intelligent Tracking Protection (ITP) have made the hidden iframe redirect option less viable.

Reconstituted Sessions

It can be disruptive to users to have their session timeout frequently in heavily used applications if they have to reenter several selections every time they reauthenticate. An application that needs a session timeout and falls in this category may want to provide an improved user experience by offering a session that can be reconstituted after session timeout. With this scheme, upon session timeout, the system invalidates the session for further use, but retains a memory of the session and the identity associated with it, so that the session state can be restored to its former state if the user actively reauthenticates. Such a session is terminated and permanently deleted by an active user logout, not a session timeout. That said, it is still desirable to have a limit for how long a session stays in a dormant state, to reduce backward compatibility issues and to avoid storing session data forever for sessions orphaned when a user deletes their session cookies.

Summary

Applications maintain sessions for users during a user's interaction with the application. If applications delegate authentication to an external identity provider, there may be multiple sessions for the user at different layers within the solution architecture. Each component maintaining a session for a user may have one or more types of session timeout. Sessions are a key enabler for single sign-on, which will be discussed in Chapter 11. First, however, we'll pull everything we've covered so far together in the next chapter and discuss a sample application and how it uses OIDC and OAuth 2 together to authenticate users and authorize access to APIs.

Key Points

- A user's interaction with an application for a duration of time is a session.

- Session state may contain data about the user and authentication event.

- In solutions with single sign-on, a user may have multiple authentication sessions.

- Sessions may be subject to an idle and maximum timeout.

- Session duration is typically based on the sensitivity of the resources accessible from the session, the application delivery platform, and the type of application.

- A continuous authentication session can be used to remember and reconstitute user sessions which have expired.

Notes

i. https://redis.io/

ii. https://datatracker.ietf.org/doc/html/draft-ietf-oauth-
   security-topics-21#section-2.2.2

CHAPTER 10

Using Modern Identity to Build Applications

It's not just what it looks like and feels like. Design is how it works.

—Steve Jobs, founder of Apple Computers, as quoted in "The Guts of a New Machine," *New York Times Magazine*

The past chapters covered how certain identity protocols provide a solution for authentication, API authorization, and application authorization. It may seem daunting at first to learn these identity protocols, but using them will reduce the work you have to do in the long run. In this chapter, we'll describe how we created a sample application to demonstrate how OpenID Connect (OIDC) and OAuth 2 can easily be applied to identity challenges faced by modern applications.

The source code for this book is available on GitHub via the book's product page, located at `https://github.com/Apress/Solving-Identity-Management-in-Modern-Applications`. This repository contains the sample application discussed in this chapter.

Sample Application: Collaborative Text Editor

We chose to demonstrate how modern identity protocols can be used to build an application by modeling a collaborative document editor. The application involves a stateless back-end API serving a single-page application (SPA). This architecture is very popular at the time of writing, and learnings from it can be carried over to mobile applications, which require a similar separation of concerns between the client and API Server.

© Yvonne Wilson, Abhishek Hingnikar 2023
Y. Wilson and A. Hingnikar, *Solving Identity Management in Modern Applications*,
https://doi.org/10.1007/978-1-4842-8261-8_10

Note   Discussing every detail of how to build and deploy modern applications is far beyond the scope of this chapter; thus, we will focus here on the identity-related aspects of the application.

The application offers the following features and services:

- Allows the user to create an article, using rich text – via Markdown.[i]

- Articles belong to the author (user).

- Authors can share an article with others.

- Authors can invite others to collaboratively edit an article.

- Authors can invite others to view the contents of an article in read-only mode.

The demo doesn't support multiple users editing the same article at the same time. Furthermore, a new version is created every time a document is saved. Thus, if Jon created an article, and Jessie were to edit it, Jessie would get their own copy of the version, which is a full copy of the document, and any subsequent edits by either will be in their own history and branch. We kept the user interface quite simple, with minimal validation and error checking, to keep the focus on identity management. Now that we've covered the obligatory caveats about what isn't included, we can discuss what the application will do.

Discovery

In Chapter 1, we suggested several questions to ask about your project that would help you better understand your identity management requirements. Let us now revisit those questions for this sample application. We share the following answers to clarify the application requirements for the demo application.

Who Are Your Users: Employees or Consumers?

Our sample application provides all types of users the ability to create and share documents. Therefore, both consumers and employees should be able to log in.

How Will Users Authenticate?

Our sample application allows a user to sign up for an account using a username and password and optionally offers the ability to use a social authentication provider. If a user tries to use more than one way to authenticate, they are prompted to link their accounts, in order to reduce confusion and offer a better experience.

Can Your App Be Used Anonymously?

Users can start out anonymously and create an anonymous document. To keep the application simple, if a user subsequently signs in, their anonymous documents are not converted to named-owner documents and are not visible to the named account. If an anonymous document is edited, the application creates another copy of the document.

Web-Based or Native App Format or Both?

The sample application will provide a web-based single-page application. This question helps us understand the scope of the project and argues for creating an API that encapsulates the back-end business logic needed by front-end applications. Such an API would make it easier to add a native application in the future. If you are writing a native application, many of these paradigms will remain the same.

Does Your Application Call APIs?

Our application will call our first-party API, which provides access to users' articles. There is no use of third-party APIs at this time. The front-end application and back-end API are logically part of the same entity.

Does Your Application Store Sensitive Data?

The sample application assumes that the data in a user's article might be sensitive.

What Access Control Requirements Exist?

The sample application provides anonymous authors with the ability to write and share documents. These documents are visible to everyone and such documents can be edited by the document author or cloned by anyone else.

Registered users can view documents shared with them, create new documents, edit the documents they created, and share their documents with others by specifying an email address or domain name. Documents can be shared with an individual user via their email address or with a group of users via a domain name. Basing document sharing on an email address's Internet domain name allows us to demonstrate a simple implementation of group-based sharing.

How Long Should a User Session Last?

The application offers a three-day maximum session timeout. There is no inactivity timeout implemented on the application. Instead, the application uses ephemeral access tokens issued by the identity provider. This is discussed further later in this chapter. After session timeout occurs, a user must reauthenticate.

Will Users Need Single Sign-On (If More Than One Application)?

In our sample scenario, there is only one application. However, we have implemented single sign-on into Discourse,[ii] a popular tool that is used for community documentation and support forums. This allows us to demonstrate a common scenario where users have single sign-on between an application, documentation, a public community, and some kind of support center.

What Should Happen When a User Logs Out?

When a user logs out, their application session should be terminated, and the user should be returned to a home page from which they could log in again.

Are There Any Compliance Requirements?

We assume no compliance requirements. The sample does not include a privacy notice, nor does it support any privacy requirements such as the right to erasure. We can only do this because it is a sample and can only run on a developer's machine. Real applications have to consider privacy requirements, and we encourage investigating them early in a project to understand the scope of work required.

Platform, Framework, and Identity Provider

In order to keep the application simple and easy to understand, it is implemented using the popular React Framework[iii] for the front end and Express.js[iv] on the back end. All the code is written in JavaScript. This decision was made as the learnings from javascript can be translated easily to many frameworks in many different languages. The application components can be easily deployed to a hosting platform such as Heroku[v] or Vercel.[vi]

Design

Based on the answers to the requirements questionnaire, we made a list of identity-related and application-related tasks in our design. The categorization for your application might not be as simple as our sample, but we recommend doing this exercise as it helps identify identity management requirements. Our list of tasks is shown in Table 10-1.

Table 10-1. *Identity-Related and Application-Related Tasks in Sample Application*

Identity-Related	Application-Related
Authenticating users	Reading/writing documents
Issuing tokens	Performing checks on documents
Revoking sessions/tokens	Access to documents
Logout	

From the preceding list, it's clear that we have a lot of identity-related tasks to implement. We would like to *abstract* out the identity-related tasks as much as we can. There are different approaches for doing this, such as using a library and building individual components or using an identity provider server or service. Instead of building an identity provider from scratch, we chose to leverage a third-party identity provider service for the identity-related tasks. This allows us to focus more of our time on the core functionality of our application.

Buy vs. Build

A useful analogy for this buy vs. build decision is someone needing to write a paper. A computer buff with experience building computers as a hobby might enjoy designing and building a custom computer for document editing. It would take a lot of time, possibly more time than writing the paper itself. If it is their hobby, they might not mind the time required, and since they have significant experience, they would be able to design a reliable computer and fix anything that breaks down later.

Most people, however, would just want to focus on writing the paper. They would not have the time or expertise to build a reliable custom computer. It would make a lot more sense for them to buy a computer so they could immediately get to work on their writing. If the computer malfunctions, they could get help more readily for a standard computer than one they built themselves. For similar reasons, we'll leverage a third-party identity provider rather than build our own identity provider. It enables us to focus on our application's features and reduces our future support burden.

There are several third-party identity providers available. We chose Auth0[1] as we are familiar with it, but there are several good identity providers to choose from. Third-party providers enable applications to integrate with them using common identity protocols.

Industry Standard Protocols

Industry standard identity protocols play a very important dual role here. While they provide features such as single sign-on, user federation from social or employer accounts, and authorization, they also facilitate the use of third-party identity providers. They have probably undergone more thorough security review than custom code, and it may be easier to hire engineers to work with industry standard protocols than custom code. We strongly recommend using open, industry standard identity protocols and a third-party identity provider rather than building your own identity provider from scratch. While it may seem daunting to learn the protocols at first, it reduces complexity, liability, and maintenance burden in the long run, as we will see in the next few pages. When picking an identity provider, we strongly recommend using one that supports open, industry standard protocols to integrate with your application.

---

[1] At the time of writing, the authors worked for Auth0.

Architecture

Choosing to use industry standard protocols and a third-party identity provider allows us to refactor our solution. Figure 10-1 shows our application architecture with a third-party identity provider.

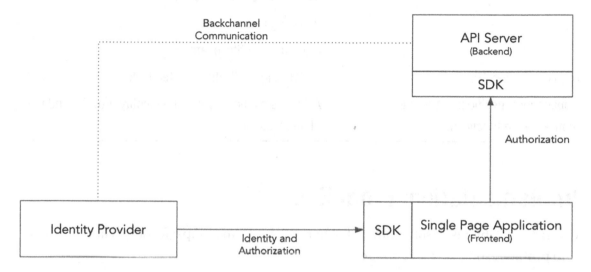

***Figure 10-1.** High-Level Design of the Sample Application*

With an Identity provider in the picture, we can reshape our original problem space into the following questions from an identity perspective:

- How is my application going to trigger a login and logout?

- How is my application going to establish who the logged-in user is?

- How is my application going to call the API?

- How can the API ensure the request it received is valid/authorized?

- How can my API ensure the requested user has sufficient authorization to perform this task?

We will focus on implementing these details in the next section. From an architectural point of view, we recommend writing a thin "glue" layer to abstract these details out from your core application code into a set of convenience functions that handle the identity calls. This can simplify your application code and make it less tightly coupled to a specific identity provider. With an identity layer, our solution can be divided into three components, shown in Table 10-2.

Table 10-2. *Architectural Components for Our Application*

Component	Responsible for
Identity Provider	Authenticating users
	Managing service-wide session
	Providing logout
	Providing identity federation
Application and API	Performing application-related tasks
Application-specific identity layer (convenience functions)	Acting as a glue between the identity provider and the API/application

Implementation: Front End

Our list of problems to solve can be further split into two groups: front end and back end. The problems on the front end are

- How is my application going to trigger a login and logout?

- How is my application going to establish who the logged-in user is?

- How is my application going to call the API?

The answers are obvious: using modern identity and access management (IAM) protocols of course! We are going to be using OpenID Connect (OIDC) to communicate between our application and the identity provider. At a high level, the identity provider will issue an ID Token to our application to convey information about the user and an access token to grant our application access to the API.

To start, we should mention that our application needs to be registered as an OIDC client on the identity provider. Different identity providers have various means of doing this. The registration process assigns a client ID to an application and allows the application to specify a callback URL, among other things. The registration process is important to establish a trust relationship between the application and identity provider. The information exchanged is used during the protocol interaction to mitigate the risk of various types of attacks. Registering our application at the identity provider gives us information, such as the client ID, that we will need to include in calls to the identity provider.

You may recall from previous chapters that integrating OIDC in your application requires constructing a URL, redirecting the user to the identity provider, and handling the callback from the identity provider. Fortunately, there are many OIDC-compliant client SDKs that will do the heavy lifting of this detailed protocol interaction for you. We chose an SDK from our identity provider because it simplifies the OIDC interaction and we knew it would be supported for use with the provider.

We then created our application's identity layer of convenience functions to call the identity provider SDK. This allowed us to abstract the protocol details into more use case–driven tasks, which map directly to our list of problems to solve on the front end. Our solution's front-end identity layer needs four convenience functions, as shown in Table 10-3.

Table 10-3. *Front-End Functions Needed*

Function	Purpose
login	To authenticate the user using the identity provider.
getToken	To get a token to call an API with specific scopes.
logout	To end the current authentication session via the identity provider.
getProfile	To get information about the current user.
handleCallback	To handle redirection back from the identity provider, mostly needed for redirect-based flows on browsers.

Depending on your identity provider, the protocol in use, and the user/application/API model, the exact signatures for these functions might vary. The tasks they need to perform, however, will likely be roughly the same as ours. For instance, the login() function might handle the details of storing the current application state and redirecting to an identity provider. At the identity provider, the redirection is typically handled by a method called "authorize," which in our case requires parameters for an "audience" and "scopes". Our *login* convenience function therefore requires such parameters to call the identity provider SDK.

Beyond the functions shown in Table 10-3, we need some kind of in-memory persistence layer in which to store the data received from the identity provider, such as user profile data or access tokens. This can reduce the frequency with which our application has to call the identity provider and improve the responsiveness of our application. Some applications store the user profile data fetched from identity providers on client storage (e.g., LocalStorage). However, any sensitive data, such as access tokens, must only be placed in adequately secure storage. The storage options available vary based on the type of application and platform used. In your identity abstraction layer, you should try to reuse as much functionality from the identity SDK as possible. If your identity SDK offers some type of storage, you should prefer using it. However, if your identity SDK provides only the bare-bones methods for abstracting OIDC, your methods would need to be doing something like that described in the following sections.

login( ) and handleCallback( )

Login in OIDC usually involves implementing the redirection flow using the "authorization code" flow. Implementing this two-step process as one "logical" unit has advantages. For instance, consider a scenario where a user who has never logged in navigates to a document at /articles/foo/1 via a hyperlink shared to them. At this point, we'd like to redirect the user to the identity provider and then redirect them to /articles/foo/1 after they have logged in successfully.

To solve this, we can include state data such as the user's desired document URL and any additional metadata on client-side storage and then "refer" to it via a string key, which we pass to the identity provider as a *state* parameter. Upon successful authentication of the user, our application will receive the *state* parameter back and would be able to use this data to redirect the user to the desired document URL.

To send such a key of state data, we usually use the *state* parameter in OIDC. One thing to stress here is that when using *state* it must be an opaque string. One simple storage solution could be to use localStorage and JSON in the browser as shown in the following code snippet:

```javascript
// encoding

function encodeState(data) {
    const state = randomBytes(32);
    const serializedData = JSON.stringify(data);
    localStorage.setItem("state_"+ state, serializedData);
    return state;
}
```

```
// decoding
function decodeState(state) {
    const stateKey = "state_"+ state;
    if (!localStorage.hasItem(stateKey)) {
        throw new Error("State not found");
    }

        const storedState = JSON.parse(localStorage.getItem(stateKey));
        localStorage.clearItem(stateKey);
        return storedState;

}

// Then use it when redirecting

.authorize({ state: encodeState({ returnTo: "/articles/foo/1" }) });

// On callback

// Assume parsedResponseUrl is URL Object
const state = parsedResponseUrl.search.state;

const storedState = decodeState(state);

window.history.push(storedState.returnTo); // replace with your library
/ router
```

The key things to look for in an identity SDK for login() and handleCallback() are

- How does the identity SDK create the authorization URL? This may
  be exposed as a method named "login," "authorize," or something
  similar.

- How does the identity SDK receive the data that is returned by the
  identity provider?

- Does the SDK handle the implementation details of redirecting the
  user and handling the response?

- What information are you responsible for storing and providing
  to the SDK?

- Does the SDK implement verification of the ID Token or not?

Once you have those details, then the flow to implement *login* can be

- Serialize your application state and generate any parameters needed to call the SDK.

- Call the method to generate the /authorize URL and redirect to the OpenID Provider in the SDK.

- Resume flow when redirect occurs using .handleCallback.

- Perform necessary validation steps, such as checking the ID Token is valid.

- Perform any additional required steps, such as redirecting to the original page, prefilling a form, etc.

Invoking ".handleCallback" should occur on a dedicated route in your web application such as /user/auth/callback, which is registered on the identity provider's configuration as the callback URL for the application. The callback handler should be written to process both successful and unsuccessful authentication cases to avoid unexpected behavior when an identity provider doesn't return with a successful status.

Note   There are some differences between authentication in a native app and a web-based app in terms of how authentication is delegated to the identity provider. On the Web, it is natural for a web-based application to redirect the user's browser to the identity provider in order for the user to authenticate there. For native apps, both iOS, MacOS and Android offer system browser integrations for doing this securely, and such redirection has become a widely accepted user experience on such platforms.

---

getToken( ) and getProfile( )

As a part of the login method using OIDC, the application will receive an ID Token and an access token. These should ideally be stored in a javascript variable (in memory) effectively acting as if they are cached until they expire. The getToken and getProfile convenience functions would primarily work on top of this cache, fetching the user profile and access token from it as needed.

The access token received will expire at some point. When it does, you will need to communicate with the identity provider and obtain a new token to continue accessing the API, as described in Chapter 6. There are two strategies available for getting a new token after the original token has expired. If your application is using refresh tokens, it would be able to get a new access token using the refresh token and the refresh token grant. If your application is not using refresh tokens, it would need to redirect to the identity provider to get a new access token. As described previously in Chapter 9, this can be done in a hidden iframe to improve user experience. OIDC SDKs and identity providers may implement this using response_mode "web_message".

Things to look for in an identity SDK for getToken() and getProfile():

- Does the SDK support the web_message response type?

- Does the SDK support refresh tokens and refresh token rotation?

Note   Long-lived, nonrotating refresh tokens are effectively sensitive credentials and should not be used on public, web-based clients due to the higher risk of exposure and compromise. If refresh token rotation is not available in an SDK, you'll need to implement the logic to receive a new refresh token each time a refresh token is used and store this new refresh token for the next request. This logic can be added on top of your token management logic, which would be responsible for checking when you need new access tokens or ID Tokens.

Once you have chosen the strategy for renewing expired access tokens, the implementation for both *getToken* and *getProfile* includes the following:

- Check if cached content is available.

- If not, use the refresh token, or do a hidden redirect flow to get a new access token and any other necessary information from the identity provider.

- If an error is raised, handle it. For example, if the error requires user interaction, handle it by redirecting the user to the identity provider.

- Once all data is obtained, for *getToken* return the access token, and for *getProfile* return the contents of the ID Token.

A Detailed Note on Token Management in SPAs

We abstract token management in the *getToken* method for the front end. When the token is acquired, the application uses the "expires_in" element of the response to compute an expected timeout for the token. All this information, along with the audience, scope, and other metadata associated with the token, is stored in memory. Later, when the application needs an access token with specific scopes, the *getToken* method simply returns an access token from the in-memory cache, until the token expires, at which point the application needs to request a new access token.

When using refresh token rotation, there are three possible flows to request a new access token (with our identity provider's feature set), as shown in Table 10-4.

Table 10-4. *Steps for SPAs to Obtain New Access Tokens*

Scenario	Steps
A refresh token is in memory.	Request a new access token using refresh token rotation.
A refresh token is not available (no longer in memory).	Try to retrieve a new access token from the identity provider using a hidden iframe. This may fail with browsers implementing tracking protections.
A refresh token is not available, and a redirect via hidden iframe fails.	Fully redirect the user's browser to the identity provider with prompt=none. If a session exists, the browser will be redirected back to the application with new tokens.

Implementing this can be challenging, especially since doing so in a browser where the user has never authenticated or is not authenticated will create unnecessary overhead for your identity provider. To simplify that, we recommend using some kind of a localStorage flag or variable, such as _lastSessionValidated_, which would represent the likelihood of a session being available on your identity provider. Based on this variable, you could execute the logic for the second and third flows, as appropriate.

In our case, we abstract *getToken* using the *getToken* method in our identity provider's SDK, auth0-spa-js.[vii] The auth0-spa-js library offers a cache implementation as well, so we do not reimplement it in the application. However, we do provide an example class that represents what such a cache requires.

.logout( )

Logout is implemented by clearing any tokens available to the application from memory. This includes tokens received during the user's session as well as any cookies and session state set by the application. In addition, when logging out, we redirect to the OpenID Provider's logout endpoint. This terminates the identity provider session as the provider will log the user out when the logout endpoint is invoked. The implementation for logout and session termination is vendor specific, and we recommend checking your identity provider's documentation for their specific implementation of any logout-related features.

Things to look for in an identity SDK for .logout():

- How to invoke the OIDC (Relying Party) RP-Initiated Logout[viii]

- Methods to clear any meta state the SDK might have stored for the user session

Implementing *logout* is pretty straightforward in our case and includes

- Clear all tokens in memory

- Remove all other locally stored information about the user

- Redirect the user to the identity provider's OIDC Logout endpoint via the SDK

An additional consideration is how to handle access tokens at logout. Identity providers that issue opaque access tokens may provide a mechanism to revoke access tokens. If provided, this can be used within a logout function. With a JWT access token, however, it is not possible to revoke the access token unless the issuing identity provider supports a blocklist feature or provides an introspection endpoint to check the status of the current token. It is possible to maintain a blocklist at your resource server, but synchronizing these blocklists can be challenging. If not revoked or blocklisted, the access tokens will stay valid until they expire. In practice, it's often more convenient to use a short token expiration than to call the provider for each token to check for blocklisting.

Our provider uses a JWT-format access token. The access tokens for our API are configured in the identity provider to have a sufficiently short expiration period so we can avoid the development work and performance impact of checking for blocklisting. We recommend checking for the recommendations from your chosen identity provider on how to terminate access associated with security tokens it has issued, as the process may vary by the provider.

Closing Note

In the preceding sections, we've described an approach for writing an identity layer of convenience functions that call an identity provider's SDK. We did this to simplify our application code and isolate the details of a particular identity provider's SDK in the identity layer. Even if an identity provider offers a higher-level SDK, we still recommend writing an identity layer as a simple wrapper on top of the SDK. This makes it easier to update your code if the SDK's API changes in the future. It can also facilitate testing, debugging, and Continuous Integration/Continuous Deployment (CI/CD) workflows without having to call the identity provider during your tests because you can stub out the convenience functions with a dummy implementation.

In our sample application, Auth0's auth-spa-js SDK is doing most of the heavy lifting for the identity protocol interaction with the identity provider. For additional learning, we have included a sample using OAuth4WebAPI which is a pure OpenID Connect Client to implement capabilities mentioned earlier. You can find this sample in the code repository in examples/oidc-spa-js.js.

Implementation: Back-End API

So far, we've been happily building the front end and haven't talked much about the back end. A strong separation of concerns between the front end and the back end allows them to be implemented with some independence. The advantage of developing with well-designed, industry standard identity protocols is that you can largely develop a front end and/or a back end as long as they agree upon the identity protocol. The front ends, whether native, browser-based, or web applications, will be able to access the back end, or many back ends, as long as they have the appropriate access token for the specific back end.

With that, let's start designing and implementing our back end. Just like the front end, there are the two major problems to solve:

- How can the API ensure the request it received is valid/authorized?

- How can my API ensure the requested user has sufficient authorization to perform this task?

The first task is primarily dependent on the client via the identity provider. The access token issued by the identity provider must be included in all requests from the client application to the back-end server, as a bearer token. Identity Providers have different ways of representing an API, but, in general, you'll register a back-end server/ API with an identity provider, which will issue it a unique identifier. A client application can then request an access token for a specific API using that identifier. In our case, the identifier for our registered API is used with the "audience" parameter in the client's authorization request to Auth0, our identity provider. (This parameter may be called the "resource" parameter in some implementations.)

Depending on the identity provider, you may receive an opaque access token that is validated by checking with the identity provider via an API call. Alternatively, you may receive a JWT-format access token, which is a self-contained token that includes the proof of its legitimacy cryptographically attached to it. JWT-format tokens are common, and there is now a defined "JSON Web Token (JWT) Profile for OAuth 2.0 Access Tokens."[ix] We use JWT access tokens that use the RS256 signature algorithm. Doing so allows us to validate the JWT using the public key hosted by the identity provider on a well-known URL. This avoids the requirement to store a secret symmetric key on our API servers to validate the signature of JWT access tokens as would be required with HS256. This reduces risk, because if the secret key were compromised, it could be used by a rogue element to issue unauthorized tokens.

Once a JWT is received by an API and extracted from the request header, the API server should decode it and perform a quick assessment on whether the JWT uses one of the approved algorithms and is issued by an approved identity provider for the API. The API back end should then fetch and cache the public key from the identity provider and validate the signature on the JWT access token before trusting the contents of the token.

Most languages and development frameworks provide a library for JWT access token validation. The website `https://jwt.io` lists a large number of these libraries. Your identity provider or SDK vendor might provide a more specialized library for this task.

You will need to ensure the audience, issuer, and algorithms are valid, by having an approved list on your API Server. You should not trust the incoming information in the access token without validating it. For example, if the issuer ID on your identity provider is `https://foo.bar`, then any requests to your API using access tokens from another issuer must receive an HTTP 401 response (unauthorized). Another example is that tokens with "none" as the algorithm must be rejected.

The second problem to solve in the back end can be divided into two major tasks, namely, identifying who the user is and what they are allowed to do. We can convert these into methods, like we did on the front end, and then focus on implementing them. Table 10-5 shows the API Helper Functions for our application.

Table 10-5. *API Helper Functions Needed*

Function	Purpose
function getUserId(token) {}	Takes a token and extracts the user_id
function canPerform(token, resource, action) {}	Given a token check a specific action can be performed using the token

.getUserId( )

This function is rather simple to implement. The claim "sub" in a JSON Web Token is often used to represent the user. Since we are using the Express framework,[x] we can extract this claim and populate this as an additional property on the request object.

As recommended in Chapter 4, we use an internal, application-specific identifier for a user in all application and API logic and use separate identifier attributes for display and notification. This enables a user to change the value of attributes such as their display name or notification email address without impacting articles tied to their identity. To keep the program simple, we didn't implement functionality to let them actually make such changes, but this may serve as a fun modeling problem for the future.

The things to look for in the identity SDK for getUserId are

- How will it perform JWT validation?

- What contents are returned?

.canPerform( )

This method is an abstraction of authorization and requires a lot more explanation. The attributes needed to answer the authorization question need to be available either in the incoming request to the API or via some form of secondary storage that is referenced by information in the incoming request.

In our case, however, we needed access control at a very granular level, namely, each individual document. In our implementation, permissions for a document are stored on the document itself. Each document is stored on disk with an additional field that encapsulates who has access to the document. As a result, we elected to handle access control enforcement within our API. This meant the API needed to receive information about the user in each request for a document. The *canPerform* method therefore accesses a document resource's metadata and then returns true or false depending on whether the resource is accessible by the user.

To model permissioning, the metadata for document resources is an array of access control which represents the following:

- The type of access granted, whether based on a user or a domain (discussed later)

- The benefactor of this access

- A list of the permissions that the benefactor has ("owner," "editor," "reader")

A simple implementation of *canPerform*, which ignores the domain-based access is

javascript

```
/**
 * Simple implementation of canPerform
 */
canPerform(token, resource, action){
        const userId = getUserId(token);

        if (resource .type !== "Document") return false;

        const {acl} = Documents.read(resource.id);

        return acl.some(access => access.userId === userId
&& access.permission.includes(action)
);
}
```

Using OAuth 2 Scopes – for API Authorization

OAuth 2 defines scopes as a means for an application to indicate the specific privileges it requests for an API call. We defined access scopes for the applications around the API endpoints and functions the applications would perform. This resulted in the following scopes that the applications can request:

- get:article

- post:article

- patch:article

- patch:profile

- get:author

Note that these are the privileges that the front-end applications will use with the API, and not privileges that will be granted for individual users. The advantage here is that we could now expose our API to third-party applications, or even other first-party applications, and customize the access granted to each one, based on the defined scopes, without having to modify our API implementation. To reiterate, the scopes are used to grant application clients the ability to make various requests to our API. We will discuss authorization of users later in this chapter.

As a final note, the access policy for our demo application is extremely simple and easily expressed using the scope parameter. If we had a different application with a significantly more complex access policy, we would have considered using a Rich Authorization Request (RAR), as described in Chapter 8. At the time of writing, this is still a draft specification, so timing and support from identity providers would be factors to keep in mind against the capabilities this specification offers.

Linking Accounts

The benefit of having abstracted the identity aspects of our application is that we can handle challenges like user duplication, where a user may inadvertently create more than one account, by using a different way to authenticate than the one they initially used.

One option is to avoid the issue by simply enforcing a constraint that they must register first with a username/password account. However, such an approach proves to reduce the efficiency offered by using a social provider. In our case, we used an extension feature in the identity provider to add an additional constraint in the login procedure. When a user is authenticating, if we determine that the email address is already registered, we prompt the user to link their existing identity. It is important that we verify the original identity and that the current user has access to the original identity before linking the accounts. Otherwise, we would open up a vulnerability whereby a compromised social account could propagate into potential account takeovers, even if the user had never used the social provider to log in to our app. Further discussion of account linking can be found in Chapter 18.

In the case of our identity provider, adding additional logic during the login process can be done by running additional javascript code, post login. An extension is provided to accomplish this task. Most identity providers have some means of accomplishing this type of linking. As a last resort, you might be able to query the user record on the first login, bring it into your application, and handle this linking challenge in your application instead.

Anonymous Access

In our API, the core of the data model is a document on which CRUD (Create, Read, Update, Delete) operations are performed. We modeled those as HTTP "verbs" that map to POST, GET, PATCH, and DELETE functions.

By decoupling the business logic from the user information and implementing just these operations, our application could be fully functional without the notion of a user. As a bonus feature, in our case it would allow anonymous access, which might entice users to try out the app who might otherwise balk at having to sign up for an account first.

However, if we enable a user to create documents anonymously and the user later signs in, documents created before logging in will stay anonymous and public. The trade-off we made is that allowing a user to start anonymously means that if they upgrade to a full user later, we miss out on the ability to integrate the information about the user with content created anonymously.

Applications may choose to offer anonymous access or require mandatory user authentication from the start. In our sample, we chose to allow anonymous use as it felt natural to encourage users to try out the application with the least amount of friction.

To make this work with our JWT validation strategy, the application sends the Bearer value of "anonym." This is a special value that means the user is untrusted. The *.canPerform* method can then be adapted to grant "create only" access to all documents, with anonymous identifiers.

Granting Access Based on Domains

One of the features that we find really convenient today is being able to grant access to an entire domain. This is a simple version of the feature to share a document with an entire team on Google Workspace. Solving this is outside the domain of OAuth 2 and OIDC. However, this allows us to highlight how easily solutions can be built on top of these standards.

In the previous sections, we loosely defined the access model for our application. In practice, we store permissions in the document metadata, similar to how files have permissions associated with them in Unix-like operating systems.

Files can be shared using the full email address "user@domain.com" or using "@domain.com" identifiers which must start with the @ symbol. A file permission of "@domain.com" provides a simple way to grant access to a team and allows all users with an @domain.com email to access the file. The creator of a file has full access to the file, and to keep things simple, only the creator of a file is able to grant "share" privilege to others.

To implement this, each file has an array in metadata with the following shape:

```
{
        Type: "DOMAIN"|"INDIVIDUAL"
        identifier: String,
        permission: Permission[],
}
```

The "identifier" attribute is either an email address or a domain name, while "permission" is one or more of the following, "read," "write," "share," and "owner." In the current permission model, a complete email will be matched in its entirety with the user's email. In the interest of privacy, instead of sharing the full email, only a salted hash of the information is stored.

This brings us to another problem. So far, our application has no means of fetching the user's hashed email or their hashed email domain in the access token. To work around this, we add custom claims in the JWT access token issued by the identity provider. To convey information about the authenticated user to an API, it is very useful to have an identity provider that offers some means of adding custom claims to the access tokens it issues.

A nonstandard claim, such as "https://dev.doc/team", is used to indicate a team's email domain, and "https://dev.doc/email" is used to indicate the salted email address of an individual user. An extensibility feature in our chosen identity provider allows us to use custom code logic to augment the claims in the access token. We used a snippet of code like the following to add a claim:

```
export async function (user, context, callback) {
    user.app_metadata = user.app_metadata || {};
    user.app_metadata.teamId = user.app_metadata.teamId || async
    hash(getDomain(user.email));

    context.accessToken["https://dev.doc/team"] = user.app_metadata.teamId;
    callback(null, user, context);
}
```

We have found that access policies vary quite a bit, and it is very common for applications to have unique access requirements. For this reason, we recommend checking for extensibility features when selecting your identity provider, as well as carefully evaluating a provider's support for your application's access control requirements. If your identity provider doesn't support either your requirements or such extensibility, you'll need to handle more logic on your application back end or add this in the provisioning step. In our case, this is conveniently handled for us out of the box with extensibility features in our identity provider, giving us more time to focus on our business logic.

The same need for extensibility applies to front-end customization as well, as most applications will want to customize consent screens and need tailored consent management or approval logic. Having an identity provider with some form of front-end extensibility for functions like login, sign-up, and consent can reduce what you have to build in your application.

Other Applications

In addition to the application that we developed, we are also using Discourse as a second application to demonstrate single sign-on. The Discourse application is registered separately with the identity provider and uses the Authorization Code Flow to authenticate users. The instructions about this are documented at the Discourse Documentation. One of the advantages of using an industry standard protocol like OIDC, OAuth 2, or SAML 2 is the benefit of support for single sign-on with third-party services like this one.

If you have an application that has a native application counterpart, the native application should also be registered at the identity provider as a second application. There are many benefits of doing so. It reduces the chances of potential abuse by limiting the impact of a bug, vulnerability, or misconfiguration. It can also improve visibility of users' usage patterns, enable implementing different access control for the two client applications, as well as provide flexibility for branding and customization.

Additional Note on Sessions

In the modern identity world, a session for a user may be in turn a series of sessions, interconnected. Even for our simple user application, there are two layers of session. There is an application session for the user as well as an identity provider session for the user. There may be additional sessions, as shown in Figure 10-2, when a user's account in one identity provider is federated to an account in a remote identity provider. Sessions A, B, and C are independent sessions, managed by each application.

The single-page app relies on the identity provider session for a user and, as such, does not store data locally, beyond storing the tokens it receives in the in-memory cache. This simplifies the application but comes with the disadvantage that every time the application is started in the browser, it has to check with the identity provider for the status of the user's session.

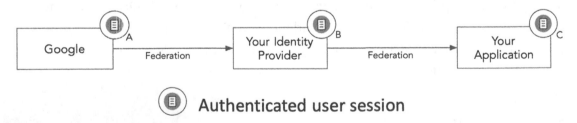

Figure 10-2. Sessions Illustrated

Luckily, it is very simple to make this transparent and perform this activity in the background. The SDK we use abstracts this for us. However, it can be achieved simply by storing some information about the user, like name and picture URL, rendering the UI optimistically, and performing the authentication in the background. This can be done by redirecting to the identity provider and fetching the response from the identity provider in an iframe, at least for first-party applications. The ability to run the authentication in the background is subject to being supported by your identity provider, but has usually been made available via "web_message" response mode or via the OpenID Connect Session Management specification.[xi]

As you learned in Chapter 9, in a typical SSO deployment, a user may have multiple sessions including an application session, identity provider session, and an additional session in each of any other applications they've authenticated to via the same identity provider. It is desirable in some cases to have a binding between the session at an identity provider and all the relying party applications it serves, so that a given application can be aware of changes to the user's session in the identity provider and vice versa. At the time of writing, there is no reliable, standard way of achieving this with OIDC. There is a recently finalized specification for session management which we elected not to use for reasons described in the following section.

Browsers, Trackers, and OAuth 2

Modern browsers deploy powerful defenses to prevent the monitoring of a user without their consent, despite being constantly challenged by tracking companies. In the past few years, in order to protect the user from being tracked by such third parties, many modern browsers now remove cookies placed by third parties and limit access to cookies in iframes. Some browsers even go so far as to remove any cookies placed by websites that use CNAMES to refer to other domains (e.g., a CDN Service) after seven days. All of this has had a cascading effect that limits the background detection of session status as described in the OpenID Connect Session Management specification.[xi]

In response to the additional security added by browsers to thwart third-party trackers, the OAuth 2 specification now recommends the use of refresh token rotation in browsers. This involves using a short-lived, refresh token. Each consumption of the refresh token results in a new refresh token being issued, such that each refresh token is only used once. The utility here is that since this refresh token is short-lived, the risk of exposure is limited, and it makes the programming model almost the same as for native applications. Additionally, OAuth 2 recommends adding token reuse detection and revoking sessions in case of a token reuse being detected, to further improve the user's security.

Summary

We've covered in this chapter how we designed and built a sample application that uses OIDC for user authentication and OAuth 2 for API authorization for our custom API. In this scenario, both functions are handled by our identity provider, which serves as an OpenID Provider and an OAuth 2 authorization server. We shared some key design decisions and implementation points involved in creating the application. The following chapters will discuss additional aspects of identity management that applications have to handle after the user has been initially authenticated, starting with single sign-on.

Key Points

- OIDC is used to authenticate users and obtain an ID Token with claims about the authenticated user.

- OAuth 2 is used to obtain an access token to authorize the application to call our custom API.

- To obtain access tokens for our custom API, we need to obtain and configure our own identity provider to protect it.

- We used customization features from the identity provider to add custom claims to the access token to provide additional information to the API about the user. The custom claims enable the API to enforce user-level access policy. Customization features vary by identity provider.

- Both applications use the OIDC authorization code flow with PKCE for a user's initial authentication.

- Our application uses a library that uses the web_message response mode for renewing access tokens for a better user experience.

- The native application uses a refresh token to obtain a new access token if the previous access token has expired.

- Registering the single-page and native versions of our application separately at the identity provider allows us to distinguish between the two application versions for access control, branding, and logging.

Notes

i. www.markdownguide.org/getting-started/

ii. www.discourse.org/

iii. https://reactjs.org

iv. https://expressjs.com

v. https://heroku.com

vi. https://vercel.com/

vii. https://auth0.com/docs/libraries/auth0-single-page-app-sdk

viii. https://openid.net/specs/openid-connect-rpinitiated-1_0.html

ix. https://datatracker.ietf.org/doc/html/rfc9068

x. https://expressjs.com/

xi. https://openid.net/specs/openid-connect-session-1_0.html

xii. https://openid.net/specs/openid-connect-session-1_0.html

CHAPTER 11

Single Sign-On

A ripple widening from a single stone Winding around the waters of the world.

—Theodore Roethke, American poet, from *The Far Field* (1964)

Now that we've covered some protocol basics and a sample application, we can discuss single sign-on (SSO), starting with what it is and why it is valuable. We'll also cover how it works and considerations for attributes of single sign-on sessions to help you design SSO for your projects.

What Is SSO?

Single sign-on is the ability for a user to authenticate once and access multiple applications without having to log in again. It is usually enabled by using an identity provider. This chapter will focus on SSO and assumes a set of applications that use either OIDC or SAML 2, use the same identity provider, and are accessed via the same browser, or, in the case of native applications, at least use the same browser when delegating authentication to the identity provider. Once authenticated, a user enjoys single sign-on access to applications as long as their identity provider session (SSO session) has not expired or been terminated.

Single sign-on can aid a variety of scenarios. In consumer-facing environments, for example, a user might enjoy single sign-on across multiple applications that allow the user to log in via Google Sign-In.[i] In an enterprise environment, an employee might enjoy single sign-on across internal and cloud applications that leveraged their company identity provider for authentication. In universities, students, professors, and administrators might enjoy single sign-on across university applications leveraging a university identity provider.

© Yvonne Wilson, Abhishek Hingnikar 2023
Y. Wilson and A. Hingnikar, *Solving Identity Management in Modern Applications*,
https://doi.org/10.1007/978-1-4842-8261-8_11

Single sign-on offers many benefits. For users, single sign-on offers the convenience of not having to authenticate as often, fewer usernames and passwords to remember, and no exposure of their credentials to applications. Application owners can delegate to the identity provider the work for implementing login pages, credential validation, secure storage of credentials, and some account recovery features. For a business or organization, single sign-on additionally provides a single place at which to implement and enforce authentication policy, different forms of authentication, account recovery, logging, and account termination. It's easier to enforce best practices in a single place than in many individual applications. SSO also improves security to the extent that users with only one password to remember are less likely to write it down on the proverbial sticky note or whiteboard.

There are, however, a few trade-offs with single sign-on. Implementing single sign-on creates a gateway to your application with the potential to be a single point of failure. A centralized service also provides a single point of attack. To mitigate these risks, it's essential to select an identity provider that is designed to be highly available and implements security best practices. An identity provider also has greater visibility of user activity and the ability to track users across sites, which can be a privacy concern. When selecting an identity provider, you should perform due diligence evaluation of the privacy features and security certifications of a provider before entrusting your application's authentication to it.

How SSO Works

Single sign-on is possible with the authentication protocols discussed in this book because an identity provider maintains a session for a user it has authenticated. Using the example shown in Figure 11-1, a user visits application 1 which redirects their browser to an identity provider with an authentication request. The identity provider authenticates the user, establishes a session for the user, and creates a cookie in the user's browser with information about the session. Then it redirects the user's browser back to the application with security token(s) which contain data about the authentication event and authenticated user. The application can then create or update its own local session (and possibly a cookie) for the user as appropriate for the type of application.

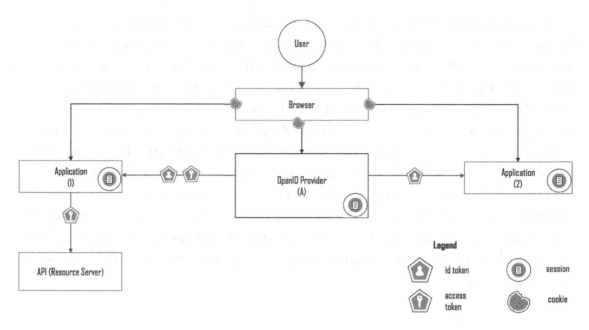

Figure 11-1. *Single Sign-On*

If the user then visits application 2 with the same browser, the second application detects that the user has not yet logged in to it and redirects the user to the identity provider. The user's browser includes the identity provider cookie with the request, so the identity provider uses the cookie to detect the user already has an authenticated session at the identity provider. It checks if the user's session is still valid and, if so, redirects the user's browser back to the second application with the requested security token(s) without prompting the user for credentials. The second application then creates or updates a local session for the user (and possibly a cookie) as appropriate for the type of application it is. The user can continue to access subsequent applications or come back to the first two, without signing in again, as long as their session at the identity provider, often called their SSO session, remains valid.

There are various reasons that the user's session might become invalid. It might have timed out as described in Chapter 9. Alternatively, the session might have been terminated at the identity provider by an administrator or if the user logged out of the identity provider. The user might have even logged out of another application that triggered a logout request to end the identity provider session. We'll cover more about logout scenarios in Chapter 13. Regardless of the reason, if a user is redirected to an identity provider with an authentication request and their session is no longer valid, the identity provider will prompt the user to reauthenticate (unless the request contained authentication request parameters to suppress active authentication).

Even with a valid SSO session, there are situations where the user still has to interact with the identity provider. If the user visits an application that requests API authorization to call an API on the user's behalf, and the identity provider is also the authorization server for the API, the identity provider will prompt the user for consent for the API access. If the user visits an application that requires a stronger or different form of authentication than that used to establish their existing session, the user will be prompted to meet the new application's authentication requirements. If an application includes in its authentication request a parameter to force authentication, the user will need to reauthenticate. Similarly, a parameter can be used to specify a maximum length of time that can elapse between active authentications, and this may trigger a need for a user to reauthenticate as well. In the absence of such special cases, SSO enables a user to access multiple applications after authenticating once, until their authentication session expires.

SSO Configuration

When implementing single sign-on with an identity provider you control, there are typically several features to configure, from session duration to the strength of the authentication mechanisms used as well as login page branding and circles of trust for each identity provider.

SSO Session Duration

The length of the SSO session, often specified in terms of maximum and idle timeouts, should be configured, keeping in mind the sensitivity of the applications relying on the SSO session; however, it is possible to accommodate applications with different requirements. If an application using OIDC requires a user to actively authenticate more frequently than an identity provider session would require, the "max_age" parameter in the authentication request can be used to specify the maximum allowed time, in seconds, that can elapse since the user was last actively authenticated. The use of this parameter requires the identity provider to actively authenticate the user again if the value of max_age in an authentication request is less than the elapsed time since the user last authenticated. Applications should still check the auth_time claim in the ID Token to ensure the requested max_age was followed.

An application can enable a user to remain active in the application without reauthenticating for a longer time than an identity provider session by using a longer application session timeout.

Authentication Mechanisms

An identity provider should be selected and configured to support the specific authentication mechanisms required by the applications leveraging the session. Applications can use parameters in the authentication request to specify desired classes of authentication mechanisms. For example, one application might require only a username/password login, whereas another application might require a stronger form of authentication such as a one-time password. Stronger forms of authentication are discussed further in the next chapter.

Login Page Branding

In terms of user experience, the login page for an SSO session should make it clear what the user is logging in to. For example, if an employee is redirected to a corporate identity provider, it is helpful for the login page to be branded to identify it as the corporate login page. We'll talk more about logout in Chapter 13, but it should be easy for users to terminate the sessions created when they log in. If the user's login creates an SSO session, but the application only performs a local application logout, users may not realize another step is needed to terminate the SSO session. In designing or configuring login pages, it should be clear through branding and other means what the user is logging in to and how to terminate any sessions when done.

Multiple Identity Providers

If SSO is implemented using an authentication broker that allows for the configuration of multiple identity providers, the broker should be configured to ensure that users from each identity provider can only log in to the applications appropriate for them. This is sometimes called the Circle of Trust (CoT) for an identity provider. For example, if a company has an authentication broker with one identity provider configured for employees and another configured for partners, the configuration should ensure that partners cannot get access to applications intended only for employees. This scenario is illustrated in Figure 11-2. In this example, Application 1 should only be accessed by users authenticated by Identity Provider A. Application 2 should only be accessed by users authenticated by Identity Provider B. An SSO session established by a user logging in to Identity Provider B should not enable access to Application 1.

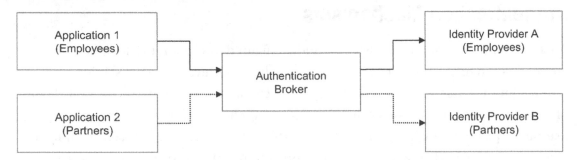

Figure 11-2. *Authentication Broker with Multiple Identity Providers*

Summary

Single sign-on is the ability to log in once and access multiple applications that rely on the same identity provider without having to reauthenticate for each application. Single sign-on offers convenience to users and provides a centralized administration point for authentication policy. Application owners should ensure the characteristics of a single sign-on session at an identity provider are compatible with their requirements for factors such as session duration and the strength of authentication required. We'll cover authentication strength in more detail in the following chapter.

Key Points

- Single sign-on is the ability for a user to authenticate once and access multiple applications that delegate authentication to the same identity provider without the user reauthenticating to each application.

- Single sign-on with an identity provider avoids exposure of user credentials to applications and can reduce the number of passwords for users to remember.

- The use of an identity provider may relieve developers of the work to build login pages and account recovery mechanisms in each application.

- The use of an identity provider for single sign-on provides a single place to administer authentication policy and a single account shut-off point.

- Single sign-on can create a single point of failure if not designed to be highly available as well as secure.

- Identity providers should be configured with session settings appropriate for the applications relying on the identity provider.

Notes

i. https://developers.google.com/identity/

CHAPTER 12

Stronger Authentication

Come, let us hasten to a higher plane,

Where dyads tread the fairy fields of Venn,

Their indices bedecked from one to n,

Commingled in an endless Markov chain!

—Stanislaw Lem, Polish author of science fiction,
philosophy, and satire, from *The Cyberiad* (1965)

Different methods of authentication are not considered equal. The static passwords that still enable access to many Internet services are considered a relatively weak authentication mechanism. Several stronger forms of authentication exist, and their use is recommended to better protect online resources. In this chapter, we'll discuss the issues with static passwords and how stronger forms of authentication can be used for multi-factor authentication and step-up authentication.

The Problem with Passwords

A static password is a secret string of characters used repeatedly over time by a user to authenticate to a particular protected resource. Static passwords are widely used today but have several drawbacks. Short passwords may be guessed by brute force attacks which try every possible password. Long passwords can be difficult for users to remember, but writing them down makes them more prone to being stolen. If a username and password are stolen, they can be used by someone far distant from the account owner, who may not realize the password has been compromised until it is used to do something unauthorized. Worse, if the compromised password has been used

© Yvonne Wilson, Abhishek Hingnikar 2023
Y. Wilson and A. Hingnikar, *Solving Identity Management in Modern Applications*,
https://doi.org/10.1007/978-1-4842-8261-8_12

across multiple sites, its theft can put them all at risk. The introduction of single sign-on makes the use of static passwords more problematic in the sense that a stolen password may grant access to many systems.

Stronger Forms of Authentication

To avoid the weakness of static passwords, there are several stronger forms of authentication that can be used. One widely used mechanism has been to send a one-time password (OTP) to a user via SMS text message or email. The OTP is often a numeric code that is generated by an application and sent to the user at the time of authentication. The user enters the OTP into a login screen to complete the authentication.

Alternatively, a one-time password can be generated by an application on a user device or by a specialized hardware OTP display token. As the name implies, a one-time password can only be used once, making it more difficult for an unauthorized party to use a stolen OTP than a stolen password. Examples of OTP-generating phone apps at the time of writing are Google Authenticator, Duo, Authy, and VIP Access. Apple has also added a built-in OTP generator capability in iOS 15.1. Symantec, Gemalto, and RSA are examples of vendors that produce a hardware OTP display token that generates and displays a one-time password. For some users, a phone is more convenient for OTP generation because they tend to always have their phone with them.

Another approach involves the use of a pair of cryptographic keys. A private key is securely encapsulated in a device such as a smartcard, hardware authentication device, or mobile phone. The entity wishing to authenticate the user sends a challenge nonce to the authenticator device. The secret key encapsulated in the device is used to sign the challenge nonce. With some multi-factor authenticator devices, the user has to enter a PIN or provide a biometric factor to unlock the device before it will sign the challenge nonce, providing a layer of protection against theft of the device. The authenticating entity receives a message back from the device with the signed challenge nonce and validates the signature, using a public key that corresponds to the private key on the device. The public key would have been previously registered during a setup step. If the signature is valid, this process indicates that the user (subject) attempting to log in possesses the authenticator device associated with the account. With this approach, authentication is based on possession of the device with the key as well as a factor (such as a PIN or fingerprint) to unlock the device.

An industry standard was defined for such hardware security keys called Fast Identity Online (FIDO) Universal Second Factor (U2F).[i] This initial protocol has since been extended with newer protocols that add additional features, known collectively as FIDO2. At the time of writing, Yubico provides many types of security keys compliant with FIDO U2F and FIDO2 and is a well-established vendor of such products. Newer offerings are also available from vendors such as Google (Titan key), Thetis, TrustKey, and Feitian.

Biometric factors such as fingerprints, facial scans, retinal scans, and voiceprints can serve as stronger forms of identification. Apple's Face ID[ii] and Touch ID[iii] are examples of biometric authentication, and the Android framework also enables biometric authentication.[iv]

It's worth noting that knowledge-based authentication (KBA), which involves answering security questions, has similar risks to passwords. Answers can be guessed, sourced from public information, or stolen and then used by a remote entity without the owner's knowledge. The strength of authentication methods can be classified, and one example classification scheme is the NIST 800-63 Security standard[v] which defines criteria for three levels of authenticator assurance.

Multi-factor Authentication

Multi-factor authentication requires the use of multiple authentication factors in order to authenticate. These typically include something you know as well as something you have and/or something you are. The something you *know* can be a password or passphrase. The something you *have* may be a device such as a mobile phone or a hardware security device used for one of the authentication mechanisms described in the previous section. The something you *are* can be a biometric factor such as a fingerprint, voiceprint, or facial scan.

The use of multi-factor authentication reduces the risk if any one factor is compromised. If authentication requires entering a static password as well as a one-time password generated by a mobile phone, a hacker would have to steal a user's password and unlocked phone to impersonate the user and gain access to their account. Requiring multiple factors for authentication therefore provides a stronger assurance that the person authenticating is the legitimate account owner.

Authorization policy may require multi-factor authentication for certain situations. It may be required at all times to access sensitive content such as administrative access to production cloud servers. In other situations, multi-factor authentication may only be required if an unusual situation is detected, such as a user attempting access from a new device or an atypical geographic location. Some enterprise environments may require multi-factor authentication for remote access or even in the office for more sensitive resources.

The selection of authentication mechanisms for a solution should take into account the sensitivity of the application and data involved as well as the usability of the solution because users may try to circumvent mechanisms that are too onerous or deemed overkill for a particular situation. Section 6 and specifically Section 6.2 of NIST publication 800-63-3 shows one example of how to approach the selection of an appropriate authenticator assurance level for a deployment.[vi] (NIST Special Publication 800-63B[vii] has the accompanying list of types of authentication for each authentication assurance level.)

Step-Up Authentication

When a user authenticates, an authenticated session is created with a certain level of authentication assurance that the user is the legitimate owner of the account. For example, if a user logs in with a static password, there is some chance the password was stolen and the account is being used by an imposter, so the user's session might be considered at "level one" in terms of authentication assurance. If a user subsequently authenticates with a stronger form of authentication such as a one-time password generated on their mobile phone, the confidence that the user logging in is the legitimate account owner is much higher because it would be harder for someone to impersonate the user when their phone is required for authentication. After authenticating with the one-time password, the user's session might then be considered at "level two" for authentication assurance. (Our choice of levels and names is an arbitrary example for purposes of illustration.) Step-up authentication is the process of authenticating with a stronger form of authentication in order to elevate the authentication assurance level of an existing authentication session.

Authorization policy may require authentication sessions to be at a specific authentication assurance level in order for a user to access resources or execute transactions that involve more risk. Applications with features that vary in sensitivity can use step-up authentication to require stronger authentication for more sensitive transactions. For example, a user might be able to browse a retail website anonymously, but have to elevate their session by authenticating with a password to access previously stored address information for a purchase delivery. In an enterprise, a manager might be able to access the accounts payable system with a password to run reports, but then have to step up their session by authenticating with a one-time password in order to approve a large payment. Step-up authentication facilitates a model where the strength of the authentication mechanism required for a situation is commensurate with the risk inherent in the protected resources involved.

Multi-factor Authentication and SSO

The use of multi-factor authentication can impact the user experience with single sign-on. If a user first accesses an application that only requires password authentication, and then moves on to a second application that uses the same identity provider as the first but requires a stronger form of authentication, such as entering a one-time code sent to their phone, the user will be prompted to satisfy that stronger authentication requirement. Therefore, when rolling out single sign-on deployments where applications may require different levels of authentication strength, you should avoid wording such as "login once, access everything" because users may in fact have to authenticate again with a stronger mechanism to access more sensitive applications. You can reduce user confusion by warning users in advance if a particular action requires stronger authentication. Don't make such notices intrusive, however, or they will create more exasperation than they avoid.

Session Timeouts

An identity provider may allow the configuration of multiple forms of authentication along with a classification or level of authentication assurance for each. A user's authentication session may then include information about the authentication mechanism(s) used, an authentication assurance level or authentication context class, and the session expiration. If an identity provider supports authentication sessions at different authentication assurance levels, you should consider shorter session timeouts for elevated sessions which provide access to more sensitive resources. Shorter session timeouts for more privileged sessions reduce the chances of highly privileged sessions being hijacked for malicious purposes and align with the security principle of least privilege.

Requesting Authentication Mechanisms

Applications may need a way to request an identity provider use a particular class of authentication mechanism to achieve a desired level of authentication assurance. This can be done with an authentication context class reference. An authentication context involves several factors, such as the identification processes used to create an account, the protections against credential compromise, and the authentication mechanism used. An authentication context class represents a set of authentication methods. An authentication context class reference is an identifier for an authentication context class. Authentication context classes and class references are often defined by an identity provider, but may be worked out by a service provider in conjunction with an identity provider. The following sections explain how applications can request a particular authentication context class and how identity providers can provide claims to convey the authentication context class reference and/or authentication mechanism(s) used.

SAML 2

A SAML 2 authentication request can specify an application's desired authentication context class using the <RequestedAuthnContext> element. A SAML 2 authentication response will show the authentication context class used to authenticate a user in the <AuthnContext> element of the authentication assertion, if the identity provider provides this information. Appendix C has additional information on SAML authentication requests and responses including the AuthnContext element. The application (service provider) and identity provider must establish in advance the definitions for different authentication context classes. The document "Authentication Context for the OASIS Security Assertion Markup Language (SAML) V2.0"[viii] lists several predefined authentication context classes which may be used.

OIDC

OIDC clients can request one or more authentication context classes, in order of preference, using the following parameter to the authentication request:

- acr_values – Authentication context class reference

An ID Token issued to an application can contain the following parameters to convey the authentication context class and authentication methods used to authenticate the user (subject) referenced in the ID Token.

- acr – Authentication context class reference, an identifier for an authentication context class

- amr – Authentication method reference, the identifiers for one or more methods used to authenticate a user

The application and OpenID Provider must establish the values and meaning for acr and amr values used. At the time of writing, there are specifications for standard values for these claims. The draft specification for OpenID Connect Extended Authentication Profile (EAP) ACR Values 1.0[ix] lists acr values, and the RFC8176 specification for Authentication Method Reference Values[x] lists amr values.

Step-Down Authentication

To align with the security principle of "least privilege," a user should operate at the minimum privilege level necessary for a particular task. In an environment where sessions can exist with different assurance levels or authentication contexts, with higher-level sessions that enable access to more sensitive resources, users would ideally be able to "step down" their session's authentication assurance level when they no longer need the elevated privileges. This reduces the damage that can be done if a session is hijacked as well as the risk from simple human error when operating at a higher privilege level. Step-down could be implemented with an explicit mechanism, though we have not seen this done in our experience. It is probably more practical to simply rely on short session timeouts for more privileged sessions as well as user logout for immediate termination of a session.

Deployment

There are several deployment considerations worth mentioning for multi-factor authentication (MFA). MFA of any form is an improvement over static passwords which can be stolen through a variety of means including phishing, social engineering, and malware. However, security, usability, maintainability, cost, and recovery are all factors to consider when choosing one or more forms of MFA for your project.

Sending one-time authentication codes to users via SMS messages is widely used and easy for many users to set up and use. If a user's phone is broken, lost, or stolen, the user only has to have the cellular company associate their phone number with the SIM card in their new replacement phone. Once this is done, all the user's SMS messages will come to the new phone, enabling the user to authenticate to applications using the new phone.

The use of SMS messages for authentication can involve a short delay as the user must wait for the code to arrive, and some users may incur a charge to receive SMS messages. A user must also have connectivity to receive the message. This may be a problem in remote environments, environments that restrict use of cellphones such as hospitals, or shielded environments such as underground data centers. Once the message is received, the user must enter the code from the message into a login screen. This is reasonably convenient when logging in to a separate device, such as a laptop, but can be more cumbersome for an app on the same phone.

At the time of writing, the security of SMS codes sent to phones is threatened by several types of attacks. In a SIM-swapping attack, an attacker impersonates a cellular customer (or bribes a cellular company employee) and requests that the victim's phone number be associated with a new SIM card possessed by the attacker. This enables the attacker to intercept the victim's calls and SMS messages. Other attacks have intercepted voice and SMS communications on cellular networks by targeting Signaling System No. 7 (SS7), a protocol layer in the infrastructure that provides connectivity between mobile phone networks. Such attacks are not yet widespread, but may increase in the future. One approach to mitigate this risk is to require the user to re-enter their password when they enter the code, but users may find this annoying, especially if they do not understand the purpose. Your projects should evaluate the current status of SMS attacks before deciding to rely on SMS codes for multi-factor authentication.

Specialized hardware authenticator tokens that generate and display a one-time password have been used in enterprise environments but are becoming less common. They avoid the vulnerabilities associated with SMS messages, but are less convenient because the user has one more item to carry around. The devices can break, get lost, stop working due to a drifting inner clock, or run out of battery and the ongoing cost of replacing devices can be substantial, in one author's experience. In addition, if it takes time to send a new device to a user, they may not be able to log in until they receive the new device and go through an administrative step to associate the new device with their account.

Using an application on a user's mobile phone to generate a one-time password avoids the drawbacks associated with SMS messages and specialized authenticator tokens, but has other issues. There are many OTP-generating applications and each of the different websites a user visits may only support the use of a particular one. This requires users to remember which generator application to use with each website they log in to. Furthermore, if a user's phone is broken, lost, or stolen, the user may temporarily lose the ability to log in while they get a new phone, install the generator apps on their new phone and go through an administrative process at each website they use to authenticate them through other means, remove the old phone, and reenroll with their new phone. The same applies if a user inadvertently deletes the OTP-generating application from their phone. For applications where frequent access might be critical, such as stock trading applications, being locked out of the application until a new phone is registered could have significant negative impact to users.

Authentication devices with cryptographic keys are becoming more common. The authentication secret in this case, a private key, never leaves the device. This means a user cannot be phished or tricked into revealing it. Some devices employ a fingerprint reader such that a user simply touches the reader to unlock the device for authentication. This provides a convenient user authentication experience. On the negative side, this solution involves a separate device which a user must remember to have with them when they need to authenticate. In the past, a given website may have only supported specific security keys or keys from a specific vendor, potentially requiring a user to have more than one across different websites. The FIDO2 protocols and interoperability testing should help alleviate this issue by facilitating interoperability between different vendors' security keys and different websites needing to authenticate users. Like phones, these devices can break, get lost, or be stolen, and a user may temporarily lose the ability to log in if this happens.

With OTP-generating apps on phones or hardware authentication devices, an administrative process is required to deregister an old device and associate a new device with a user's account. If the old device is available and functioning, the user can authenticate with it in order to perform this administrative step themselves. If, however, the device is not available, a user cannot authenticate. Some sites provide the ability to download a set of backup codes for this scenario. The backup codes are system-generated so they are typically long, unique to a particular site, and can only be used once. The use of backup codes, however, relies on the user safely storing the backup codes, noting the site they are for, and having them readily available if their primary authentication device is no longer usable. If a user does not have their backup codes, it is necessary to authenticate them through another means before registering a new device. This is to prevent hackers from bypassing multi-factor authentication by calling up and claiming to be the user and that they've lost their phone. In addition, an attacker who is able to steal a user's backup codes, and password if used, can potentially bypass the multi-factor authentication and take control of the user's account.

Biometric factors have the drawback that if used for authentication and compromised or damaged, they cannot be reissued. In other words, a person cannot be issued a new finger if a hacker is able to capture their fingerprint and use it with biometric fingerprint authentication. If a biometric authentication factor is compromised, it is necessary to either change the factors used or change what the authentication algorithm looks for in the existing factors. In addition, with some biometric factors such as a fingerprint scan, it may be possible for an attacker who has stolen a phone to unlock it if the user is asleep or to physically force the user to unlock the phone. As with other forms of authentication, you need to plan in advance for how to recover from likely compromise scenarios.

Beyond security considerations, be sure to consider usability and ongoing maintenance requirements. Testing multi-factor authentication mechanisms and the use of step-up authentication with users who are representative of the target user population is valuable to identify any usability issues before widespread rollout. Be sure to test failure (unsuccessful) cases as well as successful cases. For every failure case, consider what a user would need to do to recover from the situation and make sure it is reasonable. Evaluate authentication devices for their durability as well as likely battery life if applicable to avoid unexpected costs for replacing broken/dead hardware devices. Depending on the type of authenticator chosen, you may have to budget for replacing lost and damaged devices. When replacement is necessary, you'll also need a process for quickly but securely replacing lost or damaged devices to restore a user's ability to log in. Be sure to plan for secure distribution, replacement, and revocation of authentication mechanisms as part of any deployment.

Summary

Some forms of authentication are considered stronger than others. Passwords are a weak form of authentication, whereas the use of one-time passwords generated on a device or multi-factor cryptographic authentication devices are stronger forms of authentication. Multi-factor authentication requires the use of multiple authentication factors, typically something you have as well as something you know. Step-up authentication is the act of authenticating with a stronger form of authentication which elevates a previously existing authentication session to a higher level of authentication assurance. Authorization policy may require a session to be at a specific level in order to access sensitive resources. Both OIDC and SAML 2 allow applications to request that an identity provider authenticate a user with a particular authentication context class of authentication mechanisms and to receive information about the authentication context class and/or authentication method(s) used to authenticate a user. You should also plan to terminate higher-level sessions in a timely manner via shorter session timeouts or logout, and, conveniently, logout is the topic of the next chapter.

Key Points

- Static passwords are considered a weak form of authentication.

- The compromise of a static password may not be noticed until damage is done.

- It is harder for remote hackers to impersonate a user when authentication requires physical devices in the user's possession.

- Multi-factor authentication relies on multiple factors, such as something you know, something you have, and/or something you are.

- Step-up authentication involves authenticating with a stronger form of authentication to elevate the authentication assurance level of a session.

- Both SAML 2 and OIDC allow an application to request an identity provider use a specified authentication context class when authenticating users.

- To support the principle of least privilege, it may be desirable to have shorter session timeouts for elevated sessions required to access sensitive resources.

- Multi-factor authentication provides greater authentication assurance, but involves considerations of usability, maintenance, cost, and how to securely recover when a user's multi-factor authentication device is lost, broken, or stolen.

Notes

i.   https://fidoalliance.org/specifications/

ii. https://support.apple.com/en-us/HT208108

iii. https://support.apple.com/en-us/HT204587

iv. https://source.android.com/security/biometric

v.   https://pages.nist.gov/800-63-3/sp800-63b.html

vi. https://pages.nist.gov/800-63-3/sp800-63-3.html#sec6

vii. https://pages.nist.gov/800-63-3/sp800-63b.html

viii. https://docs.oasis-open.org/security/saml/v2.0/saml-authn-context-2.0-os.pdf

ix. https://openid.net/specs/openid-connect-eap-acr-values-1_0.html

x.   https://datatracker.ietf.org/doc/html/rfc8176

CHAPTER 13

Logout

Great is the art of beginning, but greater is the art of ending.

—Henry Wadsworth Longfellow, American poet and educator, from
"Elegiac Verse" (1881)

Logout is probably not something that you think about very often, if ever. It might not even be on any of your project's planned sprints, but it should be. Implementing logout can be more complex to design and test in some cases than login.

For many applications, it's important for users to have a way to terminate their session. This is especially true for shared device environments that are used to access sensitive applications, like ATMs, kiosks employed on a manufacturing shop floor, or a medical facility where many doctors and nurses access the terminals in patient examination rooms or hospital stations. Terminating a session if it is no longer needed eliminates the chance that the session can be hijacked by others. This complements other measures in a comprehensive security strategy and is beneficial for situations where devices might be stolen or confiscated. In this chapter, we'll cover why logout can be complicated, what to include when designing logout, and some implementation options.

Multiple Sessions

Logout can be complex to implement in environments with single sign-on, because there may be multiple sessions to worry about. Figure 13-1 shows three different scenarios with the resultant authentication sessions for the user in each one. At a minimum, a user has an application session (Model 1). If an application delegates authentication to an identity provider (IdP), the identity provider may have an active session for the user (Model 2). If an application uses an authentication broker, to

© Yvonne Wilson, Abhishek Hingnikar 2023

Y. Wilson and A. Hingnikar, *Solving Identity Management in Modern Applications*,
https://doi.org/10.1007/978-1-4842-8261-8_13

facilitate handling many different identity providers and protocols, the authentication broker may also have an active session for the user (Model 3). This means that a user could have sessions in up to three different tiers of a solution architecture like Model 3 after logging in. It is possible for an identity provider to delegate authentication to another identity provider, so there could be even more tiers involved, but that is not common.

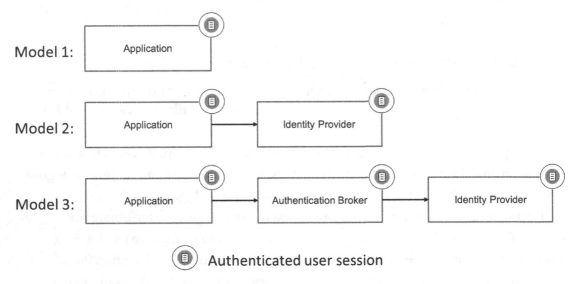

Figure 13-1. *Multiple User Sessions*

Logout is further complicated because with single sign-on (SSO), there might be even more sessions to consider. If a user can access multiple applications via SSO, there could be an additional session in each of those applications. This possibility is illustrated in Figure 13-2 which shows a scenario where applications A and B delegate authentication to an authentication broker, which in turn delegates user authentication to an identity provider. Application C delegates authentication directly to the identity provider. If a user accesses applications A, B, and C in short order, the user would have five active sessions.

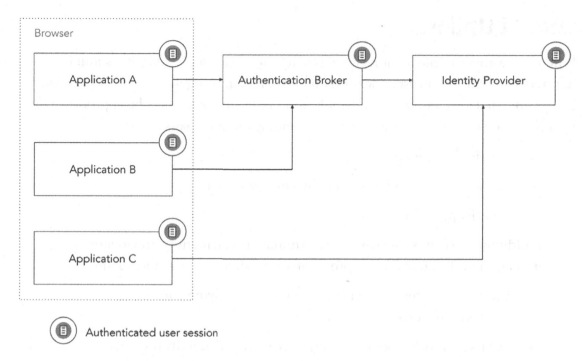

Figure 13-2. *Sessions in Relying Parties*

Logout Triggers

The termination of any of a user's sessions can be triggered by several different events. The most obvious is when a user clicks a logout button in an application. A user may also be able to trigger a logout of their session directly at an identity provider if it provides such a feature. In addition to user-initiated logout, an administrator might terminate a user's session in either an application or identity provider. Another possibility is that a user's session times out if the user has been idle or logged in for too long. Then again, an application or identity provider may receive a logout request from another component in the environment. When any of these events occur, one or more of the user's sessions will be terminated. The question is: Which ones should be terminated and under which circumstances?

Logout Options

When there are multiple sessions for a user, it is necessary to decide what should happen when any of the user's sessions are terminated. Using the models depicted in Figure 13-1, if a user's session in an application is terminated, it may be appropriate to terminate one or more of the following, depending on where sessions exist:

- Application session

- Authentication broker session (if a broker is used)

- Identity provider session

In addition, if a user's SSO session is terminated at an identity provider or authentication broker, it may be appropriate to terminate one or more of the

- User sessions for the user at any "upstream" relying parties (applications or other providers)

- User sessions for the user at any "downstream" identity providers

For example, in Figure 13-2, when the user logs out of application A, the application could send a logout request to the authentication broker. The authentication broker may have other applications (relying parties) relying on its session for the user, such as application B in the diagram. When it receives the logout request, the authentication broker could send a logout request to application B to terminate the user's session there. In addition, the authentication broker could send a logout request to the identity provider. The identity provider would see that application C relied on its session for the user and could send a logout request to application C.

The same possibilities should be evaluated if a user's session is terminated at an identity provider or authentication broker for any reason. Again using Figure 13-2, if the user's session is terminated at the identity provider, it could send a logout request to application C and the authentication broker because they are both relying parties to the identity provider. Similarly, if the user's session is terminated at the authentication broker, it could send a logout request to the identity provider and/or to one or both of the relying party applications A and B.

In designing logout, it is necessary to consider where sessions exist and which should be terminated when a user initiates a logout or if their session is terminated for other reasons. One factor in the decision is the entity owning the sessions. In enterprise environments, corporate security policy may dictate that a logout in an application must trigger the termination of an identity provider session and possibly all the user's open sessions in other applications. In a consumer-facing environment where a user logs in with a social provider, however, it may be less justified or impossible for an application logout to terminate the user's session at the social identity provider. Obviously, an identity provider or authentication broker's supported features for logout are another factor that will influence logout design.

User experience is an important factor as well. Care should be taken to avoid surprises for users. Terminating all application and SSO sessions for a user with one logout provides a convenient way to terminate all access at once. This may be desirable in an enterprise environment because if users have to log out of each application individually, they may forget one. However, if the impact of such a logout is not clear to a user, this may "pull the rug out" from under the user's other application sessions that rely on the same SSO session. An example will help illustrate this.

Using the scenario in Figure 13-2, if a user is working simultaneously in the three applications, A, B, and C, and a logout from application A triggers the termination of their sessions everywhere, that may prevent the user from completing in-flight transactions in application B or C, depending on how those applications handle session termination. The abrupt termination of sessions in other applications may cause a user to lose their work there. Whether the user can continue working in the other applications depends on how logout and session termination is implemented.

One possibility is to have the logout in application A trigger an immediate logout of the user in applications B and C. This would require that the termination of the user's session at application A triggers a logout request to the authentication broker, which is configured to send, upon its session termination, a logout request to application B. The authentication broker could also send a logout request to the identity provider, which in turn could send a logout request to application C. These logout messages would effectively terminate all the user's sessions across the three applications, the authentication broker, and the identity provider.

Alternatively, when application A sends a logout request to the authentication broker, the broker could simply terminate its own session for the user. In this case, the user can continue working in application B until the user's session in application B times out. Upon such timeout, application B would check if the user's session is valid at the authentication broker. If the user's session in the authentication broker had been terminated, the user would need to log in again to continue to access application B.

The decision regarding which sessions to terminate is specific to each environment and should take into account the entity that owns a session, the user experience, and the sensitivity of the application as well as security benefits of not leaving sessions open when not needed. The design of logout will also need to consider the capabilities of individual applications, brokers, and identity providers as their support for logout features may vary. Once logout is implemented, it should be thoroughly tested to make sure it works as designed. The best advice we can give is to allow plenty of time in your project for both designing and testing logout and to start early, as it often takes more time than expected. As shown in Figure 13-1, other entities besides applications, such as authentication brokers, may be relying parties to identity providers. In the subsequent sections, we'll therefore use the broader term "relying party" in places instead of "application" to recognize all types of entities which may be impacted by logout.

Application Logout

The simplest case to implement is local application logout, which terminates a user's session in one individual application. For application logout, when any of the logout triggers described in an earlier section occur, the application needs to delete any application session information, tokens, and browser cookies set by the application. If using OAuth 2 access tokens from an authorization server that supports access token revocation, they should be revoked via the authorization server's revocation endpoint. Refresh tokens, if used, should be revoked as well. Local application logout by itself does not impact any other authenticated sessions the user might have established at an identity provider or authentication broker, but an application can choose to send logout request messages to such other components when local application logout is triggered.

OAuth 2

OAuth 2 does not contain a logout endpoint because it is designed for authorizing an API call, not authenticating users. Nevertheless, upon the termination of a user's session, an application should clean up security tokens related to the user if possible. An application may have obtained access tokens for APIs and possibly refresh tokens as well. The OAuth 2 specification indicates that authorization servers **SHOULD** provide a mechanism to revoke access tokens, and the "OAuth 2.0 Token Revocation"[i] specification defines a standard for this. Providing an access token revocation mechanism is not mandatory, however, so some authorization server implementations may not support it.

If an authorization server supports access token revocation, an application should use its revocation endpoint to revoke access tokens authorized by a user for that application when the user logs out or their session is terminated for other reasons. If an access token cannot be revoked, an application that has refresh token(s) for renewing expired access tokens should revoke the refresh tokens. (Authorization servers must support refresh token revocation.) Without a refresh token, when a previously issued access token expires, the application will not be able to obtain a new access token.

Applications that cannot revoke access tokens must rely on the access token expiration to terminate the application's ability to call an API. This underscores a benefit of access tokens with short expirations.

OIDC

The original OIDC specification does not define an explicit logout mechanism for an application to request termination of a user's session at an OpenID Provider or a way for an OpenID Provider to notify a relying party when the OpenID Provider's session has terminated. At the time of writing, however, there are several recently finalized specifications related to OIDC logout which bear consideration. You should keep in mind that it may take time for providers to implement support for newly approved specifications. Consult your OIDC Provider's documentation and plans regarding any recent specifications and logout capability.

The OpenID Connect RP-Initiated Logout[ii] specification describes a logout flow whereby a relying party can request an OIDC Provider to log a user out. The relying party does this by redirecting the user's browser to a logout endpoint at the OIDC Provider. The OIDC Provider then asks the user to confirm they wish to log out and, if so, terminates its session for the user. The relying party can optionally specify a URL to which the user is redirected after logout at the OIDC Provider.

The OpenID Connect Session Management[iii] specification offers a solution for a relying party application to detect when an OpenID Provider session has terminated. It is designed to use a hidden iframe loaded from an OpenID Provider and which has access to browser state from the OpenID Provider. This iframe is polled from another hidden iframe loaded from the relying party application and will receive back a status of "changed" if the user's session at the OpenID Provider has changed. If this occurs, the relying party application can redirect the user to the OpenID Provider with a new authentication request using prompt=none, and if this request receives an error response, it indicates the user session at the OpenID Provider is no longer valid. The application can terminate its session for the user, if appropriate, or perhaps ask the user if they'd like to renew their session. If so, the application can redirect them back to the OpenID Provider to authenticate and renew the session. At the time of writing, however, recent browser features for tracking prevention may prevent this scheme from reliably working as designed. It is not yet clear if a fix or workaround will be developed.

The OpenID Connect Front-Channel Logout facility[iv] provides a solution for an OpenID Provider to send logout requests to relying party applications when the OpenID Provider session for a user has been terminated. Front-Channel Logout relies on an OpenID Provider rendering an iframe that contains the relying party's logout URL. The logout URL must have been previously registered with the OpenID Provider. This mechanism can enable a global logout capability but suffers from some disadvantages. At the time of writing, this specification is also impacted by recent browser features for tracking prevention. This can prevent a relying party application from being able to process the logout. In addition, if a user has navigated away from an application in their browser, a Front-Channel Logout request to the application may fail, with the user's session in the application only logged out if the user returns to it using the browser's back button.

The OpenID Connect Back-Channel Logout[v] specification provides a solution for an OpenID Provider to send logout requests to a relying party via back-channel communication directly between servers rather than via front-channel browser actions. This may provide a more reliable logout option than Front-Channel Logout when there are many relying parties. For this solution, relying parties register a back-channel logout URI with an OpenID Provider. The OpenID Provider remembers all relying parties to which a user has logged in via their OpenID Provider session. When the OpenID Provider session for the user is terminated, the OpenID Provider sends a logout request, formatted as a JWT and called a Logout Token, to each of the relying parties the user visited during the session.

The Logout Token is sent via back-channel communication (server to server) using an HTTP-POST to the relying party's back-channel logout URI previously registered with the OpenID Provider. Upon receiving and validating a Logout Token, a relying party removes its session for the user and returns a status response to the OpenID Provider. This solution requires direct connectivity between the OpenID Provider and a relying party's back-channel logout URI. This may be problematic for applications residing in on-premise enterprise environments behind firewalls unless the OpenID Provider is also in the same internal environment behind the firewalls.

It is also possible for a relying party application to detect the termination of a user's session at an OpenID Provider by periodically polling the OpenID Provider by redirecting a user's browser to the OpenID Provider with the prompt parameter in the authentication request set to "none." If the user does not have a valid session at the OpenID Provider, an error status response will be returned, and the application can terminate the user's session in the application or redirect the user again to reauthenticate and renew their session. This approach results in network traffic from the polling and has the drawback that the redirect may interrupt the user experience. As noted previously, doing the redirect in a hidden iframe to mitigate user experience issues has been negatively impacted by recent browser features for tracking prevention and may not be a viable solution for some scenarios. Repeatedly polling an OpenID Provider may also run the risk of hitting rate limits.

A common concern is the ability to quickly terminate a user's access to an application. This may be needed in corporate situations if an employee has been terminated against their will. If the OpenID Provider for an environment supports a capability to notify relying parties when a user's OpenID Provider session has terminated, this can be used. In the absence of such single logout capabilities, an application can poll an OpenID Provider periodically as previously described. If the user's account in the OpenID Provider has been disabled, the application will not receive the successful response needed to renew the session. This should effectively terminate the user's ability to use the application, at least with a tolerance period equal to the application's polling frequency.

SAML 2

With SAML 2, a service provider application can terminate a user's session at an identity provider by issuing a logout request message to the identity provider. Upon receipt of the logout request message, the identity provider terminates the session it holds for the user, identified by a subject identifier in the request and possibly a session identifier for the session. The identity provider may also update or remove its session cookie in the user's browser. The identity provider then responds to the application with a logout response message.

SAML 2 also provides a way for the identity provider to notify other relying parties if a user's session is terminated at the identity provider. Upon termination of the identity provider session or receipt of a logout request message from a service provider, the identity provider can send a logout request message to each of the other relying parties with an active session for the user. The relying parties are supposed to terminate their session and respond with a logout response message to the identity provider. If the global logout was initiated by one service provider, the identity provider returns a logout response message to the relying party that initiated the logout. This interaction is shown in Figure 13-3.

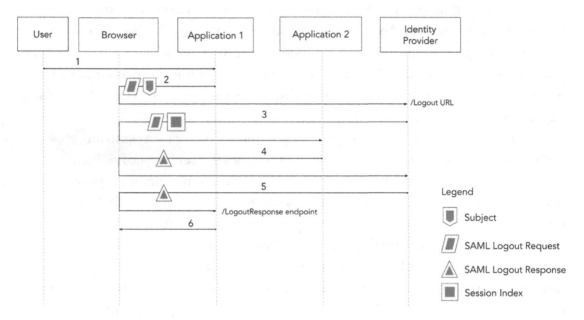

Figure 13-3. *SAML 2.0 Single Logout*

1. The user initiates the logout at Application 1 (a relying party).

2. Application 1 redirects the user's browser to the Identity Provider with a SAML Logout Request message.

3. The Identity Provider sends a SAML Logout Request message to other relying parties, such as Application 2.

4. Application 2 sends a SAML Logout Response message after processing the logout.

5. The Identity Provider sends a SAML Logout Response message back to the relying party that sent the original Logout Request.

6. Application 1 acknowledges the logout.

Steps 3 and 4 in the preceding sequence are commonly sent via the user's browser, using front-channel interaction. Many SAML 2 identity providers reside behind corporate firewalls, and using a front-channel implementation avoids issues with firewalls. In a complicated logout scenario, however, with several relying parties, the sequence may fail before it completes, leaving some sessions intact. The SAML 2 specification includes a back-channel logout mechanism which may be more reliable if logout messages need to be sent to multiple parties. However, back-channel logout may not be implemented in all SAML 2 implementations, and back-channel logout messages require direct connectivity between the identity provider and the relying parties, which may be challenging for components behind corporate firewalls.

Session Termination

There may be a need at times to quickly terminate a user's SSO session as well as application sessions. In corporate settings, this is often a requirement for situations where an employee is terminated against their will. In the absence of single logout, a user's account can be disabled at an identity provider, but they may be able to remain active in applications with open sessions until the applications next communicate with the identity provider. In the case of OIDC or OAuth 2, this may be when the application session and/or access token expires. In the case of SAML 2, it will be when the application session expires. When this occurs, the application sends a new authentication request to the identity provider, which will fail if the user's account is disabled. If user termination risk is a concern, application session duration and access token expiration should be set considering the sensitivity of applications involved and the availability of means to quickly terminate a user's sessions.

Logout and Multilevel Authentication

If step-up or multi-factor authentication is implemented such that it is possible for a user's session to be at different authentication assurance levels, based on the strength of authentication mechanisms used, it should be clear what happens when a user logs out.

A common solution is for logout to completely terminate the user's session, regardless of the authentication level it was at. Whatever logout behavior is chosen, it is important that its behavior and effect be clear to users.

Redirect After Logout

A final aspect of designing logout is deciding where to send the user after logout. If you send the user to an application home page which redirects the user to an identity provider where the user still has a valid session, the user will be returned right back into the application with a new session created for them. This effectively breaks the logout process and can waste your helpdesk's time with complaints that logout doesn't work. For a better user experience, you can redirect to a logout confirmation page or a home page that doesn't automatically redirect a user to an identity provider. In addition to carefully selecting where to send a user after logout, you should ensure that redirection is only done to a list of allow-listed URLs to avoid vulnerabilities stemming from open redirects.[vi] Planning appropriate redirect URLs for logout and including them in an allow-list will provide a good user experience and avoid open redirect vulnerabilities.

Summary

Implementing logout can be more complex to design and test than login. There may be multiple authentication sessions for a user, and you need to decide which to terminate when any user session is terminated or times out. In addition to the logout behavior, designs should specify where to send a user after logout has occurred.

We've now covered all the events that happen as a user logs in and out of systems. At some point in the life of an identity, changes may occur which require identity profile attributes to be updated. Account management enables that and is the topic of the next chapter.

Key Points

- Logout often takes more time to design and test than login.
- Solution designs should specify which authentication sessions should be terminated when a user logs out.

- The effect of a logout action should be made clear to users so they know which sessions have been terminated and which have not.

- Designs should specify where to redirect the user after logout.

- Single logout can be used to send a logout message to relying party sessions associated with a user's identity provider session.

- There are several recently finalized specifications related to logout with OIDC.

- SAML 2 relying parties can send a logout request to terminate a user's session at an identity provider.

- SAML 2 supports single logout.

- The effect and scope of any logout should be clear to users.

Notes

i. https://tools.ietf.org/html/rfc7009

ii. https://openid.net/specs/openid-connect-rpinitiated-1_0.html

iii. https://openid.net/specs/openid-connect-session-1_0.html

iv. https://openid.net/specs/openid-connect-frontchannel-1_0.html

v. https://openid.net/specs/openid-connect-backchannel-1_0.html

vi. https://cwe.mitre.org/data/definitions/601.html

CHAPTER 14

Account Management

And yet in our world, everybody thinks of changing humanity and nobody thinks of changing himself.

—Leo Tolstoy, from "Three Methods of Reform"

It may be true, as suggested by Tolstoy, that people are unwilling to make deep internal changes, but when it comes to identity information, it is quite common for there to be changes. In this chapter, we'll cover the need to support changes to an identity and its attributes over time.

Identity Attributes

You will need to consider many scenarios related to altered identity attributes.

User Profile Attributes

A user's identity information may change over time for multiple reasons. Some updates will come from users themselves, and others may come from administrators. You should assume that users may need to change almost any attribute in their profile such as their email address, street address, phone number, and even their name. Many privacy regulations, including Article 15 of the GDPR (EU General Data Protection Regulation), mandate that users must be able to access and correct data about themselves held by a data controller.[i] If you are a data processor, you may need to help provide this capability to the data controllers who use your service.

© Yvonne Wilson, Abhishek Hingnikar 2023
Y. Wilson and A. Hingnikar, *Solving Identity Management in Modern Applications*,
https://doi.org/10.1007/978-1-4842-8261-8_14

Update Process

The need to support identity profile changes depends on where the information is managed. If your application delegates authentication to social providers, the user may need to update some profile attributes at the social provider. Similarly, if your application delegates authentication to an enterprise provider, the user may need to update identity information there. In addition to updates made by users themselves, administrators or automated administrative processes may make updates to user identities. These updates often impact attributes that are controlled by the owner of the identity provider instead of the user and may involve attributes used for access control decisions in applications such as a job level, department, and roles or group memberships.

If user profile data in your application comes from multiple sources, you must make clear how and where to update each attribute. Your application may pull some user attributes from an identity provider and augment that data with additional data that is collected and managed by the application. In this case, users need to know where to update different attributes. Any administrative or support processes for your application will also need to know how and where to update each attribute.

Cached Identity Attributes

When user profile data from an identity provider is cached by an application, the necessary frequency for updating the cache must be considered. When a user authenticates, the application may receive user profile attributes in a token or assertion from the authenticating identity provider. The application will have the information during a user's login session and may store the information in its own repository for use when the user is offline. A cache, however, will become stale if the user attribute information changes at the identity provider.

Each time a user logs in to an application via an identity provider, the application should receive user profile information from the provider that is current at the time of the authentication. If an application allows lengthy user sessions without reauthentication, it is possible that a user's profile attributes at the identity provider may have changed during their application session. In an enterprise scenario, if a user's privileges, such as roles or group memberships are changed at the identity provider, it may be problematic if an application has an ID Token or SAML assertion with out-of-date profile information. The same issue holds for self-contained access tokens that contain claims with stale user profile attributes.

To mitigate the risk of outdated information, applications can request updated profile information periodically or before executing sensitive transactions which require up-to-date profile attributes. This has been done by issuing a redirect to the identity provider with a parameter that suppresses active interaction with the user for authentication. At the time of writing, however, browser changes to prevent tracking may impact the feasibility of this approach, especially for single-page applications. Future browser changes may mitigate some of the issues created by tracking prevention, but in the meantime, an alternate approach is to use a refresh token to request new tokens. Refresh token rotation should be used to mitigate the risk of compromised refresh tokens.

Applications which obtain user profile information from identity providers and store a copy in their own database have an additional challenge. If users do not log in frequently, the user profile information in the application database may get stale. This can be an issue for reports that include user profile data if the reports are run by other users, such as administrators. If up-to-date information is needed in between user logins, it may be possible for an application to query an API at the identity provider for updated information. Alternatively, if an identity provider supports a capability whereby a log entry about an altered identity profile triggers a webhook, a webhook could be written to push identity profile changes to another system. The feasibility of such an approach may be impacted by firewalls and accessibility between the systems involved. Otherwise, periodic synchronization may be needed. Historically, such synchronization has been done with proprietary solutions, but the System for Cross-domain Identity Management (SCIM) protocol[ii] was created to standardize the synchronization of identity updates across domains, typically between corporate identity providers and relying parties. Adoption of SCIM is not widespread at the time of writing and may not be supported for scenarios where individual users own their accounts at social providers, but for enterprise scenarios, SCIM may be worth considering over proprietary one-off solutions, especially if an entity anticipates having many partners with which to synchronize.

Updated Identifiers

A special case to accommodate is the situation where a user needs to update the attribute which serves as an identifier for their account at a remote identity provider. If a remote identity provider identifier for a user is changed, the next time the user logs in, the application will receive the new identifier. If the application account or data is tied to the old identifier, and the user logs in with a new identifier, the user may not be able to access the application account or data associated with the old identifier. The issue can be avoided if the identity provider delivers to applications an internal identifier that never changes, in addition to other user profile attributes. Alternatively, if explicit account linking is used, as described in Chapter 18, a user may be able to unlink the old identity before the change and relink to the new identity after the change, but this requires forethought on the part of a user which may not be realistic.

Credential Reset

Users may also need to update their credentials from time to time. An application that delegates authentication to an identity provider does not have to store credentials or implement credential reset functionality because the credentials are at the identity provider. An application can simply provide a link or instructions that point to the credential reset function at the appropriate provider. If you use an identity provider service, you should be sure to select one that supports self-service credential update and account recovery.

Account Recovery

A user may forget or lose the credential to an account. In the case of a password, the user may forget it. In the case of authenticators such as a phone or hardware security token, they may be lost, stolen, damaged, or broken. If this occurs, a user has to prove they are the owners of an account, via some mechanism other than the original credential, before being allowed to set a new credential.

In many cases, an application relying on an identity provider may be able to leverage account recovery mechanisms provided by the identity provider. It then becomes important to select provider(s) with reasonably secure self-service account recovery mechanisms. Solutions that prompt a user for answers to previously established security questions are problematic as the answers can often be looked up or guessed. They also depend on the user remembering the answers, which is not always the case. Schemes that require users to download recovery codes rely on users saving the codes in a secure place, which may not be dependable either.

A solution that sends a password reset link to an email address previously registered with the account avoids the drawbacks of the previous schemes. This depends, however, on the owner of the account being able to access the email for the email address associated with the account. Sending a one-time code via SMS to a previously registered cellphone number in the user's profile relies on the number being current and the security of SMS messages. At the time of writing, vulnerabilities persist in Signaling System 7, which connects different phone networks, that have enabled some researchers and hackers to intercept SMS messages. There have also been SIM-swapping attacks[iii] and other demonstrated vulnerabilities[iv] that allowed phone numbers to be rerouted to phones controlled by attackers. These attacks have not been widespread at the time of writing, but raise some questions about the future security of using SMS messaging. Project owners should evaluate the current state of such issues before deciding to use SMS messages in future projects. Enabling users to set up a primary and one or more backup authentication mechanisms may provide the best defense against any one authentication mechanism becoming broken or compromised.

Password Guidance

If passwords are used, you may wish to provide guidance to your users on what constitutes a good password and, where you have a choice, select identity providers that enforce stronger password policy. Interesting new research by NIST has examined the effectiveness of previous password guidelines.[v] Security advice in the past has recommended a mixture of lowercase and uppercase characters, numbers, and special characters, the longer the better. Users were also advised to change their password on a regular interval. This advice was designed to make a password hard to guess by humans or discover by a brute force password guessing approach and mitigate risk from compromised passwords. This research by NIST suggests that some elements of the past guidance may not have been as effective as expected.

Their new guidance suggests that the size of a password matters more than the password complexity as user-selected password complexity is somewhat predictable, and rate limiting on failed password attempts may be a more effective approach. Users are recommended to select a long passphrase that consists of several words but is not a common or guessable phrase. Users are recommended to change a password if there is evidence it has been compromised, but rate limits on failed passwords and checking for breached passwords may be more effective than periodic forced password resets. Authentication services should implement rate limiting on failed login attempts and check username/password combinations against databases of known breached passwords to protect against brute force attacks and compromised passwords. You'll want to use identity providers that offer such features.

Helpdesk Reset

A manual, helpdesk-assisted credential reset process is expensive to provide and can expose sensitive information. If done remotely, such as over the phone, it requires the helpdesk staff to have knowledge of secret information with which to validate an account owner. Examples of secrets that have been used in the past are a portion of a government-issued identity number, information on recent transactions, or answers to secret questions. This process has the advantage of providing human assistance, but may expose sensitive information to risk of compromise. If the sensitive information used to validate an account owner is used at other sites, a compromise of the information at one site may allow a malicious actor to take over a person's accounts elsewhere.

If assisted credential reset is handled in person, account owner validation can leverage government-issued identification documents, avoiding exposure of other sensitive identity attributes. This approach requires staff that is properly trained to check the authenticity of such documents and involves the cost of maintaining such staff. This also assumes that users can appear in person where such staff is located, and that users have government-issued identification documents, which may not be true in some scenarios. Given the drawbacks with assisted credential reset, for both cost savings and security, self-service credential reset capability should be preferred for most scenarios.

Notification

Whether a user is updating user profile attributes, resetting a password, or performing other account management transactions, it is useful to send notification of the changes to the previously registered email, phone number, or address for the account. Notifications can help users recognize if they've made an error, such as accidentally making a change they did not intend. Notifications can also provide an early warning system if an account has been taken over by an unauthorized entity. The notification message should be sent using the prior contact information when contact information has been changed and include instructions on what to do if the user did not intend or initiate the changes. To the extent that users pay attention to notifications, such messages can be a useful tool to recognize and combat fraud.

Summary

Identity information may need to be updated over time. Privacy regulations often require that users have the ability to view and correct personal information held about them. Account updates can be handled by identity providers for information managed by them. If identity information is maintained in both an identity provider and an application, account update mechanisms must help users make updates in the right place. Changes to the primary identifier for a user at an identity provider may impact a user's ability to access application accounts tied to the old identifier. Credentials need to be reset if compromised, forgotten, or rendered inoperable, but a user must be validated before being allowed to reset credentials. An application may delegate credential reset and account recovery features to an identity provider, but the integrity of the mechanisms used by the identity provider should be validated. Last but not least, confirmation notifications should be sent to users regarding all changes to mitigate the damage from mistakes or fraud. This brings us in the next chapter to the final event in the life of an identity, which is deprovisioning.

Key Points

- User identity attributes may need to change over time.

- Privacy regulations may mandate a process for users to update identity information.

- Account management may be delegated to identity providers when the attributes to be changed reside at the identity provider.

- If a user changes their identifier at an identity provider, it may impact their ability to access application accounts tied to an old identifier unless a solution is provided for this scenario.

- Credential reset and account recovery may be delegated to identity providers for many common scenarios, but exceptional cases such as account takeover may need to involve application owners as well.

- Notification messages to confirm account changes should be sent to users, with instructions on what to do if they did not intend or initiate the changes.

Notes

i.   https://gdpr.eu/article-15-right-of-access/

ii. https://tools.ietf.org/html/rfc7644

iii. www.vice.com/en/article/d3n3am/att-and-verizon-employees-charged-sim-swapping-criminal-ring

iv. www.vice.com/en/article/y3g8wb/hacker-got-my-texts-16-dollars-sakari-netnumber

v.   https://pages.nist.gov/800-63-3/sp800-63b.html#appA

CHAPTER 15

Deprovisioning

The boundaries which divide Life from Death are at best shadowy and vague. Who shall say where the one ends, and where the other begins?

—Edgar Allan Poe, American author, from *The Premature Burial* (1844)

The final event in the life of an identity is deprovisioning, when an account and associated identity attributes are deleted or disabled so they can no longer be used. When an account is terminated, there are several design points to consider related to how to delete or disable accounts, what identity information to keep, and for how long.

Account Termination

An account may be terminated for several reasons. An account may be deleted by the account owner if they no longer need to use a service. An account may also be deleted by an administrator of a service if the account appears to have been abandoned or if a customer has abused a service in violation of terms of service. With a paid service, termination may result if a user fails to pay for the service. In a university setting, a student's account may be terminated when the student graduates. In a corporate setting, an account may be terminated if an employee leaves the company's employ. Regardless of the reason, upon termination, it is necessary to render the account so it can no longer be used to access resources. As we will see in the following sections, simply deleting an account may not be an appropriate solution for this.

© Yvonne Wilson, Abhishek Hingnikar 2023
Y. Wilson and A. Hingnikar, *Solving Identity Management in Modern Applications*,
https://doi.org/10.1007/978-1-4842-8261-8_15

Best Practices

Processes for the deprovisioning of accounts and identity information should be designed with several best practices in mind. These range from ensuring it gets done in a timely fashion to protecting against accidental account deletion and from enabling customers to transfer data elsewhere to satisfying privacy rights and requests for secure deletion. The exact requirements will vary by environment. This section will describe many common requirements associated with deprovisioning to help you identify which might be necessary for your projects.

Just Do It

The best practice for deprovisioning is to make sure it gets done in a timely fashion. If an account is no longer needed, it should be immediately disabled so it cannot be hijacked by an unauthorized user. Unfortunately, deprovisioning is notoriously overlooked in settings that lack mature identity management. To minimize the possibility of abandoned or unused accounts, you should implement automation to trigger periodic account review and to deprovision accounts that are unused or no longer appropriate. In a company setting, an HR system may initiate a deprovisioning workflow when a user is terminated. In a university environment, a student information system may trigger account deprovisioning upon graduation, at least for access reserved for current students. Automation can detect accounts that have not been used for a long time and privileges that are not aligned with a user's profile. Even the best automation fails at some point, however, so a periodic manual audit of existing accounts is essential to find accounts and privileges that are no longer appropriate so they can be deprovisioned. In consumer-facing environments, it may be appropriate to consider deprovisioning accounts which have had no activity for many years.

Provide a Soft Delete Technique

Human beings make mistakes. If you provide a "delete account" button, it's almost guaranteed that someone will delete their account by mistake. To save yourself the trouble of restoring customer data when that occurs, you can make it harder to erroneously delete an account by implementing a soft delete. This can take the form of a confirmation screen ("Caution: Are you sure you want to delete your account? This cannot be undone!") and marking an account as deleted while providing a grace period before the account is truly deleted. During the grace period, an "undelete account" capability should be available. You can also send a confirmation email at the beginning of the grace period explaining that the account is marked for removal and will be permanently deleted at the end of the grace period. The email can include instructions for how to reverse the account deletion if it was done in error. While not foolproof, these ideas may prevent some accidental account removals and the work to restore mistakenly deleted accounts.

If you implement a soft delete that delays the actual account deletion, privacy compliance may require that you include in your site's privacy notice and/or Terms and Conditions an explanation that deleted accounts will not be deleted immediately and why. As privacy laws vary by jurisdiction, you will need to consult the privacy laws relevant for your application to determine what is required.

Reserve Deprovisioned Identities

When deprovisioning accounts, it is best to preserve a list of deleted account identifiers and prevent each identifier from being reused by a new owner in the future. If this is not done, a new person could create an account with a previously used identifier and might be able to request a restore of historical data associated with that identifier to get data that belonged to the previous owner of the account. If a deleted account identifier was used in a single sign-on scenario and was used to access multiple applications, the owner of a new account with the same identifier might be able to access the previous person's data in those applications. This is especially important if an email address is used as the sole identifier for an account. (See Chapter 4 for why this is problematic.) By reserving previously used identifiers and checking all new identifiers for uniqueness against both active and deprovisioned accounts, several issues can be avoided.

Preserve Account Record

You never know when unauthorized activity might be detected. It could be weeks or even months after the fact. Because a fraud investigation may arise at any time, even after an account has been closed, you need to consider whether information about deleted accounts should be kept for some period of time, including transactions, the time they were submitted, the accounts that performed them, identity data linked to the accounts, and any other information needed for forensic evidence. When an account is deleted, it may be appropriate to preserve some account identity information along with the date, time, and reason why an account was disabled or terminated. If an account is terminated due to abuse, keeping sufficient records may help identify if a user attempts to open another account, at least with the same identity data.

One caveat is that privacy regulations require that data be kept only as long as needed for legitimate business purposes, and users have the right to request that personal data about them be erased. These rights may conflict with the need to have backups and audit logs. In practice, approaches are being worked out to satisfy the intent of privacy rights as well as operational system needs. Such approaches include minimizing data that is retained, encrypting and restricting access to retained data, and following defined data retention policies and procedures. Such policies and procedures should be created with guidance from legal and privacy advisors to ensure alignment with best current practices.

Data Transfer

It may be helpful or even required to provide customers a means to download or transfer data out of your service. Users may have this right, at least for personal information, as part of privacy legislation. Providing such a feature for all of a customer's data may make customers who worry about vendor lock-in more likely to sign up because they know if they are unhappy, they can take their data and go elsewhere. Corporate customers will often request the ability to periodically obtain an extract of all their data to protect themselves against a vendor failure.

For consumer users, the most scalable option is to provide a self-service means to download customer-owned data. The feature to download data can be shown in the "Delete account" process as an option before the account is deleted. You should consider the data formats that will be most useful to customers. For sensitive data, you should have a procedure to validate the requestor before providing a data dump. Requiring step-up authentication or at least reauthentication to obtain the data is one good precaution. This protects a user's data if they have walked away from their keyboard without locking their screen.

For corporate or business customers, there are a few more points to consider. It may make sense to require the involvement of two people from the customer in the request process to prevent a lone actor from downloading sensitive corporate data for unauthorized purposes. Once suitable customer validation is obtained for the download request, it should be provided in the most direct, self-service manner to minimize the service provider's access to the customer's data. For example, if a data dump were done manually by the service provider, it might be downloaded to a person's laptop or transferred to the customer by a channel that introduces risk.

For corporate customer data that involves user identities and passwords, the passwords should have been stored in a hashed format and may not be usable elsewhere if different hashing functions are used. Chapter 4 discusses options for migrating user identity data between systems. As with consumer users, thought should be given to the data format for a transfer as well as the security of the transfer process. Even if a customer is leaving, providing a good experience may keep a future opportunity open.

Privacy Right to Erasure

When a user deletes their account, it may not be enough to simply delete data your own service holds about a user. Article 17 of the General Data Protection Regulation (GDPR) provides consumers the right to erasure, commonly referred to as the right to be forgotten, which enables a user to request that an organization delete the data it has about the user.[i] Under Article 19 of the GDPR, data controllers are obligated to communicate an erasure request to any data processors to whom they've given personal data.[ii] The California Consumer Privacy Act (CCPA),[iii] the Virginia Consumer Data Protection Act (VCDPA),[iv] and the Colorado Privacy Act (CPA)[v] in the United States contain similar requirements, and future legislation enacted by other US states will likely follow suit. Users who wish to delete their account may wish to exercise their right to erasure, which may require deleting data in an application's user repository and possibly other data processor services.

It should be noted that the right of erasure does not nullify other obligations a business or organization may have that require keeping records, including those which contain personal information. There are several exceptions to the right to erasure. Article 17, paragraph 3, of the GDPR outlines several situations where the right of erasure does not apply. These include the fulfillment of legal obligations on the part of a data controller or processor, supporting rights for freedom of information and establishing, exercising, or defending legal claims. The CCPA, VCDPA, and CPA also provide for several exceptions. Financial institutions may have legal obligations to retain records with personal information for a period of time after an account is closed. Healthcare organizations often are required to retain healthcare-related records for a period after the date of service. Even small businesses have legal obligations to retain employment and tax records for a period of time.

Privacy legislation may dictate allowed mechanisms for users to make erasure requests and timeframes in which organizations must respond as well as whether confirmation notices are required. Unfortunately for businesses, there are differences between the privacy legislation enacted in different jurisdictions. Balancing privacy rights and other legal obligations can be complex, so you should define a data retention policy and procedures for handling erasure requests, in consultation with legal and privacy experts.

Certificate of Deletion

In addition to having procedures for disabling and terminating individual user accounts for privacy reasons, corporate customers that terminate their use of a service may request that their corporate account be deleted. This can include the user data of administrative users associated with the account, application data related to the service, and user data. Customers may request a certificate of deletion that states that all their data has been deleted. If sensitive data is involved, including data about users, customers may request a certificate of secure deletion. This demonstrates their due diligence to ensure data they've given to vendors has been deleted when no longer needed, which helps protect sensitive information.

Secure Delete

It can be surprisingly complex to "completely delete" data. Simply issuing a delete command in a database or to delete a file may not completely delete the data. In some cases, such a delete simply removes pointers to the data, but does not alter the space on the disk where it was stored, allowing specially written tools to recover the data.

Various techniques have been employed to effect secure deletion. One approach is to encrypt data and throw away the encryption key. This effectively deletes the data because it can no longer be decrypted. This approach assumes the time required to decrypt the data using brute force mechanisms is significantly longer than the time during which the data is likely to be valuable to data thieves. Since it is impossible to predict how long this assumption will be true as well as the future value of data, this is not a reliable option.

Another method of deleting data from a disk or other magnetic storage media involves degaussing a disk. Information is stored on disks by magnetizing the surface of the disk with small pulses of electricity as the read/write head of the disk passes over it. A disk can be erased with a special tool called a degausser which generates a powerful magnetic field that scrambles and removes magnetic fields on a disk. This method may be feasible when all information on a disk needs to be removed, as when the disk will be completely decommissioned from use. A drawback is that degaussing, as with physical destruction of a disk, may render the disk unusable and contribute to e-waste. Degaussing to remove only one customer's data is also not feasible in a cloud service where many customers' data resides on the same disk.

When a disk stores data of many customers, one customer's data can effectively be erased by overwriting the data with random 0s and 1s. The question is how many times the data must be overwritten in order to ensure that residual magnetic traces do not allow data recovery. The US Department of Defense (DoD) 5220.22-M protocol has been cited for this. The 1995 version of this standard indicated data should be overwritten three times. This is now considered obsolete however.[vi] For specific sanitization details, it has been superseded by the National Institute of Standards and Technology's (NIST) "Special Publication 800-88: Guidelines for Media Sanitization" which indicates that for most of today's media, overwriting with a fixed pattern, such as all zeros, with at least one pass is sufficient.[vii] This technique would require a service to create features to perform the overwriting. Requirements for secure delete may vary by industry and country so researching requirements for your target customer base will provide the best guidance on secure account deletion expectations.

Consider Reprovisioning Requirements

It may be worth considering the likelihood of requests from customers to reprovision their previously deprovisioned account and establishing policies for this. It would constitute a security breach if an account were reprovisioned and given to someone other than the original authorized owner, so one option is to not support reprovisioning. If reprovisioning is to be supported, you'll need procedures for validating that a requestor is an authorized owner of the original account. Any practices to support this should also be aligned with applicable privacy legislation.

Summary

When a relationship with an employee or customer ends, you may need to do more than just delete their account. You may need to preserve the identifier for the account and prevent it from being used again by someone else. Privacy legislation around the world often includes a right to erasure of personal data which may extend to subprocessors who process or store personal data you collect. You should create a data inventory to understand the data you collect and process and then create a data retention plan and erasure procedures in compliance with both privacy and legal advice. You may also need to satisfy requirements for secure delete procedures and provide certificates of deletion or confirmation notices.

We've now covered the key events in the life of an identity that your implementation will likely need to support. Since it is common during an implementation to need to troubleshoot a few issues, the next chapter covers advice on troubleshooting techniques for authentication and authorization issues.

Key Points

- Deprovisioning deletes or disables an account and associated identity information so it can no longer be used to access protected resources.

- Deprovisioning may be initiated by either an account owner or the owners of a service where the account resides.

- Automation and periodic account review should be used to help identify accounts that are no longer needed.

- A soft delete feature can be used to reduce accidental account deletion.

- Identifiers for deprovisioned accounts should be reserved and not used for new accounts.

- Data retention policies and procedures should be developed in consultation with legal and privacy experts.

- Procedures may need to be created to enable customers to download their data for use elsewhere, as part of account deprovisioning.

- Privacy legislation often includes a right to erasure. There may be requirements for how requests are to be made, timeframes for responses, and whether confirmations are sent. There are also several exceptions describing situations where data should not be erased.

- It may be necessary to provide customers a certificate of deletion or to follow secure delete procedures as part of account deprovisioning.

- Policies should be created for whether reprovisioning of accounts is allowed and, if so, the procedures to follow.

Notes

i.   https://gdpr.eu/article-17-right-to-be-forgotten/

ii. https://gdpr.eu/article-19-notification-obligation/

iii. https://oag.ca.gov/privacy/ccpa#sectione

iv. https://lis.virginia.gov/cgi-bin/legp604.exe?211+sum+SB1392

v.   https://leg.colorado.gov/sites/default/files/2021a_190_signed.pdf

vi. www.dami.army.pentagon.mil/site/IndustSec/docs/5220.22m.pdf

vii. https://csrc.nist.gov/publications/detail/sp/800-88/rev-1/final

CHAPTER 16

Troubleshooting

> *When you have eliminated the impossible, whatever remains, however improbable, must be the truth.*
>
> —Sir Arthur Conan Doyle, British author, from *The Sign of the Four* (1890)

You've created your application, fired off your first authentication, and your hard work blows up in a roaring flame of error messages... or, worse, nothing happens, no error messages are displayed, and you don't have a clue where to start looking. Fear not, there is a methodical approach to debugging authentication and authorization issues. We'll share an approach, tools, and techniques, and soon you'll be solving authentication and authorization issues with the mastery of Sherlock Holmes.

Get Familiar with the Protocols

A working knowledge of the identity protocol(s) you are using for authentication and API authorization is helpful. These protocols involve browser redirects and/or HTTP requests/responses between several components. Troubleshooting will be easier if you are familiar with the expected sequence of interaction for a particular scenario. You can capture an HTTP or network trace for a situation and compare it to the expected interaction as described in a protocol specification and/or identity provider documentation, to identify where things are going wrong. It is particularly helpful to know

- The sequence of interaction for different scenarios

- The parameters expected by each protocol endpoint

- The responses and error codes returned by each endpoint

Y. Wilson and A. Hingnikar, *Solving Identity Management in Modern Applications*,
https://doi.org/10.1007/978-1-4842-8261-8_16

In addition to the protocol specifications, you should know the identity provider APIs and SDKs you are using. Vendors may extend a specification when they implement a protocol. Using an API testing tool to try out calls with various parameters and observing the results can give you a better understanding of the identity provider and APIs you use, which can help when debugging issues.

Prepare Your Tools

The following tools will help you debug an issue:

- An environment where you can duplicate a problem and test

- Two independent browser windows

- Tools to capture and view HTTP traces

- A tool with which to test API calls

- Tools to capture and view network traces of back-end API calls

- Tools for viewing and creating JWT and SAML 2.0 tokens

The next few sections will explain why each tool is necessary in more detail, and Appendix E contains a list of some specific tools. New tools may arise over time, so be sure to check for any new tools, including vendor- or protocol-specific solutions as well as browser extensions.

Test Environment

It is often helpful to have an environment in which to duplicate a problem. For some issues, you may be able to use your production environment to collect all the data you need. For others, you may need an environment where you can experiment and change settings as part of your investigation. You'll need a test environment with an instance of the identity provider used and with an account for a test user. Ideally, you'll have administrative access so you can alter configuration settings or create users with different profiles if needed. Having a test environment in which to test and debug an issue avoids any impact to your production system from debugging activity.

Independent Browser Windows

In addition to a test environment, it is helpful to bring up two independent browser windows. You can use two different browsers or two windows for the same browser with "Private" or "Incognito" browsing mode so they do not share cookies between them. One browser window is for testing the broken login issue as an end user. The other browser window is for accessing the administrative interface of your identity provider or application to make configuration changes. Independent browser windows ensure that activity in one window doesn't impact the other window and give you confusing results.

It is also necessary to note how each browser handles sessions, particularly whether it will save or reconstitute a previous session. When testing, it is best to start with a clean browser session, unless the issue you are debugging does not occur with a new session. A new browser session ensures that there are no cookies or state from a previous session to confuse results. Browsers now offer the ability to restore state from a previous session so it is best to use a new "Private" or "Incognito" browser session and start with a clean slate each time.

Capture HTTP Traces

You'll need a browser with the ability to capture an HTTP trace. The Chrome, Firefox, and Edge browsers offer developer tools features that provide a built-in ability to capture an HTTP trace in the "Network" tab. Safari's Web Inspector, accessible via the "Develop" menu option, enables you to capture network activity in the Network tab. Learn how to capture an HTTP trace in every browser that your service officially supports so you are prepared to debug issues on each browser.

If you are collaborating with others, it is convenient to be able to dump the HTTP trace to an HTTP Archive format file (.har file). Note, however, that a .har file will capture everything, including the cleartext value of any secret (client secret, password, API key, etc.) entered or transmitted during the capture. If you can't avoid capturing a secret by limiting a trace to only a part of the interaction, you should edit the files to remove any sensitive information and/or reset any secrets after capture so you don't expose valid secret(s). If you ask another person to send you a .har file, be sure to have them take these precautions to reduce your liability from exposure to secrets in the file.

View HTTP Traces

If you receive an HTTP Archive (.har) file from someone else, you'll need a tool to view it. A list of HTTP trace and .har file viewers as well as other useful debugging tools is included in Appendix E. The ability to view traces sent by others is useful if you cannot duplicate a problem yourself.

Make API Calls

Another valuable tool is an API client explorer that allows you to create and send API calls. This provides a convenient interface for learning, debugging, and testing API calls for identity providers as well as your own APIs. Vendors of identity services (or authors of other APIs) may provide ready-built packages with calls for their APIs that you can import into such tools. Appendix E lists some current tools in this category. You can use such tools to test and debug individual API calls which can facilitate finding the source of problems.

View API Calls

If you make API calls from a back-end application component or native application, you will need a different mechanism to capture the calls as they do not go through a browser. You can use a network web debugging proxy tool or a debugger. Appendix E lists a few tools for this purpose.

View JWT and SAML 2 Tokens

A tool to decode and view the security tokens received by your application is essential. Appendix E lists a few sites which are useful for viewing JWTs and SAML 2 requests/ responses. These tools will allow you to inspect the contents of the tokens. They may also provide you with a way to create test tokens for sending to APIs for tests. With these tools in place, you're ready to start debugging.

Check the Simple Things

You may save yourself some time by checking a few simple things before diving into a detailed analysis:

- Check the identity provider is accessible and not experiencing an outage.

- Check the credentials supplied are correct for the environment (test vs. production).

- Check the login account and credentials are not disabled or expired at the identity provider. You can do this by logging in to another application that uses the same identity provider.

- Check the application is using the correct URL for the identity provider.

- Check the client ID in the application matches that registered in the identity provider.

- Check the redirect/callback URL for the application exactly matches the URL registered in the identity provider.

- Check whether any certificates or cryptographic keys have expired.

- Check for any error messages logged by the application or identity provider to see if they provide valuable clues.

Once you've checked the simple things, if the issue is reported by someone else, ask questions to understand the problem so you can replicate it or focus your debugging on the most likely spot. Start by asking for a general description of what happens, followed by questions to elicit more details on what the user did so you can replicate the situation. Be sure to ask about any error messages displayed on the screen or in any log files. Also ask what the user expected, because sometimes users can have an incorrect expectation of how a system is supposed to work.

Gather Information

Troubleshooting is facilitated by knowing what questions to ask. Identity solutions involve many components, including your application, the user's browser, and an identity provider. There may also be APIs, an API Gateway, or an authentication hub in the mix. Any of these components could potentially contribute to a problem. The following questions will give you useful information to replicate the problem and/or narrow down the possible source of an issue.

How Many Users Impacted?

Is the issue experienced by all users or just a few? If only a few users, the issue is most likely caused by something unique to those users' profiles or their environments, such as browser configuration settings. On the other hand, if all users experience an issue, it is probably caused by something in the components common to all users, such as the application or the identity provider.

Contributing Environmental Factors?

Does the issue occur with all browsers, devices, locations, or platforms or just one? Testing with different browsers, devices, locations, and platforms can identify if there are any environmental factors contributing to the issue. Authentication and single sign-on can be impacted by browser settings for third-party cookies and tracking prevention, so you should check browser settings related to those features. If an issue occurs in multiple environments, it is probably not caused by an environmental factor, and debugging should focus on other components such as the application or identity provider. If, however, an issue occurs on only one browser or type of device, your inquiry should focus on whether the browser or device could cause the issue.

Which Applications Impacted?

How many applications does the issue affect? If there are multiple applications involved in a scenario, it can be helpful to test each to see if the problem occurs in all of them or just some applications. If all applications experience the issue, the problem may be caused by an issue at the identity provider. If only one or some applications experience the issue, it is probably caused by the application code/configuration or the configuration for the application(s) at the identity provider.

Consistent or Intermittent Issue?

Does the problem happen consistently or only intermittently? An intermittent problem will be easier to debug if you can reduce it to a problem you can reliably reproduce. If there are multiple instances of application, identity provider, firewall, or load balancer servers, for example, try checking whether one instance of a component out of several could be misconfigured, such as one application server or one firewall instance. You can do this by shutting them all down and starting them up one at a time to see if the issue occurs consistently with one.

Worked Previously?

Does the issue occur in an application that worked previously but suddenly stopped working? If so, check for recent changes, such as the following:

- Identity provider outage

- Change to the identity provider API or API used by the failing application

- Network connectivity issue

- User password expired

- Recent software upgrades

- Recent browser or device configuration changes

- Certificate expiration or key rotation

- Servers with incorrect time due to NTP[i] not running

These are common causes of failures of previously working systems.

Where Does Failure Occur?

How much of the authentication and authorization sequence of interaction completes, as observed during a login transaction or in an HTTP/network trace? Noting where the interaction stopped often suggests which component to investigate first.

Replicate the Problem

If the issue is reported by someone else, it is valuable to replicate the problem in your own environment. This can determine if the other person's environment contributes to the issue. It also provides a test environment in which to try different things to gather more information about what causes the problem to appear. This is particularly useful if the person reporting the problem is unable or unwilling to test different scenarios to aid debugging.

Analyzing an HTTP/Network Trace

An HTTP or network trace of a broken scenario is invaluable for debugging. In this section, we'll describe what to look for in a trace.

Capture a Trace

A trace of HTTP and API calls will be one of the most valuable debugging aids. Using a debugger or other tracing tool, perform the failing authentication, authorization, or logout transaction starting from the beginning and going as far as you can through the sequence. When done, stop the trace to minimize the capture of irrelevant data. If you receive a trace captured by someone else, use a suitable tool to view it.

Check Sequence of Interaction

The first thing to check is the sequence of redirects or API calls to see how much of the expected interaction succeeded. The sequence diagrams in earlier chapters may be helpful for this. For OIDC or OAuth 2, look first for a call to an "authorize" endpoint on the authorization server. For SAML 2, look for a "SAMLRequest" message to the SSO URL of the identity provider. Then look for the requests to prompt the user to log in and for a redirect or response back to the application after the user has authenticated. For OIDC/OAuth 2, this will be to one of the callback URLs configured in the authorization server. For SAML 2, this will be a SAMLResponse message to the ACS (Assertion Consumer Service) URL configured in the identity provider. If you do not see the complete sequence of expected calls and responses, the place where the interaction started to deviate from normal is a clue for where to start looking for issues. Table 16-1 provides some symptoms and possible causes.

Table 16-1. *Symptoms and Issues*

Symptom	Possible Causes
User never redirected to identity provider.	Application has incorrect URL for identity provider.
User redirected to identity provider but no login prompt.	Application sent malformed request.
	Incorrect client ID or client secret.
	Error in identity provider login page configuration.
User prompted to log in but receives error.	User error. Test with a different account.
	User password has expired.
	Wrong password for environment.
	User account does not exist.
	Identity provider lost connection to data store.
	Misconfigured login page at identity provider.
User logs in without error, but not redirected back to application.	Incorrect or invalid callback URL for application at authorization server (OAuth 2/OIDC).
	Incorrect Assertion Consumer Service URL for application at identity provider (SAML 2).
	Misconfigured extensibility feature at identity provider.
User redirected back to application but receives authorization error, or application content doesn't display.	Tokens or assertions returned to application are malformed or do not contain information expected by application.
	Exchange of authorization code for token fails.
	Application not granted necessary scopes.
	User does not have sufficient privileges in application.

Check Parameters in Requests

Check the parameters in a request. For OAuth 2 or OIDC, check the following:

- The request is sent to the correct endpoint at the authorization server.

- Correct response_type used for the desired grant type or flow.

- The scope parameter value is adequate for the requested action.

- The callback URL matches what is registered in the authorization server.

- A state parameter value is specified, if required by authorization server.

For SAML 2 requests, check the following:

- The request is sent to the correct URL at the identity provider.

- The request specifies the binding for a response, if required.

- The correct certificates and public keys have been configured.

Check HTTP Status Codes

The next step is to check the HTTP status code on the response from the authorization server or identity provider. Table 16-2 lists some common HTTP status codes for error scenarios and some possible causes.

Table 16-2. *HTTP Status Codes and Possible Causes*

HTTP Status Code	Possible Causes
400	Malformed request. Check your request has the correct parameters and valid values for them.
401	Unauthorized. Check the application or user has the necessary privileges for the request.
403	Forbidden. Check the application or user has the necessary privileges for the request.
500	Internal Server Error. Check the configuration at the authorization server or identity provider.
503	Service Unavailable. Check if the authorization server or identity provider service is running and reachable.

Check Security Token Contents

If the HTTP status code does not indicate there is an error, check the security token(s) returned. Appendix E lists tools for viewing the contents of these security tokens. Check the relevant security tokens to see if they are formatted correctly and they contain the requisite information.

For ID Tokens, check

- The ID Token contains the correct user information in the "sub" claim.

- The ID Token contains any other claims expected by the application.

For Access Tokens that can be viewed, check

- Scopes granted to the application are adequate for the request.

- The access token contains any claims needed by an API.

- Audience for the token is correct for the intended recipient API.

- The access token is valid and has not expired.

261

For SAML 2 SAMLResponse messages:

- Subject element's name identifier (nameid) element contains a user identifier expected by the application.

- Additional attribute statements expected by the application exist.

An application may need information for authorization conveyed in custom claims. If such authorization data is missing from an ID Token or SAML 2 assertion, the user may get an "unauthorized" message or possibly a blank screen. If an API you call requires custom claims in an access token, your program may get an error status from the API. You should check the contents of the access token if possible. If the access tokens are in JWT format, they can be viewed in a JWT viewer. If they are opaque strings, however, you may need to use an introspection endpoint on the authorization server to get information about the token. If the contents of the security tokens are correct, another possible cause of issues is a problem validating a security token.

Check for Security Token Validation Errors

After an application receives a security token, it must validate it. The security tokens returned by OIDC and SAML 2 are digitally signed. They may also be digitally encrypted. If an application cannot validate the signature on a security token (or decrypt it if encrypted), it should log an error. Checking application logs for such errors can help identify if this type of issue exists. You can also check whether signing keys are being properly retrieved and managed as incorrect key management can contribute to token validation errors.

Errors with security tokens can also occur at identity providers. One identity provider may delegate authentication for a user to another identity provider. If the first identity provider does not receive a valid authentication token from the remote provider, it should log the authentication failure. Identity provider logs should be consulted if errors seem to originate at the identity provider as these logs will often have the most useful information.

Collaborating with Others

The previous sections described a series of troubleshooting steps that will help you solve many common causes of authentication and authorization issues. A frequent complication with troubleshooting is that you may not own all the pieces. In such cases, you need to collaborate with others.

If you are not able to test the application personally, or can't replicate the problem, you will need to ask someone who can replicate the problem to capture a trace of the issue. A .har file or network trace can show interactions between an application and an identity provider as well as an API if used. This can include the requests made, the parameters, the timing of such interactions, and the responses received. Such traces are extremely useful for debugging issues with authentication, SSO, and authorization. When you receive a trace file, you'll need a viewer suitable for the type of trace captured. Appendix E includes a few such tools.

You should remember that a trace may capture sensitive data, including a username and password typed by a user or sensitive security tokens returned to applications. If someone sends you a trace file, you may wish to warn them about this so they can reset a captured password or invalidate any sensitive tokens. This can reduce your liability. Furthermore, invalidating any long-lived tokens captured and deleting trace files when you are done troubleshooting is another good practice.

Lastly, if you use an identity provider product, the vendor may offer support services. The staff at the helpdesk should be able to help you debug issues related to your use of their product. Be sure to take advantage of such an option where available, to speed your debugging.

Summary

This chapter described tools and approaches useful for troubleshooting many common issues. It helps to know the protocols you are working with and to have debugging tools that give you sufficient visibility into the authentication and authorization interactions of your program. Collecting data about where and when the problem occurs can narrow down the possible source of an issue. An HTTP trace, network trace, or debugger can help you analyze the flow of traffic between components as well as the parameters in the requests and responses. By obtaining the right tools, and asking the right questions, you can speed up the process of debugging an issue. This completes the set of chapters on building and debugging the code for your application. The next chapter covers some things which can go wrong beyond the code and for which you should prepare.

Key Points

- Develop a working knowledge of the specifications for the identity protocols you use.

- Prepare a suite of debugging tools.

- Check the simple things first.

- Gather relevant information about the problem.

- Replicate the problem in your own environment if reported by someone else.

- Use an HTTP or network trace to help identify where a problem occurs.

- Check the list of symptoms and causes in this chapter.

- Check for error responses from identity providers.

- Check application and identity provider log files, if possible, for clues.

- You may need to develop collaborative troubleshooting procedures with the owners of remote identity providers.

- You should ensure that troubleshooting procedures include steps to delete all trace and log files when an issue is closed as these files may contain sensitive information.

Note

  i. www.ntp.org/ntpfaq/NTP-s-def.htm

CHAPTER 17

Exceptions

An ounce of prevention is worth a pound of cure.

—Benjamin Franklin, American founding father, inventor,
politician, diplomat, scientist, and printer, from a letter to
The Pennsylvania Gazette (1735)

The previous chapters have covered many cases where things happen as expected.
There are times, however, when failures occur or things don't go as planned. Situations
involving exceptions require planning to handle them well. Examples include
accidentally deleted data, lost phones, system outages, or even a large-scale compromise
of user credentials. We can't predict every problem your project may encounter, but
this chapter should provide you with a list of exception scenarios that might apply to
your environment. You can select which you'll need to handle and define a process for
handling them. We recommend starting with the scenarios that are most likely as well as
those that would have the biggest negative impact if they were to occur. We also suggest
identifying in advance any log information necessary to help you handle the scenarios or
records to keep to monitor your response to the events. With a plan in place, your team
can respond quickly and effectively if one of these situations arises.

Accounts

The cases in this section apply primarily to accounts and may require some human
involvement to assess risk or perform due diligence evaluation of a request.

© Yvonne Wilson, Abhishek Hingnikar 2023
Y. Wilson and A. Hingnikar, *Solving Identity Management in Modern Applications*,
https://doi.org/10.1007/978-1-4842-8261-8_17

Data Restore

A customer may inadvertently delete their account data and then regret it. The likelihood of this occurring can be reduced by requiring confirmation before deleting data and implementing a soft delete as described in Chapter 15. If you support requests to restore deleted accounts, you should develop policies and secure practices for such requests so they don't provide an opportunity for a social engineering exploit. Procedures should include evaluating the requestor, the timing of the request, and the nature of the request. The requestor should be validated as a legitimate registered owner or administrator of the account in the request. Requests made weeks or months after the data was deleted or to restore data into different accounts with different owners probably need higher scrutiny than a request made only minutes after data was deleted. For business accounts with multiple administrators, it may be appropriate to require confirmation of requests from a second person. The details will vary by application, but you'll want to define policy and procedures to ensure unauthorized parties cannot get access to data via data restore requests.

Account Decommission

A request to terminate an account carries risk similar to a data restore request. You need a means to validate that the person initiating such a request is legitimately entitled to terminate the account. For consumer-facing accounts, a self-service account decommission feature may be sufficient. Such a feature may be needed as part of supporting privacy requirements as well. For corporate accounts with multiple administrators, it may be useful to require a request by two authorized administrators or implement a delay coupled with confirmation notices to all administrators in order to prevent an unauthorized, malicious delete action by one disgruntled employee. Chapter 15 has further guidance for account decommissions accompanied by requests for account data transfers.

Also in Chapter 15 is guidance to reserve the account identifier for accounts which have been decommissioned. It should not be possible for someone to create a new account with the same identifier as a previously deleted account and then request the restoration of data from a time when the original account existed. The use of an email address as account identifier does not mitigate the risk because email addresses have been recycled by some providers in the past.[i] Reserving the account identifier for a decommissioned account for a period longer than the data retention period for backups of deleted account data mitigates this risk at least for the local system.

Orphaned Account

Although rare, the person who established an account may be terminated from a company or decease. If they were the only person associated with the account, someone not previously associated with the account may request access to it. The legitimacy of a requestor making such a claim needs to be validated before they are given access to an account. For a corporate account, it may require obtaining a contact from the company's website to help in validating that a requestor is a legitimate representative for the company and authorized to take over the account. Be sure to obtain requests in writing, validate the authenticity and authorization of requestors through independent channels, and keep records of all requests, validation steps, and actions.

When a user of a consumer-facing site has passed away, policies vary. Some social media sites allow family members to request an account be terminated or memorialized. Estate executors can direct the disposition of some types of accounts such as financial accounts. Until legal guidelines and practices governing online data and digital inheritance mature, you should obtain legal guidance, especially for accounts involving financial value or health-related information. For less sensitive accounts, allowing a user to specify a contact authorized to take over an account in the event of death may be helpful.

Account Takeover

The legitimate owner of an account can be locked out of their account as a result of a compromised password, stolen phone, social engineering, or software vulnerability. If a user calls your helpdesk and claims their account has been taken over by someone else, you will need a process for determining the legitimate owner of the account, bearing in mind that an unauthorized user could have viewed account details and changed user profile information as well as passwords after taking over the account. In this case, the legitimate owner may look like an imposter because they won't know the current password or profile information. Maintaining a history of past profile information such as addresses or phone numbers, especially if not displayed in the application user interface, may help in validating a locked-out, legitimate account owner, though further validation will probably be required. Encouraging the use of multi-factor authentication, as discussed in Chapter 12, can reduce the chances of account takeover happening.

Phone Lost, Damaged, or Stolen

If your site uses an authentication mechanism that leverages a user's mobile phone, you will need a process to help customers whose phone is lost, stolen, or damaged. Depending on the authentication mechanism, a user might need to deregister an old phone and register a new one with their account and/or install an app on their new phone. If a user's phone is stolen and open at the time of the theft, the user's account may be accessible by the thief. For this case, you'll need a process to help the legitimate owner of an account terminate the phone's access to their account.

Identity Providers

This section covers cases which may involve an identity provider.

Account Recovery Requests

To assist users who've forgotten their password or lost a device needed to authenticate, an identity provider may provide an account recovery mechanism. One option is sending a "magic link" to a previously registered email address for the account. A magic link is a nonguessable URL that is valid for a single use within a short time period and allows a user to bypass authentication to access a credential reset feature. The use of a magic link can be combined with a confirmation email indicating a credential was reset, with instructions for what to do if this action was not taken by the legitimate account owner. With a magic link, the user's access to their email becomes a backup authentication factor for account recovery.

Alternate forms of authentication can serve as a secondary authentication factor as an alternative to relying on the security of a user's email account. Sending one-time codes via Short Message Service (SMS) text messages to a user's previously registered phone number has been a common solution. At the time of writing, however, there have been some successful attacks based on SIM swapping,[ii] rerouting phone numbers to unauthorized phones,[iii] and intercepting SMS messages.[iv, v] Future projects should evaluate the threats posed by these issues and available mitigations before selecting an SMS-based approach. Other approaches use a mobile app or a specialized device to generate a one-time code. An identity provider that supports multiple authentication mechanisms and having users set them up can improve your ability to quickly adapt if one mechanism becomes compromised.

An identity provider's account recovery mechanism can open up other risks, depending on how it is implemented. A password reset link which immediately invalidates the current account password could enable a person to lock someone else out of their account. If the legitimate owner of the account has not kept their email address up to date, they will not receive the password reset link and be locked out of their account. A password reset link could even be used by pranksters to trigger an account recovery SMS message or phone call in the middle of the night to wake someone up. If a user's email account has been compromised, a hacker could use a password reset feature to trigger password reset emails and gain control of the user's accounts that use that email address. Approaches to mitigating these risks include requiring some information from the user before triggering an account recovery action, reminding users to keep their notification information current and not invalidating a current credential until a reset link has been activated.

Brute Force Attacks

In a brute force attack, a hacker attempts to log in with many different username/password combinations in hopes of guessing a user's password. They may use common or known breached passwords, and their attempts are often automated. An identity provider can reduce the chances of brute force attacks succeeding by detecting a series of many successive failed login attempts or failed password reset attempts against one account from the same IP address. If either of these situations occurs, an identity provider can slow down an attacker by techniques such as blocking an account for a short time period or asking for multi-factor authentication (if configured). An alert can be sent to the site administrator and an email sent to the owner of the account to alert them about the attack. The email can indicate why the account was blocked and provide a link for unblocking the account immediately in case the failed logins were caused by the legitimate account owner.

If an identity provider detects a series of failed logins or failed password reset attempts hitting *multiple* accounts from a single IP address, this is more suspicious, and it may be appropriate to simply block that IP address immediately. However, corporate customers with many users whose traffic comes from the same IP address due to network address translation (NAT) are an exception. If enough users on the internal network mistype their password in a set time period, it could trigger a false alarm for a brute force attack. Allowlisting IP addresses for environments using NAT helps avoid false alarms for brute force attacks in this case.

One additional caution involves environments with an automated system that will access a user's account using their credentials. If the user changes their password, but the update is not provided to the automated system, it could trigger the brute force attack response. Reviewing an environment for such cases can prevent wasting time due to false alarms.

Breached Passwords

Breached passwords are being aggregated into massive databases that can be exploited by hackers, including one discovered by breached identity curator 4iQ containing 1.4 billion breached, cleartext passwords.[vi] If a user's password at your site is easily guessable or has been compromised elsewhere, it could enable a hacker to take over the user's account on your site. Fortunately, there are databases on the Internet containing information on breached passwords, such as "have i been pwned"[vii] created by Troy Hunt. An application or an identity provider can check a user's password against such databases when they sign up for an account or reset their password. If the user's password has been breached, they can be notified and asked to select a different password. An application or identity provider can perform such checks when a password is initially set, at password reset, and periodically when users log in to detect if a password has been compromised after being set. These actions will help detect, and mitigate the risk of, breached passwords.

System Outages

Evaluating the impact of identity system failures on support systems and administrative access is recommended as part of business continuity planning.

Authentication System Outage

It may be desirable to use the same authentication service for your primary website and a support site, so users have single sign-on (SSO) across the sites. However, if the authentication service is unavailable, users will be locked out of both sites. It can be annoying for customers if they are unable to access a website and then realize they can't report the problem. If you have this scenario, you should plan for how to handle support in the event of an outage to your authentication system.

One approach is to rely on proactive outbound communication during an outage. Some mechanisms to consider include a support phone number with a recorded message to acknowledge the issue and provide updated information or a public community support forum or status page where outage updates can be posted. In designing processes for business continuity during an outage of an authentication system, you'll want to ensure that alternate processes do not rely on the primary authentication system.

Admin Access

It is helpful to evaluate your use of authentication services for your internal operations and administrative access to your site. If single sign-on is used as a primary access mechanism for administrative access, such access could be blocked during a failure of the SSO system. You may need alternate authentication mechanisms to access critical administrative functions during an outage. This includes administrative access to your service, monitoring and alerting infrastructure, and the ability to post outage updates to your customers. You should of course ensure an adequate level of security on all access paths to administrative functions. Planning for an outage of authentication solutions used for administrative access will help your team respond efficiently during an actual outage.

Provisioning Systems

Provisioning processes and systems may be less critical during an outage than authentication systems, but if you have time-critical account provisioning or deprovisioning processes, it may be necessary to define alternate processes for use during an outage of a provisioning system. Once service is restored, it may be necessary to validate that all in-flight transactions at the time of the outage were completed, especially account removal or privilege removal transactions. A routine check after an outage for incomplete deprovisioning transactions can help prevent incorrect access privileges.

Cybersecurity Threats

Your application could experience any of a wide variety of cybersecurity threats, from denial-of-service (DoS) and ransomware attacks to a data breach or suddenly being notified of a vulnerability in a code library leveraged by your application's code. It is critical to have defined a cybersecurity incident response plan in advance and trained staff on the plan. An incident response plan should minimally include

- The owner accountable for leading the response

- The response team and responsibilities of each member

- Clear priorities and required timeframes for the response effort

- The steps to take, including preventing further damage, preserving required evidence, assessing the damage, documenting all findings and decisions, and identifying and fixing the root cause as well as related damage

- Reporting and notification requirements

- Follow-up actions to prevent the incident from happening again

Having an incident response team identified and a response plan defined enables staff to respond quickly and smoothly if a cybersecurity incident occurs. According to the Ponemon Institute's 2019 and 2020 Cost of a Data Breach reports, this can help reduce the impact and cost of an adverse cybersecurity event. In addition, there may be aggressive timeframes within which you must notify regulators, law enforcement, or users if a breach occurs, so it is imperative to have a thorough response plan defined in advance that includes such responsibilities.

Compromised Personal Data

If the unthinkable happens and you experience a suspected or verified breach of personal data, you need to act quickly. It is imperative that you are aware of any legal requirements related to the exposure of personal data, have a plan worked out in advance, and have retained any outside assistance needed to respond quickly. In addition to a general incident response plan described in the previous section, your plan for responding to a breach of personal data should additionally define

- When and how to engage law enforcement, if appropriate

- When and how to engage insurers

- The process to follow for user and regulatory notification

- The process to follow for public relations communications

If personal data is compromised, many privacy regulations require notification to regulatory agencies within a certain time period. For organizations subject to the General Data Protection Regulation (GDPR), Article 33 specifies that notification should be made within 72 hours of becoming aware of a breach. Breach response procedures require significant coordination. Notification may be required to multiple government organizations, law enforcement, and users. You may need to coordinate press releases and communications on social media. Communications may need to be vetted internally with legal, security, and marketing teams and with a representative from your cyber-insurance carrier if you have such a policy. The amount of communication and collaboration for a well-coordinated, professional response can only be done in the required timeframes by having a plan and process defined in advance, as well as training staff on the plan along with templates, checklists, and contacts.

Compromised Credentials

If there is a large-scale compromise of your users' authentication credentials, the legitimate users need a way to reset their credentials and recover their accounts if thieves have taken over the accounts. Relying on users calling a support center is costly and difficult to scale and requires a secret the legitimate user and the support staff know that the thief won't know. Sending a password reset link to the user's registered email address or phone number may not work if significant time has passed between the breach and its discovery because the thief may have altered authentication credentials and user profile information, including notification attributes such as a user's email address and phone number. You need a secure and scalable account recovery process worked out in advance so that you can act in a timely manner if this happens.

Compromised Secrets

A related scenario is the compromise of other "secrets" such as OAuth 2.0 client secrets or private keys used in the signing or decryption of security tokens. This can happen as a result of human error, so it is wise to prepare for this possibility. An inventory should be maintained of all such secrets used in your operations, how each is used, and recovery steps needed if any are compromised.

Your application can facilitate recovery by dynamically retrieving the public keys used to validate security tokens. This makes it easier to rotate them but may create issues for caching. If your application caches dynamically retrieved public keys for performance reasons, and invalidates the cache anytime a signature validation fails, this could enable a denial-of-service (DoS) attack by someone sending counterfeit security tokens with fake signatures. If caching is needed, it may be possible to reduce this risk using a periodic refresh and by having applications only invalidate their cache upon a validation failure once per a certain time period, rather than for each failure, and triggering an alert for human intervention if a lot of invalid tokens are received.

If your solution includes the use of SAML 2 with other organizations and a private key used to sign or decrypt SAML 2 messages is compromised, you need to update configurations with new keys. If there is no dynamic mechanism to update federation metadata, you may need to synchronize updates with another organization. You should work out recovery processes in advance for the secrets in your environment so you can execute quickly if needed.

Summary

We've covered several scenarios that involve some type of failure and the need to create a response plan for them. Some, like forgotten passwords, are likely to occur. Others, like a breach of personal data or user credentials, may never occur. The failures possible in your environment may differ from those we outlined, but our list should help you identify possibilities to consider. This enables you to create response plans, train your team, and test your preparedness periodically to ensure you are ready if something happens. Be sure your response plan identifies any logging and records necessary to facilitate or monitor your response. Besides these failure/exception cases, there are also use cases that are simply less common, and they are the topic of the next chapter.

Key Points

- It's essential to plan for what can go wrong in an environment.

- You may need a process for restoring accidentally deleted data.

- You need a process for customers who wish to decommission their account.

- You should have a process to handle an orphaned account.

- Users may forget or lose credentials and need an account recovery mechanism.

- You need a process to check for and fix accounts whose password has been compromised.

- You need a process to identify the legitimate account owner if account takeover has occurred.

- If your support system or administrative access depends on a single sign-on system, you should plan for how to handle an outage to the single sign-on system.

- You should have an incident response plan in place for responding to cybersecurity threats, including compromised personal data, user credentials, or private keys.

- In planning how to handle exceptional events, be sure to consider logging data that could facilitate your response or records to keep of your response actions to demonstrate proper handling of an event.

Notes

i. https://thenextweb.com/news/microsoft-can-recycle-your-outlook-com-email-address-if-your-account-becomes-inactive

ii. https://www.pcmag.com/news/fcc-to-create-rules-to-stop-sim-swapping-attacks

iii. www.vice.com/en/article/y3g8wb/hacker-got-my-texts-16-dollars-sakari-netnumber

iv. https://usa.kaspersky.com/blog/ss7-hacked/17099/

v. www.theguardian.com/technology/2016/apr/19/ss7-hack-explained-mobile-phone-vulnerability-snooping-texts-calls

vi. https://medium.com/4iqdelvedeep/1-4-billion-clear-text-credentials-discovered-in-a-single-database-3131d0a1ae14

vii. https://haveibeenpwned.com

CHAPTER 18

Less Common Requirements

Two roads diverged in a wood, and I— I took the one less traveled by, And that has made all the difference.

—Robert Frost, American poet, from "The Road Not Taken" (1916)

Previous chapters covered common identity management use cases. In this chapter, we'll share some less common requirements that may apply to your project. Identifying the need for them early in a project can help you avoid surprises and project delays. We've organized these scenarios loosely around people, accounts, and environments.

People

Several requirements stem from activities, changes, or relationships in the life of people.

Family Accounts

With services that can be shared between members of a household, such as movie streaming, it may be necessary to associate multiple family members with a family account. For accountability purposes, it is often better to allow the association of different user accounts, each with their own login credential(s), with a family or shared account rather than encouraging multiple users to log in with the same user account. This sharing requirement can apply to insurance, digital libraries, cellular service providers, healthcare, or other services traditionally shared among members of a family or household. In addition, one family member may need to be informed about, or

© Yvonne Wilson, Abhishek Hingnikar 2023
Y. Wilson and A. Hingnikar, *Solving Identity Management in Modern Applications*,
https://doi.org/10.1007/978-1-4842-8261-8_18

communicate on behalf of, another person such as a minor child or an elderly adult. For such family-oriented services, applications may need to recognize all family members associated with an account as well as what each family member can do for others.

Temporary Positions

In corporate settings, temporary accounts are sometimes needed for contractors, interns, or partner workers. If temporary accounts are not governed by a company's normal account management processes, they might not be terminated when the temporary working relationship is over. A best practice is to set an expiration date for temporary accounts and require the manager of a temporary worker to periodically approve renewal of the temporary account. If the account is not renewed, it should be disabled. The sensitivity of the privileges allowed by the temporary account's access can determine the appropriate frequency for account review and renewal.

Status Transition

Another corporate requirement involves a person who transitions from working in one capacity to another, such as a temporary contract worker transitioning to full-time employee status or vice versa. If temporary workers are registered and administered separately from employees, but all sources feed into one identity provider, it might be possible for two accounts for the same person to exist at the same time which might cause ambiguity at best or unauthorized access at worst. If a person can transition from one status to another, processes should be designed to avoid duplicate accounts for the same person.

No Email Address

Many applications expect an email address attribute in a user's profile. There may be cases, however, where users don't have email addresses. Some businesses do not issue email addresses to employees who have no need to read email on the job. Parents of younger children may not allow them to have an email address. Some organizations may provide their users an email address but have privacy guidelines that prohibit the use of email addresses as account identifiers. Applications may need to accommodate users who do not have email addresses or restrictions on where an email address can be used.

Identity Defederation

It may be necessary to support account defederation while otherwise leaving an account intact. For example, when a person terminates their relationship with an employer, they may need to use a personal account to access resources that they previously accessed via an account at the employer's identity provider. If a company provides to employees a pension program, employees might sign in to the external pension website via their employer's chosen identity provider. If an employee quits their job, their account at the corporate identity provider will cease to exist. The user will need their account at the pension system to be defederated from their employer's identity provider so they can log in with an individual account local to the pension system, or perhaps federated to another identity provider operated by a government entity or a social provider. In general, defederation is needed when a user can sever a relationship with an organization, but is still entitled to access resources there that they previously accessed via a federated identity operated by that organization.

Accounts

Another category of requirements is associated with users' accounts.

Mergers and Acquisitions

Mergers and acquisitions can create identity management challenges. It is advantageous for a company to have a single identity repository against which all users are authenticated. When a company acquires or merges with another company, it is common for the identity repositories of the two companies to be merged, which may require resolving duplicate usernames to achieve username uniqueness in the new merged entity.

Changing usernames to eliminate duplicates may impact applications. When a user is authenticated by a centralized identity provider, an identifier for the user is passed to applications. If an application maintains a user profile or data records that contain the user's identifier, the identifier passed to the application from an identity provider must match the identifier for the user in the application. If a user's identifier is changed as part of a merger, (mary@domain1.com becomes mary@domain2.com or "mary" becomes "mary.smith"), an identity provider may need to translate identifiers so the user can authenticate with a new identifier but have their former identifier passed to legacy applications still using the old identifier.

Alternatively, user identifier changes can be implemented in applications. This should be done with care, however, as it may require updating data records within the application besides the user's profile. This can become complicated, so it may be easiest to have an identity provider pass old usernames to legacy applications until the legacy systems are replaced.

This scenario demonstrates why it is a bad idea to use a user's email address (or other attributes which might change) as an account identifier throughout an application's data records. It is better to use an internal account identifier throughout the application's data records and treat the user's email address as a user profile attribute that is used for communication purposes. This way, if the user's email address or external identity needs to change, it can be changed in the user profile without impacting the rest of the application. Chapter 4 contains further discussion about decoupling user profile attributes that serve different purposes.

Account Linking

A common requirement, particularly in a consumer-facing environment, is to allow a user to sign up for an application account, entering user profile information required by the application, and then add the ability later for the user to log in to their local account via a social identity provider. This requirement can come about for several reasons, including

- An application has a legacy data store of identities but wants to offer users the convenience of logging in via a remote identity provider, most commonly a social identity provider.

- A user wants to try out a new application without granting the application access to their profile at a social identity provider. If they like the application, the user would later want to leverage their social identity provider account to log in to the application.

Applications typically want to remove as many barriers to usage as possible. Allowing a user to log in via a remote identity provider means the user can log in with credentials they may use frequently and are more likely to remember than an application-specific credential. Furthermore, if the user has an existing authentication session with the identity provider when they access the application, the user may get right into the application via single sign-on, for even more convenience.

Account linking can be used to link remote accounts to a local application account. Linking is useful because accounts are associated with a particular context. For example, a local application account with identifier "mary@gmail.com" is a different account than an account at a remote identity provider that uses the same identifier. If a user signs up for an application account using identifier "mary@gmail.com" and then logs in with the identifier and credentials specified at sign-up, she will access the local application account created as a result of her sign-up. However, if Mary then signs in to the application via a social identity provider, the application will receive a security token with various claims about Mary. The claims might include an internal identifier specific to that provider and a claim about her email address. However, Mary might have used a different identifier or email address at the social provider. Unless the application has a way to associate the social provider account attributes with the user's local account, the user won't be able to access their existing application account when they sign in via the social provider.

It is risky for an application to make an automatic association between accounts based simply on matching attributes because a remote account may not have validated user profile data. Therefore, it is best for any linking between accounts to be made explicitly using a process such as the following, which requires a user to authenticate to both accounts to prove ownership of each, before the accounts are linked:

- The user logs in to a local application account, proving ownership of that account.

- The local application provides a list of remote identity providers supported for linking.

- The user selects the remote identity provider for a second account to be linked, such as a social provider.

- The application triggers an authentication request to the remote identity provider to authenticate the user.

- The user authenticates to the remote identity provider, proving ownership of their account at the provider.

- The application receives a security token from the remote identity provider with claims about the user.

- The application uses claims in the security token to associate an identifier for the remote account with the local account for the user. It may add a user identifier from the security token to the local account's user profile as a secondary identifier.

- When a user authenticates, if the user selects local authentication, the application searches through the primary account identifier, and if the user logs in via a remote provider, the application searches through any secondary, linked identifiers in the user profiles to find the appropriate account for the user.

In this example, the linking steps establish a link between a user's account at a social identity provider and their previously established, local account in an application. The user must authenticate to both accounts to prove ownership of them and give the application the user's identifier at the remote identity provider. The authentication to the accounts to be linked can be done in any order, but it must be done, to prevent the risk of account takeover via account linking. It's important to note that automatic linking of accounts that have the same value for a profile attribute such as email address, without the explicit dual authentication step, should be avoided, to prevent the possibility of unauthorized account takeover. If automatic account linking is done between accounts with unvalidated attributes, such as an email address, accounts could be erroneously linked that belong to different people. Lastly, if account linking is implemented, it should be possible for users to unlink accounts they have previously linked, in case the user wishes to stop using a linked account for some reason. This might occur if an account is compromised or if a user wants to stop using a particular identity provider. Implemented properly, account linking can provide a convenience for users to log in via different identity providers and still access the same account.

Progressive Profiling

Progressive profiling can be used to avoid having to collect a lot of information from a user at once. A user can sign up for an application account with minimal information, and progressive profiling can then add to that data over time. The gathering of additional profile attributes can be done upon subsequent uses of the application or when it is needed for a specific type of transaction. A user can even sign in to an application using a remote identity provider, and the application can create a local account for them with information from the remote provider. A user can then be prompted to supply additional profile attributes either before or after they are redirected to that identity provider, with information from both sources merged into the local application's profile for the user.

Impersonation

Impersonation is defined as the ability of one person to log in to an application as if they were another person and perform any task as that person. The most common use case is the need for support personnel to log in to an application as another user and see what the user experiences in order to troubleshoot an issue. Unfortunately, such a capability has the potential to be abused, and it can be challenging to retrofit secure, restricted impersonation capabilities into an existing application. Rather than building impersonation capabilities directly into a primary application accessible by your entire user population, you can reduce risk and liability by creating a separate application with a subset of features needed by the impersonators and making it only accessible to such users.

For example, to reduce the risk of unauthorized or accidental activity by support staff impersonating real users, a separate troubleshooting application can be created that is restricted to viewing only the data needed for troubleshooting. For example, it could provide view access to customer account configuration and data, for troubleshooting, but not the ability to modify customer data or initiate transactions. The troubleshooting application should log all activity for audit purposes. In addition, automatic monitoring of logs for anomalous activity should be implemented. Ideally, consent should be obtained from account owners before the troubleshooting application allows access to an account. Needless to say, the troubleshooting application should be protected with rigorous security measures and accessible only by authorized staff, with the list of authorized users reviewed frequently. This approach can reduce the risk of unauthorized activity via impersonation.

Delegation

Another use case sometimes referred to as delegation is when one user needs to grant another user the ability to act on their behalf, for a specific subset of tasks or data. A busy executive, for example, may delegate some chores to an executive assistant. The executive's assistant would be granted access to perform tasks on their behalf. A variant of this is when an employee goes on vacation and needs to delegate ownership of their tasks (such as support tickets) to another person while they are away. In both cases, one user needs to be granted access to perform specific actions on behalf of another user. Such capabilities are best designed into an application as the granting of delegation privileges is quite application specific. For example, an executive may wish to delegate to an assistant the ability to approve expense reports, but only up to a certain amount. Application logging should be delegation-aware so that all activity done by delegates is logged and shows both the delegating and delegated identities involved, for a full audit trail. The task-specific nature of delegation and need for audit logging makes it best implemented within an application itself.

Environment

Last but not least, we have a few use cases related to an application's environment.

Shared Workstations

There are some environments where users log in to shared kiosks or workstations. Such environments provide a shared device that is used by many users. Examples can be found on manufacturing shop floors, medical offices, and point-of-sale systems. With the same device used by multiple people, it is important to have each user log in when they start a session and log off when they complete a session.

In some environments, such as food service, it may be necessary to support a very fast transition between users where users simply enter a four-digit PIN to begin a session. Such PINs share the weaknesses of short passwords. Requiring users to remember and enter long passwords may be infeasible, and issuing users a badge with a stronger credential requires them to remember to bring the badge to work each day, which may also be infeasible. In environments that experience high employee turnover, issuing and decommissioning such badges could be expensive. Biometric solutions may be too expensive for businesses with low margins and involve the risk of a biometric factor being compromised or spoofed. The right solution for a particular environment will need to consider the sensitivity of data or actions involved, the user population, and costs.

Having users log in at the beginning of a session is easy enough, but ensuring that a user logs out is more challenging because users may get distracted and forget to log out before walking away. Implementing a session timeout after a short period of inactivity can help protect users. Bank ATM machines provide a good example, asking after every transaction if the user wants to do another, and if there is no response within a short period of time, the session is immediately terminated. For applications that run in a browser, it is helpful to use a browser that supports ephemeral sessions and to set browser policy to force ephemeral sessions so that information from previous users' sessions is cleaned up. If your application may be used on shared devices, it's also important to consider if information could be leaked through other means, such as temporary files, and mitigate any risks found. Such steps can prevent user sessions and data from being compromised on shared devices.

Identity Provider Discovery

With an employee-facing environment, there is usually one identity provider to authenticate all users. In other scenarios, such as a multitenant application used by many businesses, each business may have its own identity provider configured, and the application may need to determine the appropriate identity provider for a user needing to log in. This has been called identity provider discovery or home realm discovery. When there are multiple possible identity providers, mechanisms to identify which to use for each user include

- The user selects the appropriate identity provider from a list.

- The user selects or enters information about their organization, and a lookup is performed to determine the correct identity provider.

- Derive the identity provider from an environment factor such as the originating application or domain.

- Obtain the identity provider from information in a browser cookie, if available, and revert to one of the previous methods if not.

If an application has multiple identity providers configured for authenticating users, one of these options can help determine the correct identity provider for a user.

Multitenant Applications

Multitenant applications serve multiple tenants with a single running instance of the application, where a tenant is a group of related users sharing access to a group of resources managed by the application. While multitenant applications themselves are quite common, they pose some unique challenges related to identity management. Users are typically authorized to access specific tenants. Scenarios where a user might need to access multiple tenants include consultants working for multiple corporate clients or administrative employees needing access to test and production tenants of a corporate application.

If a given user is authorized to access multiple tenants, the appropriate tenant can be determined by mechanisms such as

- Requiring users to have a different identity for each tenant

- Providing a tenant selection mechanism before or after login

The first option may not be very convenient for users. The second option is often achieved by including the tenant name in the URL by which a user accesses the application or by providing a tenant selection mechanism for the user. Obviously, there needs to be an access check so that only authorized users can select or access a tenant.

In addition to routing a user to a specific tenant, there may be a requirement to enable different authentication policies across tenants. For a business-facing application, it may be necessary to allow the administrators for each tenant to configure different identity-related preferences, such as password strength requirements, the identity provider(s) by which to authenticate users, or the allowed length of single sign-on sessions. It may also be necessary to support the ability of customers to retrieve log data but only for their tenant. In short, a multitenant application has to satisfy all the usual identity-related requirements, but may have to provide the ability for each tenant to have their own identity-related configuration settings as well as access to identity-related log data for their tenant.

Summary

We've covered several less common use cases that might apply to your environment to help you identify such requirements early in a project. In the next chapter, we'll cover some mistakes that have led to breaches to help you avoid a similar scenario.

Key Points

- Applications may need to accommodate family relationships, temporary accounts, users changing status, and users who may need to defederate their identity.

- Users in some scenarios may not have email accounts.

- Merging of identity repositories during company mergers may require changing usernames and supporting legacy applications' need for old usernames.

- Account linking allows users to link multiple remote identities to one local account and authenticate with any of them to use that account.

- Progressive profiling enables an application to build up user profiles over time.

- Impersonation for support purposes has potential for abuse which can be mitigated with customized troubleshooting applications.

- If an application supports multiple identity providers, a discovery mechanism is needed to determine the correct identity provider to use for each user.

CHAPTER 19

Failures

Those who cannot remember the past are condemned to repeat it.

—George Santayana, Spanish philosopher, poet, and novelist, from
The Life of Reason, vol. 1 (1905)

We have covered several aspects of identity management relevant to an application development project. Writing an application with perfect identity management will be for naught, however, if flaws in your environment or processes introduce a vulnerability, especially one that compromises sensitive identity data. It is often said that one can learn a lot from failure. When it comes to identity management, however, we think it is preferable to learn from others' failures rather than your own. Inspired by George Santayana's advice about the need to learn from the past, we've collected stories of past security breaches and their causes to help you avoid making such mistakes in your environment.

This chapter describes failures that resulted in significant breaches or exposure of identity data. There may be some wonderfully interesting and obscure cryptography bugs that have caused a breach somewhere. We won't be covering any here because, sadly, many breaches have been caused by very simple failures. While there are many attack vectors, the annual Verizon Data Breach Report[i] provides some valuable statistics on the top causes behind breaches. Hacking, malware, human error, and social engineering topped the lists in the 2020[ii], 2021[iii] and 2022[iv] reports. You'll see those and more in the following stories. Take note of the root causes in each story and avoid them in your projects!

© Yvonne Wilson, Abhishek Hingnikar 2023
Y. Wilson and A. Hingnikar, *Solving Identity Management in Modern Applications*,
https://doi.org/10.1007/978-1-4842-8261-8_19

Pay Attention to Process

Our first case doesn't involve technology or a breach of identity data, but we included it because it underscores the importance of securing not just technology but also processes. In 2015, Edward Hornsey, an enterprising young businessman, hit upon the idea of buying used iPhones, many of which were stolen, and returning them to Apple to take advantage of their liberal return policy. He received shiny new replacement phones in exchange, which he was then able to sell at a handsome profit. Surprisingly, he managed to do this 51 times before Apple caught on. At the time, Apple did not check to see if a returned phone had been reported stolen or was being returned by the registered owner of the phone. Nor did Apple have any check on the number of phones returned by a single person. This demonstrates the necessity of designing appropriate anti-fraud mechanisms and identity checks into business processes. In case you are wondering, Apple did catch on and fix its processes, and Mr. Hornsey was duly convicted of fraud and sent to jail. Don't try to replicate his scheme at home.

Another classic example of an attack that involved no technology beyond charm and chocolate, yes you read that correctly, chocolate, is the 2007 social engineering attack by a perpetrator who purloined 21 million euros of jewels from safe deposit boxes at ABN AMRO Bank in Belgium.[v] The thief's charm and gifts of chocolate were apparently used to obtain safe deposit box keys and information about the diamonds. Don't shortcut security processes, even for charming, chocolate-bearing customers!

Another failure occurred in 2006 when office workers employed by *The Boston Globe* newspaper mistakenly printed out lists of subscribers' credit card and bank routing numbers. Rather than shred the printouts, the workers placed them in a recycling bin. This environmentally conscious newspaper used recycled paper for routing slips for the bundles of newspapers they distribute to newspaper vendors. As you suspected, the recycled printouts with customer credit card and bank information were used to wrap bundles of newspapers that were then distributed all around the city of Boston.[vi] The newspaper certainly earned an "A" for environmental awareness, but an "F" for data protection that day. If you handle any identity information, avoid printing sensitive information except where absolutely necessary. In addition, provide shredders and train all staff regularly on data protection procedures, including shredding printouts with sensitive information. These examples highlight the need to analyze any of your processes that touch identity data and other sensitive information to ensure there are adequate process safeguards to prevent breaches.

Beware of Phishy Emails

Don't take the bait when someone is phishing! Continuing the unfortunate tale of breaches is Anthem which suffered a breach in 2015 impacting 78.8 million records including social security numbers, birthdays, addresses, email, and income data.[vii] The Anthem breach is suspected to have originated in a single employee inadvertently clicking on a link in a phishing email containing malware. At the time, Anthem had on the order of 50,000 employees and a single person clicking a dodgy email may have opened up a door for hackers. Sadly, the list of breaches caused by phishing attacks continues unabated. In 2018, UnityPoint Health fell victim to a phishing attack, resulting in the exposure of 1.4 million patient records including names, addresses, medical data, and possibly social security numbers and payment card information.[viii] Aultman Health Foundation was compromised by phishing, impacting over 42,000 patients.[ix] MedSpring Urgent Care in Austin Texas compromised over 13,000 patients' data as a result of a successful phishing attack.[x] This should underscore the importance of security training, endpoint protection software, and procedures/tools to help employees recognize phishing attacks which may come in the form of emails, text messages, or even voicemails. Implementing a comprehensive program of security measures, for defense in depth, may help reduce or contain the damage if someone falls for a phishing attack, but preventing malware in the first place is preferable.

Use Multi-factor Authentication

While the causes behind some breaches do not involve technology, there are certainly many that do. In November 2015, JP Morgan announced they'd suffered a data breach of 83 million customers' accounts.[xi] At the time, it was the largest data breach suffered by an American financial institution. This breach was the result of an attack that began with stealing an employee's credentials and then gaining access to the bank's network through a lone server that did not require multi-factor authentication. The moral of this story is one of attention to detail. Have accurate lists of servers, check that multi-factor authentication is required for access to all access points and sensitive resources, and repeat the checks regularly. Rather than rely on error-prone manual processes, use automated processes to identify servers for asset management, build servers with secure configuration, and automate regular security scans to ensure all servers remain configured to secure build standards. Scan networks and use device management regularly to find any equipment that does not meet secure configuration standards.

Stay on Top of Patches

While we're on the topic of staying on top of things, we should cover the 2017 Equifax breach. This breach exposed the personal data of 143 million people. The breach was made possible when Equifax did not act on security vulnerability notices for its technology stack. A vulnerability in the Apache Struts technology (CVE-2017-5638)[xii] was made public on March 6, 2017.[xiii] A patch was promptly made available by Apache.[xiv] Installing a patch requires time to update the impacted software and thoroughly test applications relying on the patched technology. Care must be taken to ensure the installation of a patch doesn't cause outages or other issues. In this case, however, aggressive attempts to take advantage of the vulnerability were already being reported in March.[xv] Unfortunately for the victims in this breach, Equifax failed to patch its systems for this known vulnerability. Equifax reported that its systems were breached in May of 2017, two months after the patch for the vulnerability was provided.[xvi] The lesson here is the necessity of knowing your infrastructure and technology stack, monitoring the vulnerability announcements for each technology used, and having a process to quickly triage and apply patches for critical vulnerabilities. It is challenging to identify and keep up with patches even in small environments, so leveraging automation, at least for identifying vulnerabilities, is essential.

Secure Your Cloud Storage

Just because you use cloud services with rigorous security practices doesn't give you a free ride. If you use a cloud service, you must configure and use it securely. In 2018, MBM, which runs a company called Limoges Jewelry (a Walmart partner), exposed the personal information of 1.3 million customers via an improperly secured Amazon S3 bucket. This S3 bucket contained a database backup file and left this information publicly exposed for many weeks. The compromised information included names, addresses, phone numbers, email addresses, plaintext passwords, and encrypted credit card information.[xvii] A similar incident, in 2017, this time by a Verizon partner, exposed personal information and PINs of up to 14 million Verizon customers via an improperly secured S3 bucket.[xviii] Continuing the pattern, Uber exposed the personal information of 57 million users in a vulnerable S3 bucket.[xix] A Florida credit repair firm, National Credit Federation, exposed data including names, addresses, driver's licenses, dates of birth, social security numbers, and credit reports for tens of thousands of customers in a similar fashion.[xx] Learn from these examples and check the configuration of any S3 buckets you use, but don't stop there. There were a surprising number of discoveries by security researchers from 2019 through 2021 of improperly secured cloud databases. VoIP Provider Broadvoice inadvertently left an unsecured Elasticsearch database exposed to the Internet that contained more than 350 million records. The data involved included caller names, phone numbers, city, state, and, in some cases, call transcripts.[xxi] At the time the breach was reported, it was unclear if the information had been accessed and misused by unauthorized parties. The country of Thailand inadvertently exposed personal information including names, passport numbers, visas, and residency status of over 106 million travelers in an unprotected Elasticsearch database containing ten years of information. Thailand promptly addressed the issue when discovered by cybersecurity researchers and announced that the unsecured database had not been accessed by unauthorized parties.[xxii] Cybersecurity analytics firm Cognyte exposed an Elasticsearch database to the Internet without authentication required for access. The database contained more than five billion records of data culled from previous breaches, which included names, email addresses, passwords, and the original source breach. It is unclear if the data was accessed by unauthorized users.[xxiii] Furthermore, researchers discovered numerous mobile applications with improperly secured Firebase databases.[xxiv] An easy way to reduce the likelihood of a costly data breach is to simply take the time to periodically check the configuration of any cloud storage you use, such as S3 buckets, Elasticsearch, MongoDB, and Firebase.

Encrypt Sensitive Data

Another critical lesson can be learned from the breach of Sony PlayStation Network. The Sony attack involved 77 million accounts, 12 million of which had unencrypted data. This resulted in the compromise of names, emails, passwords, addresses, and credit card numbers.[xxv] The lesson here concerns the need to protect data. If you handle sensitive data, and identity data is by definition considered sensitive, you should encrypt the data at rest and in transit. This protection should extend to backups and log files. In addition, logs should be scanned to ensure sensitive data isn't leaked to log files. Twitter learned this lesson the hard way when a bug inadvertently wrote out cleartext passwords to log files and they didn't discover the issue for months.[xxvi] Legislators around the world are reacting to public outrage about data breaches and enacting privacy legislation with sanctions for companies that fail to adequately protect personal data. In the event of a breach, these fines may be avoided, or at least significantly reduced, if data is protected by proper encryption.

Do Not Store Cleartext Passwords

It is risky to store passwords in cleartext. Unfortunately, numerous breaches of cleartext passwords show that many sites have run this risk, to the detriment of their customers. The third largest data breach in Finnish history resulted in the compromise of usernames and cleartext passwords of 130,000 users of the New Business Center, a site for entrepreneurs.[xxvii] A breach of ClixSense, a site for viewing ads and surveys, resulted from an unsecured older server with access to a primary database. This breach exposed personal information such as names, email addresses, dates of birth, and IP addresses as well as the cleartext passwords of 6.6 million users.[xxviii] A service called "Teen Safe," designed to allow parents to track their children's phone activity, compromised the data of tens of thousands of customers. The data exposed included parent emails as well as children's Apple ID and cleartext password for the Apple ID. This incident was caused by improperly secured servers in Amazon Cloud, but the impact of the breach was compounded by passwords stored in cleartext.[xxix] All we can say is, when it comes to storing passwords in cleartext, just don't.

Provide Security Training to Developers

Secure infrastructure and practices won't help if applications themselves contain coding vulnerabilities. A good place to start for advice on secure coding practices is the most recent version of the Open Web Application Security Project (OWASP) Top 10 security and coding guidance.

- OWASP Top 10 – 2021[xxx]

This site contains advice about the most common coding vulnerabilities and how to avoid them.

Heartland Payment Systems suffered a data breach in 2008 that exposed 134 million credit cards and was caused by a SQL injection attack.[xxxi] This type of attack takes advantage of applications that do not properly validate input that is subsequently used to form queries against back-end data systems. The Heartland breach in 2008 might have been prevented had they heeded the 2007 version of the OWASP Top 10, which showed injection-style attacks as number two in the list.[xxxii] They are easy attacks to perform and automate but can be prevented with proper input validation. To reduce vulnerabilities in application code, ensure that developers are thoroughly trained on the current OWASP Top 10 application security risks and how to prevent them. In addition, to mitigate the risk of human error, institute code reviews and automated software vulnerability scanning to identify vulnerabilities in your application code.

Vet Your Partners

Many companies today use a dizzying array of vendors, and if their access is not properly managed and segregated, the results can be disastrous. The retail company Target announced in 2014 that it had been attacked, resulting in the exposure of 40 million card numbers and personal data of 70 million customers. This attack is suspected to have originated in the compromise of Target's HVAC (heating, ventilation, and air conditioning) contractor via a phishing attack which installed a Citadel Trojan. Unfortunately, there was inadequate separation between the network access granted to the HVAC vendor and other systems on Target's business network. The attackers were able to leverage the access provided to the HVAC vendor to access vulnerable systems on Target's network and from there to access POS (point of sale) systems where they collected credit and debit card data. While Target had installed security tools such as FireEye and Symantec, key monitoring features were either turned off or not monitored.[xxxiii] The lesson to learn from this breach is to thoroughly validate the security practices of all partners on an ongoing basis and ensure adequate network segregation between low sensitivity systems and systems with highly sensitive data. Applying the principle of least privilege by granting the minimum necessary access to each actor in an environment can provide another layer of defense. Last but not least, ensure monitoring systems are turned on and pay attention to alerts from security monitoring systems.

There are several more examples of breaches related to business partners. [24]7. ai, a customer service and chat vendor used by several retailers such as Sears, Kmart, Best Buy, and Delta, caused a breach in 2018 resulting in exposure of personal data and credit card information for hundreds of thousands of customers of each of these large companies.[xxxiv] In 2017, Deep Root Analytics, a small professional services company used by the Republican National Committee, mistakenly put the data of 200 million voters on a publicly accessible server.[xxxv] Volkswagen announced in 2021 that personal data on over 3.3 million Audi customers or prospective customers was compromised by a business partner that left the data exposed sometime between 2019 and 2021. The data involved was part of a dataset used between 2014 and 2019 and included first and last names, email addresses, and phone numbers as well as any cars bought or leased.[xxxvi] To avoid a repeat of these cases, make sure to track all partners you use, vet their security practices and certifications, and ask for information on whether they share your data with any of their partners and how they've vetted their partners.

Insider Threat

Some breaches are caused by insiders. The Verizon Data Breach Investigations Report for 2018 indicated that 28% of attacks were perpetrated by insiders.[xxxvii] The same report for 2022 shows this has declined slightly since 2018, but is still around 20%.[xxxviii] While the motivation in most cases remains financial gain, perhaps the most infamous example of insider threat was not. Edward Snowden, a systems administration contractor working at the US National Security Agency (NSA), was able to exfiltrate thousands of top secret documents from a Defense Intelligence Agency network. The exact scope of the breach may never be known, but the impact to political strategy as well as to offensive national cybersecurity interests will be felt for years. Snowden apparently accessed 1.7 million files using automated web-crawling software on networks to which he was legitimately given access or obtained credentials to access. He configured the software to look for specific topics. His activity was apparently not detected in part because he worked in a field office that had not yet upgraded systems to implement the latest security controls which might have detected his activity.[xxxix, xl]

The Snowden incident illustrates the threat of a malicious insider. Several lessons can be learned from the Snowden incident. The first is to implement the classic security principle of granting each person the least privilege required to do their job and to design access models to enforce segregation of duties. Admittedly, this is challenging in smaller organizations where each person has many responsibilities. A second protection is to encrypt data at rest and in transit and implement adequate protection of the encryption keys. A third technique is to employ security monitoring software that can detect anomalous activity (especially high-volume data retrieval and exfiltration). It usually takes significant time to tune such solutions so that they do not generate a time-wasting volume of false positives. Data loss prevention (DLP) solutions, which are designed to prevent exfiltration of data by detecting anomalous traffic out of a network or device, can also be used. Unfortunately, none of these techniques can guarantee protection against data theft. However, if there is a breach and such solutions are not in place, it will look much worse for the victimized organization.

Summary

This chapter was a very sobering chapter to write. The number and magnitude of breaches seem to continually get bigger and bigger. The root causes are often basic issues that seem easy to avoid in theory, but are proving to be stubbornly challenging in the scale and demands of real-world environments. George Santayana, the Spanish philosopher, poet, and novelist, said, "Those who cannot remember the past are condemned to repeat it." We hope the lessons from past breaches help you avoid following in the footsteps of the many companies featured in the preceding sections. If you are writing an application that contains or uses identity data, you have an obligation to protect that data. Unlike the game of golf, there is unfortunately no handicapping system to give beginners a break. If you are creating an application, you must follow security best practices for the coding, deployment, and environment of the application as well as people, processes, and partners involved in the project.

Furthermore, in today's world, it's not good enough to just implement security technology. You need to be able to demonstrate diligent adherence to security- and privacy-related policies and procedures, which is related to compliance, the topic of our next chapter.

Key Points

- Processes, in addition to infrastructure, should be analyzed for vulnerabilities.

- Train users to recognize and avoid phishing attacks to reduce risk of malware.

- Use multi-factor authentication to mitigate the risk of compromised passwords.

- Monitor for software vulnerabilities and apply patches when vulnerabilities are announced. Leverage automation and tools for this process where possible.

- Follow secure configuration guidelines for all cloud-hosted components such as Amazon S3 buckets and cloud databases such as Elasticsearch, Firebase, and MongoDB.

- Encrypt sensitive data at rest and in transit, including backups and log files.

- Avoid storing cleartext passwords.

- Provide security and secure coding training for developers.

- Vet partners by checking certifications and conducting due diligence evaluation of security practices.

- Mitigate the risk of insider threat by granting minimum needed privileges and frequently reviewing access grants as well as logs.

Notes

i.   https://enterprise.verizon.com/resources/reports/dbir/

ii. https://www.verizon.com/business/resources/reports/2020-data-breach-investigations-report.pdfx

iii. https://www.verizon.com/business/resources/reports/2021-data-breach-investigations-report.pdfx

iv. https://www.verizon.com/business/resources/reports/2022/dbir/2022-data-breach-investigations-report-dbir.pdf

v.   https://www.independent.co.uk/news/world/europe/thief-woos-bank-staff-with-chocolates-then-steals-diamonds-worth-163-14m-5332414.html

vi. www.computerworld.com/article/2560335/security0/
security-snafu-at-boston-globe-exposes-
subscriber-data.html

vii. https://nakedsecurity.sophos.com/2019/05/13/two-chinese-
hackers-indicted-for-massive-anthem-breach/

viii. https://www.hipaajournal.com/unitypoint-health-phishing-
attack-1-4-million-patients/

ix. https://www.healthcareitnews.com/news/phishing-hack-
ohio-provider-breaches-data-42000-patients-month

x. https://www.databreaches.net/tx-medspring-urgent-care-
notifies-13000-patients-after-phishing-attack/

xi. https://archive.nytimes.com/dealbook.nytimes.
com/2014/12/22/entry-point-of-jpmorgan-data-
breach-is-identified/

xii. https://nvd.nist.gov/vuln/detail/CVE-2017-5638

xiii. https://www.imperva.com/blog/cve-2017-5638-new-remote-
code-execution-rce-vulnerability-in-apache-struts/

xiv. https://cwiki.apache.org/confluence/display/WW/S2-045

xv. www.imperva.com/blog/cve-2017-5638-new-remote-code-
execution-rce-vulnerability-in-apache-struts/

xvi. https://www.wired.com/story/equifax-breach-no-excuse/

xvii. https://www.retailtouchpoints.com/features/news-briefs/
walmart-partner-exposed-personal-data-of-1-3-million-sho
ppers

xviii. https://threatpost.com/third-party-exposes-14-million-
verizon-customer-records/126798/

xix. https://www.techtarget.com/searchsecurity/
news/252488361/The-Uber-data-breach-cover-
up-A-timeline-of-events

xx. https://www.zdnet.com/article/national-credit-
     federation-leaked-us-citizen-data-through-
     unsecured-aws-bucket/

xxi. www.comparitech.com/blog/vpn-privacy/350-million-
      customer-records-exposed-online/

xxii. www.infosecurity-magazine.com/news/data-of-106-million-
       visitors-to/

xxiii. https://www.hackread.com/cybersecurity-firm-expose-data-
        breach-records/

xxiv. https://cybernews.com/security/research-popular-android-
       apps-with-142-5-million-collective-downloads-are-leaking-
       user-data/

xxv. https://www.extremetech.com/gaming/84218-how-the-
      playstation-network-was-hacked

xxvi. www.zdnet.com/article/twitter-says-bug-exposed-
       passwords-in-plaintext/

xxvii. https://thehackernews.com/2018/04/helsingin-
        uusyrityskeskus-hack.html

xxviii. https://thehackernews.com/2016/09/plaintext-passwords-
         leaked.html

xxix. https://www.theverge.com/2018/5/21/17375428/teensafe-
       app-breach-security-data-apple-id

xxx. https://owasp.org/Top10/

xxxi. https://www.computerworld.com/article/2522155/heartland-
       pays-amex--3-6m-over-2008-data-breach.html

xxxii. https://owasp.org/www-pdf-archive/OWASP_Top_10_2007.pdf

xxxiii. https://arxiv.org/pdf/1701.04940.pdf

xxxiv. https://www.cybergrx.com/resources/research-and-
        insights/blog/top-11-third-party-breaches-of-2018-so-
        far-data-breach-report

xxxv.   https://gizmodo.com/gop-data-firm-accidentally-leaks-
         personal-details-of-ne-1796211612

xxxvi.   www.zdnet.com/article/volkswagen-audi-disclose-data-
         breach-impacting-over-3-3-million-customers-interested-
         buyers/

xxxvii. https://www.verizon.com/business/
         verizonpartnersolutions/business/resources/reports/
         DBIR_2018_Report.pdf

xxxviii. https://www.verizon.com/business/resources/reports/2022/
         dbir/2022-data-breach-investigations-report-dbir.pdf

xxxix.   https://www.nbcnews.com/news/world/how-snowden-did-it-
         flna8C11003160

xl.   https://www.venafi.com/blog/deciphering-how-edward-
         snowden-breached-the-nsa

CHAPTER 20

Compliance

"Compliance" is just a subset of "governance" and not the other way around.

—Pearl Zhu, from *Digitizing Boardroom* (2016)

Mention the word "compliance" to an application development team, and you may get some quizzical looks. What exactly is compliance and why does it matter to application developers? This chapter will provide a brief overview of compliance, why it's needed, how it benefits application providers, and how to approach it.

What Is Compliance?

Compliance is conforming to a rule, such as a specification, policy, standard, or law. Organizations set goals for, and aspire to achieve, compliance to ensure that their policies and practices are in conformance with relevant laws, policies, and regulations or relevant standards. While compliance may be mandated and enforced differently across the globe, it is designed to check that measures are in place to protect the privacy of individuals and the confidentiality, availability, and integrity of services and data. One way of categorizing different types of compliance is

- Compliance required by legislation
- Compliance required by an industry
- Elective compliance

For compliance that is required by legislation or a particular industry, you must determine if the compliance requirements apply to your project and take steps to comply if so. For elective compliance, you can determine if it is advantageous to you to comply. A later section will explain why compliance can be beneficial for your project. If you are part of a larger company, compliance requirements may be given to you by a compliance

© Yvonne Wilson, Abhishek Hingnikar 2023
Y. Wilson and A. Hingnikar, *Solving Identity Management in Modern Applications*,
https://doi.org/10.1007/978-1-4842-8261-8_20

team, possibly in conjunction with outside auditors. If you are part of a small startup building a new application, you may wish to hire an auditor to help you understand the requirements that apply for your type of project.

Government-Mandated Compliance

Many governments have established legislation regarding privacy and data protection.[i] Perhaps the most well known is the GDPR (General Data Protection Regulation).[ii] Enacted in the European Union, it took effect in May of 2018. It contains 99 articles which describe the principles underlying the GDPR, the specific provisions of the GDPR, supervisory authorities, penalties for nonconformance, and practical matters related to implementation. The GDPR describes a legal basis for processing personal data, outlines the obligations of organizations which collect and process personal data, and establishes the rights of data subjects whose personal data is being processed.

The scope of applicability for the GDPR is any product or service that processes (e.g., collects, stores, uses, transmits, deletes) personal information (PI) of EU residents regardless of where such information is held. This includes companies in countries outside the EU who merely hold or process data about people in the EU. It applies to companies of any size, though Article 30 of the GDPR outlines some recordkeeping exemptions for companies with fewer than 250 employees and who meet additional criteria for data processing. The GDPR also requires that the latest technology be used for developing applications, privacy must be embedded into the design of the application, and the application is released with privacy default settings. If your service is likely to be used by residents of the EU, you need to understand and comply with the requirements stemming from this legislation.

The GDPR is the most comprehensive change to data privacy legislation in over 20 years. Its effects are being felt globally, and other countries are establishing similar changes. In the United States, the State of California passed the California Consumer Privacy Act (CCPA), a bill that enhances consumer rights for residents residing in the state. The CCPA went into effect in January 2020 and entitles residents to know what personal data is being collected, whether it's sold or shared, the right to opt out to the sale or sharing of their personal data, access to their data, and equal service and price even if they exercise their opt-out choice. The California Privacy Rights Act (CPRA) adds to and amends the CCPA. It adds, among other things, a right for consumers to correct inaccurate personal information about themselves and a right to limit the use and disclosure of sensitive personal information. Most of its provisions will take effect on January 1, 2023.

Many other states have privacy legislation in the works. In 2021, the state of Virginia passed the Virginia Consumer Data Protection Act (VCDPA) which takes effect on January 1, 2023, and Colorado passed the Colorado Privacy Act (CPA) which takes effect on July 1, 2023. Both provide comprehensive privacy legislation and offer many rights similar to the CCPA and CPRA, but each has minor differences in definitions, applicability, compliance, and enforcement. Over half of the US states are considering their own consumer privacy acts.

At the US federal level, the Federal Trade Commission (FTC) Fair Information Practice Principles (FIPP)[iii] is designed to ensure that the practice of collecting information is fair and provides adequate information privacy protection. It is based on the principles of Notice/Awareness, Choice/Consent, Access/Participation, Integrity/Security, and Enforcement/Redress. The FTC gives recommendations for maintaining privacy-friendly, consumer-oriented data collection practices which are self-regulated. These principles form the basis for many sectoral laws, including the Fair Credit Reporting Act and the Right to Financial Privacy Act.

Similarly, HIPAA (Health Insurance Portability and Accountability)[iv] and HITECH (Health Information Technology for Economic and Clinical Health)[v] are US legislation which apply to the handling of healthcare-related data. These frameworks may apply to you if you process, store, or transmit any electronic healthcare data for your customers. These are just a few examples of government-mandated requirements.

Industry Compliance

Compliance requirements can stem from an industry when a consortium of companies in an industry creates a standard and a means of enforcing it. The payment card industry requires all organizations that handle payment card data, including credit and debit cards, to comply with a set of standards, known as PCI DSS (Payment Card Industry Data Security Standard).[vi] This set of security standards was created by the PCI Security Standards Council, which was founded by five international credit card companies (AMEX, Discover, JCP, Mastercard, and Visa).[vii] The standards are designed to protect payment card data held or processed by companies. The standards are updated periodically and documents for PCI DSS v4 are now available.[1]

---

[1] www.pcisecuritystandards.org/document_library/

Compliance with PCI DSS is enforced by the individual payment brands (the five financial institutions that founded the PCI DSS). The PCI DSS controls apply to systems which process, store, or transmit cardholder data or authentication credentials and also apply to any systems connected to an environment that directly contains or processes such cardholder data. If your organization accepts, handles, or stores any type of payment card data, or if you outsource payment processing to a third-party vendor but can impact the security of the payment transactions in some way, you likely have obligations under PCI DSS.

Elective Compliance Frameworks

There are other security-related standards for which compliance is elective. Companies can choose to be audited against these standards to demonstrate their practices and operations follow the standard. For example, a company can elect to comply with the ISO 27000 (International Organization for Standardization 27000 family of standards for information security management systems).[viii] Another elective security standard is from the CSA STAR (Cloud Security Alliance Security Trust Assurance and Risk) Program.[ix] The CSA STAR program provides a comprehensive list of controls known as the Cloud Controls Matrix (CCM). Compliance with these or other elective standards is a choice. Companies can weigh the cost and level of effort for compliance against the benefits, which can include achieving competitive advantage, expanding into new markets or industries, supporting a brand image, or responding to customer audit requests efficiently.

Why Compliance

Compliance required by legislation or an industry is typically mandatory. Recent years have seen the passage of privacy- and security-related legislation as a reaction by governments to the alarming number of security breaches that have occurred. If your project falls under the jurisdiction of legislation which requires compliance, you must comply. Elective compliance, however, is a choice. There are several reasons why companies choose to be certified against a set of security or privacy standards:

- Protect the sensitive data they process or hold
- Use certification as a competitive sales tool

- Show due diligence to minimize penalties in the event of a breach

- Cost savings and efficiency in handling customer audit requests

Each of these reasons can offer significant benefits, as described in the following sections.

Data Protection

The first reason for pursuing compliance with an elective standard is to ensure your organization is doing its due diligence to protect the data for which you are under contract to protect. This is essentially the "sleep well at night" argument for compliance. The process of preparing for an audit initiates a thorough review of security- and privacy-related practices. This identifies any lapses from policy or defined procedures that might lead to vulnerabilities, so they can be fixed. Regular audits reinforce security best practices as your organization grows and changes. Of course, passing an audit does not guarantee an absence of security incidents. The retail store chain Target was certified against the PCI DSS standard and unfortunately still suffered a significant breach.[x] However, a properly implemented compliance framework and certification should reduce the risk of a security incident and subsequent impact should an incident occur.

Competitive Advantage

A second reason to obtain a compliance certification is because it can be used as a competitive sales tool. With so many breaches in the news, and penalties for data breaches increasing, customers are demanding more security assurances from their vendors. Having a certification from an independent, third-party auditor can help assuage customer concerns. This can reduce delays related to security concerns during the sales cycle and may help close deals. Vendors with security-conscious customers may find certification valuable for this reason.

Reduce Penalties

Another good reason to obtain certification is to reduce penalties in the event of a breach. For example, with the GDPR, the existence of a previously earned certification is one factor taken into account when a fine is levied on an organization related to a compromise of personal data. A certification is no guarantee against a breach, but if you have audit evidence of due diligence in implementing best practices, you may receive lower fines than if you do not have a certification in place.

Efficiency

A final impetus to earn certification is efficiency and cost reduction. A given cloud service today typically uses many components in its software stack and relies on a number of cloud services. Many of the cloud services used by a company may have visibility into its sensitive data including personal data of its customers. In order to provide a secure service to customers, a company must ensure that every third party it uses protects the data it shares with them. The challenge is how to obtain such assurance efficiently from the vendors.

In the absence of any standards for privacy and security, each company would need to define privacy and security standards and examine each of its vendors against them. Such an examination would need to review a wide range of artifacts such as policies and procedures for managing employees, assets, access, physical and environmental security, software development practices, operations, network security, incident management, and business continuity. The examination would also need to check evidence that policies and procedures for all those areas are being followed and the organization's documented controls are operating effectively. This is a lot of information to analyze.

The field work for such an audit can take a week or more. Even a small company will typically have several vendors to review, and because there is always entropy in organizations, it is wise to repeat audits at least annually. It would be very costly for a company to conduct its own audits of every vendor it uses. From a vendor's perspective, it would be time-consuming to provide such evidence individually to each of their customers. In the absence of standards, different customers would request different data and perhaps in different formats, making the work to provide evidence to every customer unmanageable.

Security- and privacy-related standards provide a standard list of practices and a consistent expectation for evidence to demonstrate compliance with the standard. This enables a company to hire an independent third-party auditor to conduct a review and certify the company's practices against a standard. A company's customers can then rely on the independent auditor's assessment instead of conducting their own audit. A vendor undergoes one audit (for each type of assessment) and can then share the official audit report with all of its customers. Customers can use an auditor's report as evidence that they've done their due diligence to ensure they are using vendors who provide an adequate level of data protection. The entire process is made more efficient and manageable for vendors and customers alike.

Compliance Landscape

Compliance frameworks are often divided into privacy and security categories, but privacy frameworks typically include some form of security requirements because security is a prerequisite for privacy.

Security Compliance

Security compliance frameworks are mandatory for some industries. Compliance with PCI DSS is required for the payment card industry. Compliance with HIPAA and HITECH security rules is required in the United States for the healthcare industry. FISMA (Federal Information Security Management Act) is required for US government agencies and FedRAMP (Federal Risk and Authorization Management Program) for cloud providers providing services to US government agencies. Companies can also elect to be certified for elective security compliance frameworks. A list of some security-related compliance frameworks is provided in Appendix G.

Privacy depends on security, so it is common for privacy-related legislation to contain security requirements. The GDPR contains articles that require security of data and privacy by design. HIPAA in the United States has a "Security Rule" that similarly requires data stewards to adequately protect healthcare data. Also in the United States, the Gramm-Leach-Bliley Act requires financial institutions to safeguard, and conform to privacy practices for, customer financial information. When creating a security compliance road map, be sure to include security requirements stemming from any privacy-related obligations your project may have.

Privacy Compliance

Many countries have now enacted privacy-related legislation to protect the rights of individuals with respect to how their personal data is handled. In fact, over 100 countries around the world have enacted some sort of privacy legislation.[xi] A few data privacy laws and sources for identifying more are listed in Appendix F. Your project may be subject to a region's privacy laws if you receive, collect, process, or store data about people in that country. In other words, you may need to comply with a country's legislation, even if your business does not have a legal presence in the country, as with the GDPR (General Data Protection Regulation) in the EU. The same holds for privacy legislation enacted by individual states in the United States.

The role you play in handling data influences your obligations. Privacy legislation often differentiates between the responsibilities of a data controller and a data processor. A data controller controls how personal data is used as documented in a contractual agreement or policy. The data controller collects data from end users and has obligations such as providing privacy notices, obtaining user consent for the use of their data, and providing users with certain access to their data as well as the ability to correct it. A data processor, on the other hand, processes data in accordance with instructions from a data collector in a data processing agreement. Knowing your role as data controller or processor is essential to understand your privacy obligations.

It is also important to determine privacy obligations early in the project cycle, because they can impact the application design in order to give notice about the purposes of data collection, obtain and record consent for how data is used, manage data retention, and implement data correction and erasure features. Knowing such requirements early in the project cycle is critical for a realistic project plan.

If you are writing an application that has any personal data about individuals, you should understand the locations of your users and the privacy requirements that apply for the jurisdictions applicable to your user population. You should also check security- or privacy-related legislation for your industry. You need to know your role in the handling of data, whether data collector or data processor, and the requirements for your role. Once you have your compliance requirements, it's time to prepare for and pursue certification.

Assessment and Certification

Some standards rely on self-assessment, but most require an audit by an independent third-party organization certified to conduct the particular type of audit. Self-assessment requires an organization to examine their policies and practices against the standard and remedy any gaps. The CSA STAR framework's first level of compliance is one example that involves self-assessment. Even if insufficient for official certification, self-assessment can be a useful first step in preparing for an independent, third-party audit.

For many other standards, an independent, third-party audit of policies, practices, and operations against the standard is a requirement. The ISO 27000 family of standards, for example, requires an independent audit for an organization to be considered certified against these standards. When third-party assessment is required, the organization creating a set of standards for compliance will typically certify auditors or establish the standards for certifying them. Certified auditors then conduct the assessments, in accordance with audit standards, to evaluate whether an organization complies with the standards. Auditor certification ensures audits are carried out in a rigorous, standard, and unbiased way and the use of certified auditors is required for many certifications.

There is a lot of overlap between different cybersecurity-related compliance frameworks. The Cloud Controls Matrix (CCM) created by the Cloud Security Alliance (CSA) provides a useful mapping of controls relevant to cloud security and privacy across different frameworks. Organizations wishing to pursue more than one certification can easily see how a specific control, such as having an established change control and configuration management process, will satisfy requirements in different compliance frameworks.

How to Proceed

Once you've identified relevant compliance frameworks for your project, you need to plan the work required to implement and demonstrate compliance. The following list of activities can help you understand and organize the effort:

- Identify the national, state, or industry-specific privacy legislation applicable for the regions in which your business operates.

- Research privacy and security requirements for the countries or regions in which your users reside.

- Identify cybersecurity requirements applicable for your industry.

- If you supply services to public sector organizations or process government data, check for applicable government requirements.

- Identify elective security standards which may be beneficial to demonstrate your security practices to prospective customers.

- Consult with legal, privacy, or security experts if you have any questions about which legislation or security requirements apply.

- Create a data map that describes the data elements of all data repositories and data flows for all data you handle.

- Note all data elements in the map which involve personal data.

- Document the reason for collecting the data and the data processing activities to be performed with the data.

- Review data processing to ensure your application collects the minimum data required in accordance with your privacy statement.

- If available, use a self-assessment tool for a compliance standard to identify gaps that must be mitigated before an official audit.

- Retain a secondary auditor for advice on what to expect or an informal assessment before an official audit to help you meet audit requirements without wasting time on unnecessary tasks.

- Know the scope of evidence required for an audit. For some certifications, a year's worth of past evidence is required.

- Make a list of audit evidence required, and identify owners within your organization for each category of evidence.

- Periodically check that owners understand the evidence required and their teams are generating the evidence needed for an audit.

- Select a reputable third-party auditor with experience in your domain and who will provide both an official audit result and an internal report on recommended improvement activities.

- Prior to an audit, get the official list from the auditor of evidence required. Work with owners to obtain the requested evidence.

- During the audit, additional information is often requested. Have parties ready to gather additional evidence.

- Conduct a postaudit assessment after an audit to identify what went well and how to improve the process for the next audit.

- Focus on one certification at a time.

Summary

Privacy-related compliance is usually mandatory, by virtue of government legislation to protect people's privacy and personal data. Security-related compliance may be elective in some cases, but is undertaken for several reasons: as a sales tool, to efficiently satisfy customer demands for audits, to demonstrate due diligence and reduce penalties in the event of a breach, or simply to help you sleep at night. There are myriad privacy laws and security standards, but there is a lot of overlap across them. Once you've passed a certification for one, you will likely be able to reuse some of the work to satisfy the requirements of additional compliance frameworks. This chapter concludes our advice for current projects, so in the last chapter, we'll share our ideas about why we think identity management will be even more important and necessary in the future.

Key Points

- Compliance involves assessing and demonstrating adherence to a set of controls.

- Privacy- and security-related compliance may be required by legislation or industry.

- Security-related compliance can be chosen for security and business advantage in scenarios where it is not mandatory.

- Privacy-related legislation is mandatory for entities which meet the criteria set out in the legislation.

- Over 100 countries have enacted privacy-related legislation.[xii]

- In the United States, privacy-related legislation is being enacted by many states as well as industry sectors.

- Certification against privacy- and security-related compliance frameworks

  - Demonstrates due diligence in protecting data you manage

  - Can be used as a competitive sales tool

  - May lessen fines in the event of a breach

  - Is an efficient way to respond to audit needs of individual customers

- A critical first step for compliance is building an inventory of systems and the data they contain, along with the reason for collecting any personal data and how the data is processed.

- The Cloud Security Alliance's Cloud Controls Matrix provides a useful mapping of controls across different security-related compliance frameworks.

Notes

i.   https://unctad.org/en/Pages/DTL/STI_and_ICTs/ICT4D-Legislation/eCom-Data-Protection-Laws.aspx

ii. https://ec.europa.eu/commission/priorities/justice-and-fundamental-rights/data-protection/2018-reform-eu-data-protection-rules_en

iii. https://www.fpc.gov/resources/fipps/

iv. www.hhs.gov/hipaa/for-professionals/index.html

v.   www.hhs.gov/hipaa/for-professionals/special-topics/hitech-act-enforcement-interim-final-rule/index.html

vi. www.pcisecuritystandards.org/

vii. https://www.pcisecuritystandards.org/about_us/

viii. www.iso.org/isoiec-27001-information-security.html

ix. https://cloudsecurityalliance.org/star/#_overview

x. https://blogs.gartner.com/avivah-litan/2014/01/20/how-pci-failed-target-and-u-s-consumers/

xi. https://unctad.org/en/Pages/DTL/STI_and_ICTs/ICT4D-Legislation/eCom-Data-Protection-Laws.aspx

xii. https://unctad.org/en/Pages/DTL/STI_and_ICTs/ICT4D-Legislation/eCom-Data-Protection-Laws.aspx

CHAPTER 21

Looking into the Crystal Ball

The future cannot be predicted, but futures can be invented. It was man's ability to invent which has made human society what it is.

—Dennis Gabor, Hungarian physicist, 1971 Nobel Prize winner in physics for inventing holography, from *Inventing the Future* (1963)

If we had a crystal ball, what would it show for the future of identity management? As the swirling mists parted in our all-seeing globe, we believe it would undoubtedly show identity management becoming increasingly necessary in the future for several reasons. First, it is unlikely that hackers will stop hacking, which means we'll continue to need security measures to protect against increasingly diverse and potentially more automated threats. At the same time, there will be many innovative new services and devices that will be beneficial in our lives, but they'll need adequate identity management to reduce the risk of them being used against us. We'll also see a rise in autonomous entities requiring identification, authentication, and authorization just like humans. The notion of identity will need to spread from humans to all manner of devices, agents, and robots acting on our behalf, and such entities will need identity management as part of their defenses against malicious attacks. In addition, the Covid-19 pandemic has greatly increased the number of employees working from home or other locations outside the corporate network. This has accelerated a shift from older enterprise security models that depended on a network perimeter to a different approach, based on Zero Trust principles,[i] that relies more heavily on identity and access management to control access to digital resources that reside both within and outside a

© Yvonne Wilson, Abhishek Hingnikar 2023
Y. Wilson and A. Hingnikar, *Solving Identity Management in Modern Applications*,
https://doi.org/10.1007/978-1-4842-8261-8_21

corporate network. For all these reasons, the need for identity management in the future will be more important than ever before, and we'll need to find ways to make it easier to implement and manage effectively.

In this chapter, we'll share our thoughts on where identity management will be needed in the future as well as some of the top lessons we've learned from the past that we think will apply in the future.

Continued Security Challenges

For starters, it doesn't take a crystal ball to predict that we will continue to face ever more diverse security challenges in the future. The targets and types of cyberattacks will continue to diversify as hackers are inspired with new ways to obtain and take advantage of stolen data and breached resources.

Ongoing Breaches

The number of breaches and data records reported every year as compromised shows no sign of letting up. The number of confirmed breaches covered by the Verizon Data Breach Report for 2021 rose to 5258 and for 2022 to 5212 compared to 3950 in 2020 and approximately 2000 from 2015 to 2019.[ii] A top target of cyberattacks is often credential theft, with the primary motive behind attacks being financial and the perpetrators frequently involved with organized crime groups. It's important to remember that any statistics about security incidents and breaches depend on the events being discovered and voluntarily reported so these numbers may not represent the whole picture. A large breach can also skew the numbers from one year to the next. However, both common sense and the numbers reported each year indicate that the need for cybersecurity is not going away anytime soon, and identity management solutions that mitigate risk from credential theft can help minimize the damage of an attack.

Evolving Targets

The targets and methods by which stolen data is monetized have been evolving. As one industry or avenue of theft comes under attack, consumers and service providers implement mitigations, causing cybercriminals to pivot to easier targets. The financial industry was an early target, but as financial institutions implemented more defenses, the entertainment and retail industries came under increasing attack, often as a source for stolen credit card data. Recent years have seen increased attacks on healthcare and small/medium-sized businesses and a focus on credential theft as well as an increase in ransomware attacks.

With the introduction of an EMV microchip in credit cards, and the increasing use of multi-factor authentication in financial services, some hackers have shifted their focus to stealing identity data and creating new ways to monetize it. Fraudsters have used stolen identity data to obtain medical services, commit insurance fraud, apply for tax refunds, and even redeem loyalty club points. Hackers have successfully exploited vulnerabilities in the Signaling System 7 (SS7) system that allows interconnection between phone networks, in order to intercept SMS text messages commonly used for multi-factor authentication to protect access to financial accounts and other targets of value.[iii] Malicious actors often seek and take advantage of undisclosed or unknown vulnerabilities which gives them the advantage of surprise against defenders. The constant adoption by attackers of new targets and techniques will require commensurate ongoing evolution in security defenses, including identity management mechanisms, to protect consumers and businesses.

Increasing Complexity

As the world becomes ever more connected, software systems are similarly becoming more interconnected and more complex. Greater integration and complexity increases the risk of a vulnerability, either within an individual component or in the interfaces between components. At the same time, identity information and other sensitive data is increasingly collected and shared between systems, putting it at risk when a vulnerability is found and exploited by hackers. Developers and administrators will need to continually adopt more effective solutions and practices to securely develop and manage large, highly integrated software systems.

Diversifying Motives

While early hackers often hacked into systems for entertainment and bragging rights, the motives for hackers have diversified over the years. Financial motives dominate today, with the 2022 Verizon Data Breach Report indicating that financial motives were behind well over 80% of the breaches studied.[iv] Recent years have also seen attacks with other motives including hacktivism, industrial espionage, cyber espionage by nation states, election tampering for political gain, and cyberwarfare as a political tool or in support of physical warfare. The development of comprehensive threat models and mitigation plans will need to consider a widening array of actors and motives in addition to many new types of targets.

More Targets

There is a dizzying array of new technology available to benefit many aspects of our life, which unfortunately also creates many new types of targets that require protection. A wide offering of products, from home security cameras and baby monitors to smart speakers and HVAC systems, as well as car entertainment systems, health monitoring devices, and robots, has increased the possibility that malicious actors can threaten our homes, businesses, cars, and even our bodies from afar. Better security, including identity management, will be required to protect the devices in our homes and businesses so they're not used against us.

Homes and Businesses

Smart devices for homes and businesses offer many conveniences, but require security to prevent them from being used against their owners. Security cameras and baby monitors have been hacked to spy on people in their homes.[v] Even smart dolls such as the My Friend Cayla doll and Furby, designed to interact with children, have been found to have significant privacy and security issues, being hackable via Bluetooth connection.[vi, vii] Smart devices have also been used to enable attacks against other resources on the same network. A particularly eye-opening example is the hack of a network-attached sensor for an aquarium heater for a large fish tank in a Las Vegas casino lobby.[viii] The sensor provided a conduit for hackers to infiltrate the casino's network and exfiltrate data. Without adequate security, the Internet makes it possible for hackers anywhere in the world to leverage vulnerable network-attached devices, even innocuous-seeming fish tank heaters, for malicious purposes.

Cars

Cars now offer new infotainment systems with an increasing number of helpful services. Passengers can view movies and play video games. Drivers benefit from onboard navigation systems, and services like OnStar can provide communication, weather information, emergency assistance, and remote diagnostics.[ix] Along with these valuable services, however, has come a new attack surface, and security researchers have demonstrated several exploits against it.

In July 2015, news broke of an attack against Jeep Cherokee where two security researchers demonstrated taking control of a car driving down a highway 10 miles away.[x] By exploiting a vulnerability in the Uconnect system which controls the car's entertainment system, they were able to send commands from their laptop to the car's dashboard, steering, brakes, and transmission.[xi] This incident was alarming by demonstrating the potential for a security vulnerability to be exploited to inflict physical harm on a car's occupants. Since then, researchers have demonstrated additional vulnerabilities by compromising a Tesla key fob to steal a Tesla, unlocking and remotely starting cars with OnStar RemoteLink, and taking control of navigation systems in Volkswagen and Audi vehicles.[xii] Cars and the services delivered to them will need to be designed with adequate security to protect the privacy and physical safety of occupants.

Medical Implants and Monitoring

A wide variety of medical devices help us treat chronic conditions and live fuller lives. Remote patient monitoring (RPM) technologies can be used for monitoring factors such as blood pressure and pulse, blood sugar levels for diabetes, and even heart function.[xiii] Implanted cardiac devices, for example, connect to the heart and provide relief for several heart conditions including hearts that beat too slowly, too fast, or unevenly. A monitor often connects wirelessly to retrieve data from the device. Remote monitoring with implanted cardiac devices provides the ability for doctors to assess patients without physical visits and detect problems earlier. The technology designed to improve our health, however, could potentially be used against us if not adequately secured.

In March 2019, a security vulnerability was announced for Medtronic implantable cardiac devices (implantable cardioverter defibrillator).[xiv] The devices rely on the Conexus protocol, which was not designed with any form of authentication, authorization, or encryption. Data was transmitted in the clear, potentially allowing an eavesdropper to gather information about a person's condition. Most alarming, however, was the possibility that an attacker within 20 feet could reprogram the cardiac device. The small size of these devices means they may not have the memory or processing power to run some of the security protocols used in less constrained environments. Further innovation and education will be needed to design and deploy efficient but lightweight security protocols on extremely small capacity devices.

Robots

Robots and industrial automation technologies are being designed for many industries and offer promises of efficiency, accuracy, scale, and performing tasks in environments dangerous to humans. Robots have been designed for surveillance, monitoring, routine chores such as vacuuming, disaster response, education, entertainment, manufacturing, medical applications, autonomous mobility, and research.[xv] The breadth of applications for which robots have already been designed is incredible. However, security researchers have also demonstrated security vulnerabilities in several types of robots.

Security research firm IOActive described a worrying list of security issues in robots in a paper about a recent investigation they conducted.[xvi] They evaluated robots used in homes, businesses, and industry settings, and despite it being a limited study, they found almost 50 vulnerabilities, including inadequate authentication and authorization, allowing unauthorized access to robots as well as the ability to install software on the robots. Communications involving sensitive data were not secured, and encryption of data was either missing or improperly implemented. The devices were often not secure by default, and best practices such as changing default administrative passwords were difficult.

Given the likely widespread use of robots in the future, this should be fairly alarming. Microphones and cameras in robots can be taken over for cyber espionage purposes to steal personal information or proprietary corporate information. The security of a network can be threatened by vulnerable devices attached to the network, meaning inadequately secured robots could potentially provide a conduit for attackers. Robots could also be taken over and weaponized, disabled, or held for ransom. Significant damage could be done if robotic technology is not hardened.

Erosion of Perimeter Protection

The computing infrastructure used to deliver services to consumers and businesses alike has been moving from individual data centers to cloud services and involves logic running on myriad new types of devices and edge computing servers. At the same time, the employees involved in creating and managing such services are increasingly working from home or locations other than a corporate network. This has decreased the effectiveness of the security once provided by enterprise network perimeters. As a result, organizations have been moving toward architectures based on Zero Trust principles, making identity and access management services critical to protect the access to individual infrastructure components. Organizations utilizing many services will need efficient solutions to provision and manage identities and access privileges across a widening portfolio of services and devices.

The combination of ongoing threats, evolving targets, a widening circle of actors and motives, and the bypassing of traditional network perimeter protections result in an increased need for effective identity management. At the same time, we're seeing an explosion in the number and types of entities which need an identity in order to securely participate on the Internet and access services.

Identity – Not Just for Humans

Most of the examples in this book have featured a human user, but there will be more nonhuman devices and agents in our lives in the future. They will need identities and the ability to authenticate themselves much like human users. They will also need to authenticate the services with which they communicate. Some of them may need to be associated with their owner's identities, and identity management will be needed to adequately secure them as well as the services they interact with. The following sections provide a few examples.

Personal Agents

Virtual personal assistants, customer assistants, and employee assistants will become more capable and connected. Applications on smartphones can use virtual personal assistants such as Siri or Google Assistant through APIs, enabling users to access app features and shortcuts from the lock screen or in hands-free mode. Users will be able to go beyond having assistants do simple tasks like taking notes, setting alarms, and calling friends to enabling them to perform tasks in applications on their behalf, such as making purchases or sending payments. Concierge applications might use information about our habits and preferences to help with tasks like making dinner reservations or purchasing airline tickets. Without requiring our interaction, smart applications could help with routine chores like making preventive doctor appointments, regular purchases, or texting a friend with whom we have a meeting to let them know we're running late. In corporate settings, virtual employee assistants could help with tasks such as scheduling meetings, diagnosing problems, or analyzing data. As virtual personal assistants act more autonomously, they will need to be authenticated and authorized just like a human user to ensure they perform authorized tasks and not those of a hacker. They'll also need to be capable of authenticating the services with which they interact, to avoid disclosing sensitive information to incorrect parties.

Autonomous Vehicles

Autonomous vehicles will significantly change transportation, but lack of a driver will shift some identity requirements from drivers to other entities. Humans may need to identify and authenticate autonomous vehicles that give them a ride as part of mobility as a service. Entrance gates to secured facilities may need reliable mechanisms to authenticate autonomous delivery vehicles, rather than drivers, when goods are delivered. Smart cities may want to authenticate and monitor autonomous vehicles on bridges, in tunnels, or near critical infrastructure. Autonomous vehicles may even need to identify and authenticate each other and validate the integrity of software controlling a nearby car, especially in tight spaces or at high speeds. Just as some networks only allow managed devices with validated configuration to connect, cities or highways may want to only allow authenticated and properly secured autonomous vehicles in sensitive areas.

IoT Devices

The potential applications for Internet of Things (IoT) devices are enormous. Smart thermostats, cameras, TVs, lighting, appliances, toys, medical devices, and a fascinating array of data-collecting sensors are just a few examples. IoT devices that have an IP address with which to communicate on the Internet will also need to authenticate themselves to remote servers and use adequate transmission encryption before transferring data to protect sensitive data as well as the integrity of uploaded remote datasets. They will also need to authenticate requests coming from administrative applications to mitigate the risk of malicious commands and the upload of malware to the devices. Without identity management and security measures, IoT devices can potentially be used to spy on their environment and corrupt datasets or, worse, be hijacked or rendered inoperable for malicious purposes.

Robots

Robots will need identities for the same reason as other IoT devices. They will need to authenticate themselves to services with which they interact, and they will need to authenticate incoming requests to prevent the robot from being taken over for unauthorized purposes. Robots will, in general, have significantly more capabilities and processing power, and therefore the potential for how they can be turned to malicious purposes may be greater than with smaller, simpler IoT devices like sensors. In addition to being used for espionage, robots can potentially be taken over and weaponized to cause physical harm.

On the Horizon

There are several promising solutions which bear attention. Efforts by governments and private consortiums to establish strongly validated identities, more standardized strong authentication, and new protocols for constrained devices will be rolled out and tested in real-world scenarios and will benefit identity management.

e-Identity

We expect to see more electronic identity initiatives around the world. Governments face the same pressures as businesses to deliver services more efficiently to distributed populations, which typically drives pursuit of online delivery for services. At the same time, many government services must be protected against fraud, which means their online delivery requires well-validated electronic identity information and stronger forms of authentication than simple passwords. This is likely to increase interest by governments in government-issued electronic identities (e-identity) or public-private sector collaboration for e-identities.

Several governments have already embarked on national e-identity initiatives. Estonia has a well-established e-identity program that issues a digital identity to citizens and residents and is used to streamline functions such as accessing government services, paying taxes, coordinating healthcare, and voting.[xvii] Estonia is even working on expanding this to create a digital nation, offering select services to remote e-residents.[xviii] Belgium has issued a national digital identity which can be used for identification, digital signature, and access with public services online.[xix] A consortium of mobile phone network providers and banks in Belgium, called Belgian Mobile ID, have created a mobile application called itsme that enables those with a Belgian e-identity (eID) and mobile phone to register at participating websites, authenticate, confirm payment transactions, and digitally sign documents.[xx] In yet another model, Sweden offers access to some public services via electronic identities issued by banks.[xxi]

Electronic identity programs will face some adoption challenges. Cultural distrust of governments or the banking industry in some countries may hinder and slow e-identity initiatives. Privacy and security concerns with electronic identity schemes will also need to be addressed. The constitutional validity of India's ambitious Aadhaar electronic identity program, for example, faced a lengthy Supreme Court challenge which hinged on security and privacy concerns.[xxii] However, the need for governments to deliver public services efficiently and securely, the desire by some businesses to leverage more strongly validated identities, and the preference by citizens and customers to conduct more transactions online will likely drive continued efforts by governments and private sector consortiums for citizen/consumer-facing e-identities. In addition to validated identity information, such identities will need to support stronger forms of authentication.

Stronger Authentication

We will doubtless see increased adoption of stronger forms of authentication to mitigate the risks associated with static passwords. The W3C Web Authentication (webauthn) specification creates a more standardized level of abstraction between applications and specific authenticators. Developers will be able to implement authenticator-agnostic strong authentication, and users will gain the ability to use authenticators of their own choosing, whether hardware security tokens or biometric factors collected by their device. This standard is likely to facilitate the adoption of stronger forms of authentication and reduce the use of passwords as a sole authentication factor.

Solutions for Smaller Devices

We anticipate ongoing evolution in solutions and protocols to support smaller, constrained IoT devices that need protections such as authentication, authorization, message integrity validation, and encryption. Devices with small amounts of memory and which need to minimize power consumption to conserve battery life need protocols that are lightweight and use techniques such as minimizing round trips and overhead as well as using cryptographic algorithms that enable the use of smaller keys and/or certificates. Entities which need to validate the likes of security messages and certificates depend on having accurate time as well as solutions for detecting certificate revocations, but existing solutions may not work on constrained devices. The Constrained Application Protocol (CoAP),[xxiii] Transport Layer Security (TLS) 1.3,[xxiv] and Datagram Transport Layer Security (DTLS) 1.3[xxv] may prove useful for solutions involving such devices.

Asynchronous Online Interaction

With digital transformation driving more services and interactions online, we are likely to see innovation and AI driving more autonomous and asynchronous interaction between digital services. Users may want to facilitate automation by authorizing third-party entities to perform tasks on their behalf or to access their data. For example, when applying for a loan online, a lender might require information about an applicant's income, credit score, ratio of debt to income, past tax returns, and credit card statements. An online lender will want to obtain information electronically for efficiency and to facilitate the use of artificial intelligence in evaluating applicant data. A user could authorize the loan site to obtain information about their salary from an employer, data on their credit history from a credit reporting agency, and perhaps credit purchase history from their credit card company, but such checks would likely occur asynchronously, triggered by a cascade of online transactions once the applicant submits their request.

Specifications such as the "User Managed Access grant for OAuth 2.0"[xxvi] from the Kantara Initiative[xxvii] may contribute to making such use cases feasible, in parallel with efforts to explore the risk, liability, and privacy rights applicable for such scenarios. This standard allows a user to authorize access to their content to a third-party while decoupling the timing of the authorization from the access request. A third party can initiate a request to a resource server without the user's synchronous involvement.

The third party interacts with the authorization server to obtain claims to satisfy access policy specified by the owner of the requested data. Solutions for autonomous and asynchronous interaction will require work on technical protocols and products as well as work on business, social, and legal feasibility, and identity and access management will be an important enabler.

Easier Adoption

We need better resources created to make correct implementation of identity management easier for developers. The specifications we have discussed total over 800 pages. This is a lot for developers to absorb especially when you consider the number of specifications involved, requiring developers to go back and forth between multiple documents to coalesce advice and figure out how to apply the technology correctly in their application and environment. Libraries will be needed that are well documented, support a good user experience, and help developers implement the protocols/ frameworks correctly. To be successful, this will require collaboration between parties creating or promoting specifications, platform/device vendors, user agent vendors (for devices with browsers or other user agents), security analysts, and those creating libraries and SDKs. A sentiment from John Dickinson's 1768 "The Liberty Song" says it best: "By uniting we stand, by dividing we fall."[xxviii]

Lessons Learned

Knowing that identity management will be critical in the future to help secure our homes, businesses, civic infrastructure, and all manner of devices in our world, we close with some of the lessons we've learned from working on many identity management projects and deployments.

Always Look Forward

During our years of working with customers, engaging with product and solutions teams, and building identity solutions for projects, we have come to appreciate that what starts with just a simple login box can quickly grow into a primary line of defense between your application and threat actors, yet can also serve as a key driver for customer conversion.

Authenticating a user today requires validating their credentials and additional factors, intelligently assessing risk associated with the authentication transaction, implementing password brute force attack protection, and more, but the sign-in box and process is also the leading conversion influencer. A large number of user abandonments in the online sales process happen at the login box for online retail sites.

Balancing the needs of security and user experience can be an accelerator for business value, but may cause tremendous overhead in technical implementation if not done efficiently and well. Being able to look ahead and develop identity features for your application as a service that can be worked on independently from your application allows you to easily integrate and expand the identity service to meet your future requirements. You may also be able to offload or even integrate with a vendor solution to provide risk-based security assessment.

Open standards play a very large role in being able to realize this vision. Following an open standard may seem daunting at first, but as we learned in Chapter 10, implementing standards-based identity management for an application can be simple and straightforward. Open source libraries and vendor-provided libraries are readily available for most of your application requirements. Leveraging standards enables you to more easily adopt open source and third-party solutions that can provide helpful features, make it easier to adapt to future trends, and allow you to focus on innovation for your application's core purpose.

Usability Is Important

Designing or deploying a complex security mechanism can be a satisfying intellectual challenge. You should ensure, however, that the resulting system can be easily used and understood by mere mortals. Users who are annoyed by overly cumbersome security measures will seek ways to bypass them. Users who do not adequately understand security technology can inadvertently render it useless through misconfiguration or erroneous usage. Make it easy for users to understand how to do the right thing and conduct some usability testing with target users to identify any usability glitches before a big deployment.

Validation Is Critical

You've probably heard the phrase "Garbage In, Garbage Out," and this certainly applies to security. Security decisions depend upon validated information as input. For this reason, be sure to correctly validate all tokens before relying upon the information they contain, and validate all input of identity and user profile attributes used in access control decisions or communication to users.

Logout Takes Time

In environments where a user may have sessions in many components or tiers of an architecture, designing, implementing, and testing logout can take longer than login. Make sure to understand the challenges involved in logout as well as session termination and allow adequate time in your project to make this feature work correctly.

Monitor Trends and Vulnerabilities

The only thing constant is change. Keep an eye on the current security guidance for the protocols, technologies, and products you use to stay aligned with best practices as they evolve. Read security industry reports, such as the Verizon Data Breach Investigations Report, to stay abreast of trends in attacks, common vulnerabilities, and how to minimize your risk. Make sure to also monitor nonsecurity trends impacting your target users, industry, or market, as they may give rise to new security challenges or requirements. Lastly, to facilitate your ability to respond to changes, be sure to allocate budget and resources for responding to unexpected vulnerabilities/incidents as well as proactively upgrading to adopt new best practices.

Summary

The future will undoubtedly bring increased and more diverse challenges to our online security. Perimeters that provided a layer of protection in times past, especially in enterprises, are increasingly bypassed. New threats will arise from the use of many innovative new services and Internet-connected devices that need to be secured. At the same time, nonhuman, autonomous entities and agents will act on our behalf and need to be authenticated, authorized, and monitored just like humans. We'll need more strongly validated identity, stronger authentication, and solutions for constrained devices as well as better resources to help developers do the right thing quickly and easily.

Key Points

- Security challenges will continue with diversified targets, actors, and motives.

- We will face more security and privacy risks from network-connected devices in our lives such as smart home devices, car infotainment, and medical monitoring.

- The number of nonhuman entities that will need identities and identity management will grow substantially, considering technologies such as personal agents, autonomous vehicles, and IoT devices including robots.

- More governments and/or private consortiums will issue electronic identities based on more strongly validated identity information.

- Passwords as a single authentication factor will continue to be replaced with stronger forms of authentication.

- Security protocols will need to accommodate the small memory, processing power, and power consumption requirements of small IoT devices to better secure them.

- Identity management will become even more important in the future to help protect innovative new services and devices.

Lessons we have learned from the past that will apply in the future include the following:

- It is essential to design for the entire identity life cycle, from provisioning/onboarding to deprovisioning, and even audit records required for accountability after deprovisioning.

- Architecting your application to treat identity management as a separable component will enable you to work on it in parallel with your application and take advantage of open source or third-party solutions where it makes sense.

- The use of open standards will give you flexibility to adopt open source or third-party solutions that can provide many important security features.

- Identity management features should satisfy both security and usability requirements.

- It is critical to validate all inputs to security decisions and policy enforcement points, including security tokens and identity profile attributes.

- Implementing logout features can take time, especially when there are multiple sessions for users across different components. Research requirements early so you can allow sufficient time to implement logout well.

- To avoid surprises, periodically monitor trends in security, identity management solutions, types of attacks, common root causes of breaches, updated guidance for how to use open standards, and nonsecurity-related trends impacting your target customer base.

Notes

i. https://nvlpubs.nist.gov/nistpubs/SpecialPublications/NIST.SP.800-207.pdf

ii. https://www.verizon.com/business/resources/reports/dbir/#archive

iii. www.telegraph.co.uk/technology/2019/02/01/metro-bank-hit-cyber-attack-used-empty-customer-accounts/

iv. https://www.verizon.com/business/resources/reports/2022/dbir/2022-data-breach-investigations-report-dbir.pdf

v.   www.cbsnews.com/news/nest-camera-hacked-hacker-spoke-to-baby-hurled-obscenities-at-couple-using-nest-camera-dad-says/

vi.   www.bbc.com/news/technology-38222472

vii.   www.nytimes.com/2017/12/21/technology/connected-toys-hacking.html

viii.   www.washingtonpost.com/news/innovations/wp/2017/07/21/how-a-fish-tank-helped-hack-a-casino/?noredirect=on&utm_term=.a22c8c331869

ix.   https://www.onstar.com/us/en/why-onstar

x.   https://www.pcmag.com/news/hackers-remotely-hijack-a-jeep-crash-it-into-a-ditch

xi.   www.wired.com/2015/07/hackers-remotely-kill-jeep-highway/

xii.   www.zdnet.com/article/these-are-the-most-interesting-ways-to-hack-internet-connected-vehicles/

xiii.   www.cchpca.org/about/about-telehealth/remote-patient-monitoring-rpm

xiv.   https://www.securityweek.com/dhs-warns-vulnerabilities-medtronic-defibrillators

xv.   https://robots.ieee.org/learn/types-of-robots/

xvi.   https://ioactive.com/pdfs/Hacking-Robots-Before-Skynet.pdf

xvii.   www.newyorker.com/magazine/2017/12/18/estonia-the-digital-republic

xviii.   https://e-resident.gov.ee/

xix.   https://eid.belgium.be/en/what-eid

xx.   https://www.itsme-id.com/why-itsme

  xxi.   https://bolagsverket.se/en/fee/e-services/swedish-e-
         identification-1.1639

 xxii.   https://iapp.org/news/a/the-indian-supreme-courts-
         aadhaar-judgement-a-privacy-perspective/

xxiii.   https://tools.ietf.org/html/rfc7252#section-9

xxiv.   https://tools.ietf.org/html/rfc8446

 xxv.   https://datatracker.ietf.org/doc/rfc9147/

xxvi.   https://docs.kantarainitiative.org/uma/wg/rec-oauth-uma-
         grant-2.0.html

xxvii.   https://kantarainitiative.org/

xxviii. http://archives.dickinson.edu/sundries/liberty-song-1768

CHAPTER 22

Conclusion

> *I didn't know I loved so many things and I had to wait until sixty to find it out sitting by the window on the Prague-Berlin train watching the world disappear as if on a journey of no return.*
>
> —Nâzim Hikmet, Turkish poet, from "Things I Didn't Know I Loved" (1962)

The world would be a strange place without identity. It's woven through much of our lives and enables us to establish trust relationships with others in order to conduct transactions. When conducting those transactions online, identity management is a core foundation of security which in turn is a prerequisite for privacy. The complexity of how to handle identity management well in the face of evolving technology and business requirements has continued to unfold over time, a bit like a Mandelbrot set. We hope this book has provided a useful introduction to identity management for those involved in projects to build applications. We hope you enjoy the challenges presented by this field and are inspired to learn more. Identity management is a broad topic, and there is a lot more to learn beyond what we could cover in this book.

We started out by introducing the types of problems faced by developers related to identity and how trying to solve them might seem like battling a many-headed Hydra. We covered the key events in the life of an online identity, from provisioning to deprovisioning, and everything in between, including authentication, authorization, policy enforcement, step-up and multi-factor authentication, logging out, and account management. We provided more information on each of these topics in subsequent chapters to provide an overview on the identity management capabilities a typical application might need. Our objective was to provide an introductory, practical overview of such topics, specifically for anyone building applications delivered via the Web or to mobile devices. We hope we've provided sufficient background information to help you get started and more easily understand other resources as you continue learning.

© Yvonne Wilson, Abhishek Hingnikar 2023
Y. Wilson and A. Hingnikar, *Solving Identity Management in Modern Applications*,
https://doi.org/10.1007/978-1-4842-8261-8_22

We've also shared some lessons learned based on our past experience, such as how to approach troubleshooting and some of the typical things that can go wrong. We've added some of the less common use cases we've come across so you can evaluate at the beginning of your project whether they might apply to your environment. Learning about additional requirements near the end of a project is never conducive to delivering on time.

There have unfortunately been many breaches that have compromised identity information. We collected information on a variety of breaches and researched the root causes to help you learn from the past. The root causes of many breaches are not complex, but they do require diligence if they are to be avoided. Pursuing a compliance certification can instill the practices needed to find cybersecurity gaps and avoid errors leading to security incidents. We added the compliance chapter to help you identify privacy- or security-related requirements you may need to comply with, why compliance can be a beneficial exercise, and how to approach it.

We closed with a summary of why we think knowledge of identity management will be even more important in the future. The need for identity management will expand to all manner of devices, bots, agents, cars, and more. That means a lot more people need to be familiar with the requirements for identity management and how to solve them. We hope the information in this book and the sample program help you understand some of the scope of what identity management entails. Most of all, we hope this encourages you to continue to learn more about the topic, to leverage the knowledge gained for your projects, and to find ways to share any new learning or techniques you discover with others. Ongoing collaboration between all of us to continually improve identity management practices and solutions will be essential to protect our data, privacy, reputation, and even our physical safety with the services and devices we use.

Appendix A: Glossary

The following is a list of terms and their definitions as they are used in this book.

Access Token – In the context of OAuth 2 and OIDC, a security token used by an application to access protected resources such as an API.

Account – A construct within a software application or service that usually contains or is associated with identity information and optionally privileges and which is used to access features within the application or service.

Application – A software application that issues requests to a server.

Application Programming Interface (API) – A software service interface that allows a client program to request resources or actions from the software service.

Authorization Code – In the context of OAuth 2 and OIDC, an intermediary, opaque code returned to an application and which represents the application's authorization by the user to call an API on the user's behalf. It is used to obtain security token(s).

Authorization Server – A service which implements the OAuth 2 protocol and enables resource owners (users) to authorize applications to access content they own at resource servers and which issues security tokens enabling the authorized access.

B2B (Business to Business) – A business model where services are targeted to businesses that use the services in some way to deliver a service to their customers.

B2C (Business to Consumer) – A business model where services are targeted to consumers who typically act on their own behalf.

B2E (Business to Employee) – A business model where services are targeted to businesses where the users are the employees of the businesses and act on their employer's behalf.

Back-Channel – Communication sent directly from one component, typically a back-end server, to another back-end server, as opposed to being sent via HTTP redirects, with a user's browser as an enabling intermediary. Compare to front-channel.

Browser-Based Application – See the definition for single-page application.

Client – In the context of OAuth 2 and OIDC, an application that requests access to protected resources on behalf of the owner of those resources.

© Yvonne Wilson, Abhishek Hingnikar 2023
Y. Wilson and A. Hingnikar, *Solving Identity Management in Modern Applications*,
https://doi.org/10.1007/978-1-4842-8261-8

Confidential Client – In the context of OAuth 2 and OIDC, an application that runs on a protected server which enables it to securely store confidential secrets with which to authenticate itself to the authorization server.

Directory Server – A repository for storing, managing, and organizing information about resources. Directory server products have often been optimized for storing information that is frequently read but infrequently modified and used to store information about entities such as users, access control privileges, application configurations, and network printers. Information in directory services has been used for authentication and authorization of users.

End User or User – A human subject using applications or services and who is authenticated and authorized when accessing protected resources.

Front-Channel – Communication sent via HTTP redirects, with a user's browser as an enabling intermediary, instead of directly from one back-end server to another back-end server. Compare to back-channel.

HS256 – Hash-based message authentication code (HMAC) using SHA256 hash function. A symmetric cryptographic algorithm that can be used for creating and validating a digital signature. It is one option for signing a JSON Web Token, but requires both the issuer and validator of the token to know the same secret.

Identifier – A single identifying attribute that points to a unique individual user or entity, within a particular context.

Identity – A set of attributes, including one or more identifiers, associated with a specific user or entity, in a particular context.

Identity Proofing – The process of vetting a user's identity and profile information.

Identity Provider (IdP) – (1) A general term for an entity providing an identity service designed to authenticate users and provide assertions about an authenticated user and the authentication event. (2) In the context of the SAML 2 cross-domain single sign-on profile specification, a server which issues SAML 2 assertions about an authenticated subject and authentication event.

Identity Repository – A collection of users stored in a computer storage system, such as a database or directory service.

ID Token – In the context of OIDC, a token used to convey claims about an authentication event and an authenticated entity to a relying party (application).

Internet of Things (IoT) Device – A network-attached device that has an IP address and is capable of transferring information over a network without human interaction.

Usually refers to dedicated-purpose devices such as sensors or smart appliances as opposed to general computing devices such as computer servers.

Least Privilege – A security principle of granting the minimum privilege level required for a task or operating at the lowest possible privilege level for a task.

Mobile Application – An application that executes on a mobile device as a native application.

Multitenant Application – An application deployment shared by multiple independent customers whose data is segmented into their own area of the application's data storage. The separation between different customers' data is enforced by the application and its storage, rather than the network.

Native Application – An application installed and run natively on a computing device.

OpenID Provider – In the context of OIDC, an OAuth 2 authorization server that authenticates a user and returns claims about the user and authentication event to a relying party (application) in accordance with the OIDC specification. Applications can delegate user authentication to an OpenID Provider.

Public Client – In the context of OAuth 2 and OIDC, an application that executes primarily on the user's client device or in the client browser and cannot securely store secrets with which to authenticate itself to an authorization server.

Refresh Token – In the context of OAuth 2 and OIDC, a token that can be used by an application to request a new access token when a prior access token has expired or become invalid. With OIDC, a refresh request can optionally return an ID Token as well.

Relying Party – An entity that delegates authentication to an Identity Provider or OpenID Provider or delegates authorization to an authorization server and, in either case, relies on the results, usually in the form of security tokens. With OAuth 2, an API is a relying party, and with OIDC and SAML 2, an application is a relying party.

Resource Owner – In the context of OAuth 2, a user that authorizes access to protected resources hosted at a resource server.

Resource Server – In the context of OAuth 2 and OIDC, an entity that contains protected resources.

RS256 – RSA Signature with SHA256 hash algorithm. An asymmetric cryptographic algorithm that can be used for creating and validating a digital signature. It is one option for signing a JSON Web Token and, unlike HS256, does not require that the issuer and validator of the token know the same secret.

Security Domain – A security domain is a logical construct that defines the boundaries of one entity's control or ownership.

Service Provider – (1) A general term for an entity providing a service, such as an application, to a user. (2) In the context of the SAML 2 cross-domain single sign-on profile specification, a client entity which requests SAML 2 assertions about an authenticated subject and authentication event.

Single-Page Application (SPA) – An application with logic that executes primarily in a browser, by dynamically altering the displayed web page, rather than making requests to a server to render new pages to respond to user actions. A SPA is assumed to be a public client, as defined by OAuth 2.

Tracking Prevention – A set of features implemented by browsers to limit the ability of third parties to track users' activity across different websites.

User – See the definition for the end user.

User Consent – In the context of provisioning an account for a user, the process through which an end user is asked to provide their consent for the collection and processing of their personal data. In the context of OAuth 2, the process through which a user provides their consent to authorize an application to access protected resources on their behalf.

Web Application or Traditional Web Application – An application with logic that executes primarily from a protected server, by rendering new pages from the server to respond to user actions. Traditional web applications are assumed to meet the definition of a confidential client, as defined by OAuth 2.

Appendix B: Resources for Further Learning

This appendix lists resources which may be helpful for further learning.

B.1. OAuth 2 – Related Specifications

OAuth 2.1 Authorization Framework (draft as of this writing) – Consolidates several OAuth-related specifications since the original OAuth 2.0 specification:
https://datatracker.ietf.org/doc/html/draft-ietf-oauth-v2-1-06
OAuth 2.0 Authorization Framework (original specification):
https://tools.ietf.org/html/rfc6749
OAuth 2.0 Threat Model and Security Considerations:
https://tools.ietf.org/html/rfc6819
OAuth 2.0 for Browser-Based Apps (draft as of this writing):
https://datatracker.ietf.org/doc/html/draft-ietf-oauth-browser-based-apps
OAuth 2.0 for Native Apps:
https://tools.ietf.org/html/rfc8252
OAuth 2.0 Security Best Current Practice (draft as of this writing):
https://datatracker.ietf.org/doc/html/draft-ietf-oauth-security-topics
OAuth 2.0 Device Authorization Grant:
https://datatracker.ietf.org/doc/html/rfc8628
OAuth 2.0 Authorization Framework: Bearer Token Usage:
https://tools.ietf.org/html/rfc6750
Proof Key for Code Exchange by OAuth Public Clients:
https://tools.ietf.org/html/rfc7636
OAuth 2.0 Token Introspection:
https://tools.ietf.org/html/rfc7662
OAuth 2.0 Token Revocation:
https://tools.ietf.org/html/rfc7009

© Yvonne Wilson, Abhishek Hingnikar 2023
Y. Wilson and A. Hingnikar, *Solving Identity Management in Modern Applications*,
https://doi.org/10.1007/978-1-4842-8261-8

OAuth 2.0 Pushed Authorization Requests (PAR):
https://datatracker.ietf.org/doc/html/rfc9126
OAuth 2.0 Rich Authorization Requests (RAR): (draft as of this writing)
https://datatracker.ietf.org/doc/html/draft-ietf-oauth-rar
JWT-Secured Authorization Requests (JAR):
https://datatracker.ietf.org/doc/html/rfc9101

B.2. JWT

JSON Web Token (JWT):
https://tools.ietf.org/html/rfc7519
JSON Web Encryption (JWE):
https://datatracker.ietf.org/doc/html/rfc7516/
JSON Web Signature (JWS):
https://datatracker.ietf.org/doc/html/rfc7515

B.3. OIDC

OIDC Specifications:
https://openid.net/connect/

B.4. SAML

SAML specifications. See especially the core, bindings, and profile specifications:
https://wiki.oasis-open.org/security/FrontPage
Security Assertion Markup Language (SAML) V2.0 Technical Overview:
www.oasis-open.org/committees/download.php/27819/sstc-saml-tech-overview-2.0-cd-02.pdf
SAML Security and Privacy Considerations for the OASIS Security Assertion Markup Language (SAML) V2.0:
http://docs.oasis-open.org/security/saml/v2.0/saml-sec-consider-2.0-os.pdf
SAML 2.0 Profile for OAuth 2.0 Client Authentication and Authorization Grants:
https://datatracker.ietf.org/doc/html/rfc7522

B.5. Multi-factor Authentication

The FIDO Alliance:

https://fidoalliance.org/fido2/

WebAuthn:

www.w3.org/TR/2019/REC-webauthn-1-20190304/

B.6. Background Information

An explanation of cookies, including security guidance:

https://developer.mozilla.org/en-US/docs/Web/HTTP/Cookies

Explanation of Cross-Origin Resource Sharing (CORS):

https://developer.mozilla.org/en-US/docs/Web/HTTP/CORS

Brief outline of different approaches to authorization and access control:

https://nvlpubs.nist.gov/nistpubs/Legacy/IR/nistir7316.pdf

OWASP Top 10 – Critical security risks for web applications and how to avoid them:

www.owasp.org/index.php/Category:OWASP_Top_Ten_Project

OWASP SAML Cheat Sheet:

https://github.com/OWASP/CheatSheetSeries/blob/master/cheatsheets/SAML
Security_Cheat_Sheet.md

Two sites on open redirects:

https://github.com/OWASP/CheatSheetSeries/blob/master/cheatsheets/
Unvalidated_Redirects_and_Forwards_Cheat_Sheet.md

https://cwe.mitre.org/data/definitions/601.html

Checking for breached passwords – I've Just Launched "Pwned Passwords" V2:

www.troyhunt.com/ive-just-launched-pwned-passwords-version-2

B.7. Privacy

A map showing the location and strength of privacy legislation around the world:

www.dlapiperdataprotection.com/

This website presents the articles of the GDPR in a convenient fashion:

https://gdpr-info.eu/

Appendix C: SAML 2 Authentication Request and Response

SAML 2 authentication request and response messages contain a lot of information. We've assumed that most developers are using an SDK or authentication broker rather than implementing SAML 2 directly in their applications, and therefore their primary need is to understand SAML 2 requests and responses for troubleshooting purposes and to understand validation steps. As explained in Chapter 16, the best way to debug issues with SAML 2 is to capture an HTTP trace, extract the SAML 2 request and/or response, and examine it. In the following sections, we'll explain which fields to examine and what to look for.

C.1. SAML 2 Authentication Request

When an application needs a user authenticated by a SAML 2 identity provider (IdP), the application redirects the user's browser to the identity provider with a SAML 2 authentication request message. An authentication request message can vary substantially as many elements are optional. A sample request without a signature might look like the following (text in bolded italics has been substituted for the actual values):

```
<samlp:AuthnRequest
    xmlns:samlp="urn:oasis:names:tc:SAML:2.0:protocol"
    Destination="IDP URL"
    ID="ID"
    IssueInstant="TIME ISSUED"
    ProtocolBinding=
        "urn:oasis:names:tc:SAML:2.0:bindings:HTTP-POST"
```

© Yvonne Wilson, Abhishek Hingnikar 2023
Y. Wilson and A. Hingnikar, *Solving Identity Management in Modern Applications*,
https://doi.org/10.1007/978-1-4842-8261-8

```
    Version="2.0"
    ProviderName="SERVICE PROVIDER"
    AssertionConsumerServiceURL="ACS URL">
  <saml:Issuer>SERVICE PROVIDER</saml:Issuer>
</samlp:AuthnRequest>
```

The request elements we have found most useful to check when troubleshooting SAML 2 are shown in Table C-1, along with an explanation for each. A given request may have more or fewer elements, depending on a particular service provider's configuration or implementation.

Table C-1. *Useful SAML 2 Authentication Request Elements*

Name	Purpose
AssertionConsumerServiceURL	URL at the service provider to which the identity provider's authentication response message should be sent. Often called the "ACS" URL.
AuthnRequest	Type of request. In this case, a request to authenticate a user.
Destination	URL for the recipient of the request, in this case, the IdP. This element was designed to prevent forwarding of messages to unintended recipients. This value must match the URL at which the request was received.
ForceAuthn	Can be used by requestor to indicate the IdP should prompt the user for credentials, regardless of the state of the user's session at the IdP.
ID	The ID is a unique identifier for each request. When an IDP responds, the value of the InResponseTo element of the response should match the ID for the request that triggered the response.
Issue Instant	The time at which the request was issued. Identity providers should reject requests that are outside a certain time tolerance.
Issuer	Entity which generated the request, namely, the SAML 2 service provider. The IdP should check to make sure a request's Issuer element matches a registered service provider.

(continued)

Table C-1. (*continued*)

Name	Purpose
NameIDPolicy	Can be used by the service provider to specify the type of identifier to use in identifying the authenticated user. Using an email address is common, but can conflict with privacy requirements.
ProtocolBinding	The requested mechanism by which the SAML response message should be sent over an underlying transport protocol. In practice, HTTP-POST is often used to avoid issues with browser URL size limits.
ProviderName	Human-readable name of entity issuing the SAML 2 request (the service provider).
RequestedAuthnContext	Can be used by a requestor to specify requirements for the authentication context used by IdP when authenticating the user. Can be used to request a type or strength level of authentication, as agreed between the service provider and IdP.
Signature	Signature information if a request has been signed by the issuer.
Subject	Used to specify the desired subject (user) for the requested authentication assertion.
Version	The version should be "2.0" for SAML 2.

A SAML 2 service provider (application) can send a SAML 2 request to an identity provider using a few different bindings. These indicate the mechanism for sending the message over underlying transport protocols. In practice, the HTTP-Redirect and HTTP-POST bindings are commonly used because they do not require direct network connectivity between the service provider and the identity provider. The HTTP-Redirect binding can be used with SAML 2 requests that are not digitally signed, but production environments are recommended to use signed requests to prevent request tampering. If a request is digitally signed, it typically needs to be sent using the HTTP-POST binding to avoid issues with browser URL size limits. The response or assertion from the identity provider must be digitally signed. Due to the size of a signed response, the HTTP-POST binding is typically used for responses.

C.2. SAML 2 Authentication Response

When an identity provider receives an authentication request, it will authenticate the user, if necessary, and return an authentication response to the service provider in the form of a SAML 2 response message which contains a SAML 2 assertion. In the case of an IdP-initiated flow, an IdP may send an unsolicited authentication response to a service provider. The SAML 2 response is an XML message with several components. The exact contents of the response can vary somewhat, depending on the nature of the request, the IdP configuration, and the information returned. Figure C-1 shows the high-level anatomy of a typical SAML 2 authentication response message to help you understand the structure of these often lengthy messages. (Note: A Signature element can be associated with an Assertion, the Response, or both. We have shown it in the Assertion for this sample.)

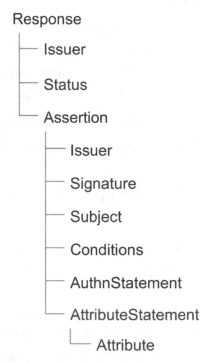

Figure C-1. *Structure of a Sample SAML 2 Authentication Response*

A sample SAML 2 authentication response is shown in the following sections. We've replaced specific values with explanatory text in bolded italics and provided a table after each snippet to indicate what's useful to check when debugging.

C.2.1. Response

A SAML 2 authentication response message starts off with "samlp:Response" and includes the information shown in the snippet that follows and explained in Table C-2:

```
<samlp:Response
      xmlns:samlp="urn:oasis:names:tc:SAML:2.0:protocol"
      ID="ID"
      InResponseTo="ID OF CORRESPONDING REQUEST"
      Version="2.0"
      IssueInstant="TIME ISSUED"
      Destination="ACS URL of Service Provider">
  <saml:Issuer
    xmlns:saml="urn:oasis:names:tc:SAML:2.0:assertion">ISSUER OF RESPONSE -
    IDENTITY PROVIDER
  </saml:Issuer>
  <samlp:Status>
  <samlp:StatusCode  Value-"urn:oasis:names:tc:SAML:2.0:status:Success"/>
  </samlp:Status>
```

Table C-2. *SAML 2 Authentication Response Elements Useful for Troubleshooting*

Element	Description
ID	A unique identifier for a response.
InResponseTo	This response element should match the ID of the authentication request which triggered the response (for service provider–initiated cases).
IssueInstant	Time at which the response was issued. This can be checked for correct time to detect time skew issues. Service providers should reject responses that are older than a configured time tolerance.
Destination	The Assertion Consumer Service (ACS) URL where the service provider receives the response. Service providers should validate that the Destination URL in the response is where they received the response.
Issuer	The issuer of the response. Should match the expected identity provider.
Status	The Status element contains the result of the authentication request. Successful authentication is required for a status of "Success."

C.2.1.1. Authentication Assertion (Beginning)

The beginning of the assertion element of a response contains an ID, the instant at which the assertion itself was issued, and the identity of the assertion issuer as shown in the following snippet and explained in Table C-3:

```
<saml:Assertion
     xmlns:saml="urn:oasis:names:tc:SAML:2.0:assertion"
     Version="2.0"
     ID="ID FOR ASSERTION"
     IssueInstant="TIME ASSERTION ISSUED">
   <saml:Issuer>ENTITY ISSUING ASSERTION</saml:Issuer>
```

Table C-3. *SAML 2 Authentication Assertion Elements Useful for Troubleshooting*

Element	Description
ID	A unique identifier for an assertion.
IssueInstant	Time at which the assertion was issued. This can be checked for correct time to detect time skew issues. Service providers should reject responses that are older than a configured time tolerance.
Issuer	The issuer of the response. Should match the expected identity provider.

C.2.1.2. Digital Signature for Authentication Assertion

The digital signature provides integrity assurance for the signed element. The IdP must sign either the assertion or the response when the HTTP-POST or HTTP-Redirect binding is used and can sign both. The typical elements to check are shown in Table C-4. Portions of this element are not shown for brevity.

```
<Signature
     xmlns:="http://www.w3.org/2000/09/xmldsig#">
   <SignedInfo>

       ...

     <SignatureMethod  Algorithm=
         "http://www.w3.org/2001/04/xmldsig-more#rsa-sha256"/>

             ...

   </SignedInfo>
```

```
<SignatureValue>DIGITAL SIGNATURE</SignatureValue>
<KeyInfo>
   <X509Data>
      <X509Certificate>CERTIFICATE</X509Certificate>
   </X509Data>
</KeyInfo>
</Signature>
```

Table C-4. *SAML 2 Assertion Signature Elements Useful for Troubleshooting*

Element	Description
SignatureMethod	Check that the signature algorithm used by the IdP is an algorithm accepted by the service provider implementation.
Certificate	Check that the certificate shown is correct for the IdP and matches IdP metadata configured at the service provider.

C.2.1.3. Subject

The Subject element identifies the authenticated user. A very common issue is that an identifier specified by the identity provider in the assertion is different from the identifier expected by a service provider (application) for the user. The typical elements to check are shown in Table C-5.

```
<saml:Subject>
   <saml:NameID
      Format="urn:oasis:names:tc:SAML:1.1:nameid-format:unspecified">
      USER IDENTIFIER
   </saml:NameID>
   <saml:SubjectConfirmation
      Method="urn:oasis:names:tc:SAML:2.0:cm:bearer">
      <saml:SubjectConfirmationData
         NotOnOrAfter="EXPIRATION FOR SUBJECT DATA"
         Recipient="SERVICE PROVIDER ACS URL>"
         InResponseTo="ID FROM REQUEST"/>
   </saml:SubjectConfirmation>
</saml:Subject>
```

Table C-5. *SAML 2 Subject Elements Useful for Troubleshooting*

Element	Description
NameID	Contains an identifier for the authenticated user.
NotOnOrAfter	Specified validity period for subject data. This time should not have already passed when the assertion is received.
Recipient	This element should match the ACS URL to which the response was delivered. Used by a service provider to ensure it is the intended recipient of an assertion it receives.
InResponseTo	This element should match the ID of the authentication request which triggered the response (for service provider–initiated cases).

C.2.1.4. Conditions

The Conditions element contains conditions on the use of the assertion which should be checked by a service provider. The typical elements to check are shown in Table C-6.

```
<saml:Conditions
      NotBefore="BEGIN VALIDITY TIME"
      NotOnOrAfter="END VALIDITY TIME">
   <saml:AudienceRestriction>
      <saml:Audience>INTENDED RECIPIENT</saml:Audience>
   </saml:AudienceRestriction>
</saml:Conditions>
```

Table C-6. *SAML 2 Conditions Elements Useful for Troubleshooting*

Element	Description
NotBefore	Start of validity period for assertion. This time should have passed when the assertion is received.
NotOnOrAfter	End of validity period for assertion. This time should not have already passed when the assertion is received.
Audience	Audience (intended recipient) of the assertion. May be specified in URN format. Used by a service provider to ensure it is the intended recipient of an assertion it receives.

C.2.1.5. Authentication Statement

The AuthnStatement element indicates when authentication occurred, and the AuthnContextClassRef can be used to return an indicator of the strength of the authentication mechanism used. This section of the response is not typically a frequent cause of issues. The typical elements to check are shown in Table C-7.

```
<saml:AuthnStatement
     AuthnInstant="2019-01-19T19:11:28.407Z"
     SessionIndex="SESSION INDEX">
  <saml:AuthnContext>
    <saml:AuthnContextClassRef>
       urn:oasis:names:tc:SAML:2.0:ac:classes:unspecified
    </saml:AuthnContextClassRef>
  </saml:AuthnContext>
</saml:AuthnStatement>
```

Table C-7. *SAML 2 AuthnStatement Elements Useful for Troubleshooting*

Element	Description
AuthnContextClassRef	If a particular AuthnContextClassRef was requested, this can be checked to see if it matches the requested value.

C.2.1.6. Attribute Statements

Attribute statements are used to convey additional user profile attributes about the user. A frequent cause of issues is a mismatch between attributes expected by an application and the attributes delivered in a SAML assertion. The specific attributes will vary across different applications and identity providers. We have shown two attributes in the following snippet, one for a user identifier and one for a user's email address. The list of attribute statements in an assertion should be checked to ensure all attributes required by an application are delivered in the assertion.

```
<saml:AttributeStatement
     xmlns:xs="http://www.w3.org/2001/XMLSchema"
     xmlns:xsi="http://www.w3.org/2001/XMLSchema-instance">
```

```
<saml:Attribute
Name="http://schemas.xmlsoap.org/ws/2005/05/identity/claims/nameidentifier"
NameFormat="urn:oasis:names:tc:SAML:2.0:attrname-format:uri">
    <saml:AttributeValue xsi:type="xs:string">
        USER IDENTIFIER
    </saml:AttributeValue>
  </saml:Attribute>
  <saml:Attribute
    Name=
"http://schemas.xmlsoap.org/ws/2005/05/identity/claims/emailaddress"
NameFormat="urn:oasis:names:tc:SAML:2.0:attrname-format:uri">
    <saml:AttributeValue xsi:type="xs:string">
        USER EMAIL ADDRESS
    </saml:AttributeValue>
  </saml:Attribute>
</saml:AttributeStatement>
</saml:Assertion>
</samlp:Response>
```

C.3. Validation

Applications must properly validate the SAML assertions they receive. We will focus in this section on validation steps for applications, as this book is targeted to application developers rather than identity provider implementers. We will further focus on validation steps that may impact troubleshooting as there are now many good SAML 2 libraries available to parse and validate protocol messages, and we do not recommend that new applications implement the SAML protocol or the validation of protocol messages themselves. We assume a simple scenario where an Identity Provider responds to a Service Provider without any intermediate proxies, transitive relationships, or further redirection to other parties.

Assuming that responses are sent to an application using HTTP-POST, validation steps include checking

- The response contains a valid, properly formatted SAML 2 response.

- The Destination element of the SAML response matches the Service Provider.

- The Issuer of the response assertion matches the configured/expected Identity Provider.

- The Status element indicates success and does not contain an error code.

- The digital signature on an assertion is valid for the issuing identity provider.

- The Subject element exists and contains the subject of the assertion, using a name format for the subject that is recognizable by the Service Provider.

- The AudienceRestriction in the Conditions element matches the Service Provider.

- The AuthnContext element of the AuthnStatement matches an application's requirements, such as for the strength of the authentication mechanism used.

- The AttributeStatements contain values for any attributes required by the application.

- The application's Assertion Consumer Service URL that received a response is the same as the Recipient in the SubjectConfirmationData element of the response received.

- The NotOnOrAfter time specified in the SubjectConfirmationData and Conditions elements in the response has not passed. It is acceptable to allow a small tolerance for clock differences between servers, but if assertions repeatedly time out, the issue should be fixed by configuring servers to synchronize clocks with time servers.

- The ID for each incoming assertion is not on a list of previously used assertion ID values, maintained by the application for the length of time the IDs would be valid (from NotOnOrAfter), to ensure that the assertion has not been replayed.

Additional validations only possible with SP-initiated flow include

- Check that the InResponseTo element in the response matches the unique ID of the authentication request sent.

- If a value was sent using the RelayState parameter, the response should contain the same value in the RelayState parameter.

Additional validations for IdP-initiated flow include

- There should not be an InResponseTo element.

The RelayState element may include a URL at the Service Provider to which the user is to be directed after a successful authentication response is received. With an IdP-initiated flow, such use of RelayState is often undertaken with a mutual agreement between the Service Provider and the Identity Provider. If no RelayState is specified, a Service Provider should have a designated default URL to which a user will be redirected after a response is received. If RelayState is used, the contents must be protected against tampering with a mechanism that supports size restrictions for this field. It should be noted, however, that the protocol does not provide a way to ensure the integrity of a SAML message and RelayState pairing. In other words, an attacker could potentially recombine a SAML message from one response with a RelayState from another response. With IdP-initiated flows, especially with the use of RelayState, it may be difficult for a Service Provider to validate that a response is legitimate and hasn't been tampered with, making IdP-initiated flows vulnerable to additional risks.

Our discussion in this section has assumed the use of general security measures such as the use of a suitably up-to-date version of TLS and secure cipher suite for the protocol communications, along with secure key management for cryptographic keys, and trusted certificate authorities for trusted bindings between public keys and identities.

Appendix D: Public Key Cryptography

This appendix provides a brief description of how public and private keys are used to encrypt and sign tokens in a public key cryptography scheme.

With public key cryptography, there is a private key and a public key. The private key is a long string of random characters. A public key is generated from the private key. The two keys are called a key pair. The owner of a key pair should keep the private key a secret, but the public key is designed to be distributed to others and used as described in the following.

To encrypt a message or object, the sender uses the public key of the intended recipient to encrypt the message. Once it is encrypted, only the recipient, who holds the matching private key, can decipher the message.

To digitally sign a message or object, the signer uses its private key to digitally sign the message. The recipient of the message uses the sender's public key to verify the signature on the message.

© Yvonne Wilson, Abhishek Hingnikar 2023
Y. Wilson and A. Hingnikar, *Solving Identity Management in Modern Applications*,
https://doi.org/10.1007/978-1-4842-8261-8

Appendix E: Troubleshooting Tools

The following sections contain tools the authors have found useful for troubleshooting issues with applications using identity protocols.

E.1. Capture an HTTP Trace

An HTTP trace is essential for troubleshooting many scenarios. The following instructions indicate how to access trace features in different browsers, at the time of writing. A search for "How to capture an HTTP trace in <name of browser>" should provide current instructions if the following instructions no longer apply:

Chrome

- Open Developer Tools.

- Click the Network tab.

- Check the "Preserve Log" option, if not already checked.

- After capturing a trace, click the Export HAR arrow button to save the trace in a .har file.

Firefox

- There is a nice extension called Live HTTP Headers that is handy with Firefox.

- Alternatively, you can open a new tab in Firefox and select "Tools" ➤ "Browser Tools" ➤ "Web Developer Tools" and then click the Network tab.

- Reproduce the issue.

- Right-click in the trace window and select "Save All As HAR."

Edge

- Press F12 to bring up Developer Tools.

- Click the Network tab. Make sure the "Preserve log" option is checked.

- Reproduce the issue.

- Click the Export HAR button.

Safari

- In Safari Preferences, Advanced, turn on "Show Develop Menu in Menu bar."

- When viewing a site, use the Develop ➤ Show Web Inspector to view.

- Click the Network tab.

- Turn on Preserve Log. Reproduce the issue.

- Use "Export" to save the HTTP trace to a .har file.

E.2. View a HAR File

If you can reproduce an authentication/authorization issue, you can view the HTTP trace of the issue in your own browser. However, if you need to view an HTTP Archive file captured by someone else, the following tools will be useful.

Caution   Remember that HTTP trace files may contain sensitive information such as passwords or security tokens. You should remove sensitive content such as passwords before sharing or uploading trace files, as well as reset credentials and revoke any tokens, as appropriate.

If the tools listed as follows are no longer available, you should be able to find new ones by searching for "HTTP Archive View" or "How to view a .har file."

Chrome

The Chrome browser supports the ability to import a .har file.

- Open the Chrome Developer Tools Network tab.

- Drag and drop your .har file onto the tab.

Google .har file analyzer

Google provides a website which can be used to view HTTP Archive (.har) files:
`https://toolbox.googleapps.com/apps/har_analyzer/`

Fiddler

Fiddler, another useful network trace tool, can also be used to view .har files:
`https://docs.telerik.com/fiddler/configure-fiddler/tasks/configurefiddler`

E.3. Capture a Network Trace

To capture API traffic originating from a back-end application component or native application, you can rely on your favorite debugger or a network trace tool such as the following:

Fiddler

`https://docs.telerik.com/fiddler`

Charles Proxy

`www.charlesproxy.com/`

E.4. View Security Tokens

The ability to view security tokens issued by identity providers greatly aids the debugging process. Table E-1 contains some of our favorites.

Table E-1. *Useful Tools for Viewing Security Tokens*

Tool	Purpose
`https://jwt.io`	Tool provided by Auth0 for viewing JWT tokens.
`https://samltool.com`	Tool provided by OneLogin for viewing SAML tokens.
`https://samltool.io`	Tool provided by Auth0 for viewing SAML tokens.

E.5. Test APIs

A tool for testing API calls, without the added complexity of a client application, can aid debugging. Table E-2 contains tools we've found helpful for testing calls to APIs.

Table E-2. *API Debugging Tools*

Tool	Purpose
`https://getpostman.com`	Tool for learning, debugging, and testing API calls.
`https://insomnia.rest/`	Tool for learning, debugging, and testing API calls.

Appendix F: Privacy Legislation

This section contains information on privacy-related legislation. Countries around the world are recognizing the need to enact legislation to protect personal information. It is beyond the scope of this book to provide a comprehensive list of privacy legislation as the list is long and new legislation is being introduced on an ongoing basis. In fact, at the time of writing, the privacy legislation in several countries is undergoing significant revision, in some cases to align more closely with the GDPR.

We will provide selected resources for learning more about the primary privacy legislation applicable to the EU, namely, the GDPR, and legislation in the United States, which takes a sectoral approach to privacy legislation. We've also provided resources to help you find legislation applicable to other countries and to stay on top of privacy changes around the world.

The information provided in the following does not constitute legal guidance, and we recommend that organizations consult with legal and privacy professionals in the development of any privacy compliance efforts.

F.1. European Union

The European Union updated its 1996 Data Protection Directive with comprehensive privacy legislation known as the EU GDPR, General Data Protection Regulation.[i] The GDPR took effect in 2018 and applies to any entity that receives, stores, or processes data about persons in the EU and includes stiff fines for noncompliance.

Note that individual countries within the EU may enact additional country-specific legislation for implementation of the GDPR.

© Yvonne Wilson, Abhishek Hingnikar 2023
Y. Wilson and A. Hingnikar, *Solving Identity Management in Modern Applications*,
https://doi.org/10.1007/978-1-4842-8261-8

F.2. United States

In the United States, there are several privacy-related laws rather than one single federal privacy law. Privacy legislation in the United States uses a sectoral approach with different laws for different industry sectors and for several individual states:

- **GLBA (Gramm-Leach-Bliley Act)**[ii] – Specifies privacy and security requirements for the financial industry governing the handling and protection of NPI (nonpublic personal information).

- **HIPAA (Health Insurance Portability and Accountability Act)**[iii] – Specifies privacy and security requirements for the healthcare industry, governing personal data as well as information about a person's healthcare, health status, and payment for healthcare.

- **FTCA (Federal Trade Commission Act)**[iv] – Protects consumers against deceptive or unfair business practices, which may include uses of personal data that do not conform to published privacy notices. See in particular the FTC Privacy Rule.

- **FCRA (Fair Credit Reporting Act)**[v] **and FACTA (Fair and Accurate Credit Transactions Act)**[vi] – Governs protection of personal data, including a person's credit score, capacity for credit, and any personal characteristics related to credit worthiness. It also obligates financial institutions to implement measures to detect and respond to suspected instances of identity theft, via the Identity Theft Red Flags Rule.

- **CAN-SPAM (Controlling the Assault of Non-Solicited Pornography and Marketing)**[vii] – Governs the use of unsolicited commercial emails whose primary purpose is advertisement or promotion of commercial products or services.

- **TCPA (Telephone Consumer Protection Act)**[viii] – Governs telemarketing calls and the use of automated calls, otherwise known as robocalls.

- **COPPA (Children's Online Privacy Protection Act)**[ix] – Governs the collection, use, and disclosure of information about children under the age of 13 for protection from unfair or deceptive practices.

It places requirements on websites or online services targeted to children under 13 or which knowingly have personal data about children under 13.

- **VPPA (Video Privacy Protection Act)**[x] – Originally established in 1988 and amended in 2012, it governs the protection of personal data related to rental or sales of videos.

In addition, a patchwork of different privacy laws is being enacted by individual states in the absence of national legislation in the United States. Examples are

- **California Consumer Privacy Act (CCPA)**[xi] – California enacted the California Consumer Privacy Act (CCPA) which took effect in January 2020. The CCPA entitles California residents to know what personal data is being collected, whether it's sold or shared, the right to opt out to the sale or sharing of their personal data, access to their data, and equal service and price even if they exercise their opt-out choice. The CCPA was the first comprehensive data privacy law enacted by a state in the United States.

- **California Privacy Rights Act (CPRA)**[xii] – This act takes effect on July 1, 2023, and expands upon the CCPA. It enlarges the definition of "personal information" to include things like cookies, browser history, IP addresses, geolocation data, and device identifiers. It defines a new category of data to be considered sensitive personal information, adds measures designed to prevent users' geolocation from being tracked, adds further protections for minors, and provides greater legal rights for users, including private right of action such as the ability to sue providers after a data breach. The CPRA also establishes the California Privacy Protection Agency to serve as an advocate for users and to oversee and enforce privacy requirements.

- **Virginia Consumer Data Protection Act (CDPA)**[xiii] – The Virginia CDPA was signed on March 2, 2021, and becomes effective on January 1, 2023. It is the second comprehensive data privacy law at the state level in the United States and establishes several requirements similar to the GDPR and the CCPA. The CDPA requires organizations to provide privacy notices and disclose if personal data is sold or used for targeted advertising and provide an opt-out mechanism. It gives users the right to view, correct, and request the deletion of their personal data held and the right to opt out of certain processing of their data. The Virginia CDPA applies to individuals who conduct business in Virginia or target services to Virginia residents as well as meet thresholds related to the number of consumers whose personal data is processed and the percent of gross revenue gained from the sale of personal data.

- **Colorado Privacy Act (CPA)**[xiv] – The Colorado CPA was signed into law on July 7, 2021, and becomes effective on July 1, 2023. It is the third comprehensive, state-level data privacy legislation in the United States and contains elements similar to the GDPR, CCPA, CPRA, and the Virginia CDPA. It applies to data controllers who conduct business in Colorado or target services to Colorado residents and meet thresholds related to the number of consumers whose personal data is processed and whether any revenue or discounts are gained from the sale of personal data.

- **Vermont Data Broker Privacy Law**[xv] – Vermont has enacted legislation that applies to data brokers that collect, store, aggregate, and sell data about data subjects. This legislation applies to brokers who don't have a direct relationship with the data subjects. The law requires data brokers to be transparent about their practices by registering with the state, secure the data they hold, and to not use personal data to harass or discriminate against data subjects. The Vermont law also requires free credit freezes to protect consumers whose identity has been stolen.

For information on other states, the International Association of Privacy Professionals has prepared a chart comparing US states' passage of comprehensive privacy legislation.[xvi] With individual states each passing their own different legislation, businesses will need to devote time to understanding how to be compliant with different states' legislation in an efficient manner.

F.3. Other Countries

For information on privacy legislation in other countries, we have found the following sites useful for identifying privacy laws in each location and tracking news on privacy changes:

- **DLA Piper** – Data Protection Laws of the World[xvii]

- **United Nations Conference on Trade and Development** – Data Protection and Privacy Legislation[xviii]

- **International Association of Privacy Professionals (IAPP)** – (Some content for members only)[xix]

In reviewing privacy legislation, it is worth noting that in some countries, there is different legislation for private sector businesses vs. public sector entities, and there may be additional legislation enacted by regional governments or for specific industries. For example, in Canada, the Personal Information Protection and Electronic Documents Act (PIPEDA)[xx] applies to private sector businesses in Canada, whereas the Privacy Act[xxi] applies to federally regulated public bodies in Canada. In addition, some Canadian provinces have enacted additional privacy legislation.

F.4. Notes

i.   https://gdpr.eu/what-is-gdpr/

ii. www.ftc.gov/tips-advice/business-center/privacy-and-security/gramm-leach-bliley-act

iii. www.hhs.gov/hipaa/index.html

iv. https://www.ftc.gov/legal-library/browse/rules/financial-privacy-rule

v.   www.ftc.gov/enforcement/rules/rulemaking-regulatory-reform-proceedings/fair-credit-reporting-act

vi. www.ftc.gov/enforcement/statutes/fair-accurate-credit-transactions-act-2003

vii. www.ftc.gov/tips-advice/business-center/guidance/can-spam-act-compliance-guide-busines

viii. www.fdic.gov/resources/supervision-and-examinations/consumer-compliance-examination-manual/documents/8/viii-5-1.pdf

ix. www.ftc.gov/enforcement/rules/rulemaking-regulatory-reform-proceedings/childrens-online-privacy-protection-rule

x. https://www.congress.gov/bill/100th-congress/senate-bill/2361

xi. https://leginfo.legislature.ca.gov/faces/billTextClient.xhtml?bill_id=201720180AB375

xii. https://thecpra.org/

xiii. https://law.lis.virginia.gov/vacode/title59.1/chapter53/

xiv. https://leg.colorado.gov/bills/sb21-190

xv. https://legislature.vermont.gov/statutes/chapter/09/062

xvi. https://iapp.org/resources/article/state-comparison-table/

xvii. www.dlapiperdataprotection.com/

xviii. https://unctad.org/en/Pages/DTL/STI_and_ICTs/ICT4D-Legislation/eCom-Data-Protection-Laws.aspx

xix. https://iapp.org/

xx. www.priv.gc.ca/en/privacy-topics/privacy-laws-in-canada/the-personal-information-protection-and-electronic-documents-act-pipeda/

xxi. www.priv.gc.ca/en/privacy-topics/privacy-laws-in-canada/the-privacy-act/

Appendix G: Security Compliance Frameworks

Security frameworks provide a list of controls that represent requirements that would reasonably be expected of an organization to adequately secure systems and information under its control. We list here some security frameworks we have had occasion to review, in two sections. The first section contains general security frameworks that are not specific to an individual country or government. The second section presents several security requirements or frameworks that are specific to the United States.

G.1. General Security Frameworks

The following is a list of security frameworks, in alphabetical order.

G.1.1. Center for Internet Security – Top 20 Controls

The CIS Controls[i] are a series of 20 foundational cybersecurity controls intended to eliminate the most common attacks.

G.1.2. Cloud Security Alliance

The Cloud Security Alliance[ii] has a mission to promote best practices for security assurance for cloud providers. CSA has a three-level certification program called CSA STAR based on a published framework of security controls known as the Cloud Controls Matrix (CCM).

© Yvonne Wilson, Abhishek Hingnikar 2023
Y. Wilson and A. Hingnikar, *Solving Identity Management in Modern Applications*,
https://doi.org/10.1007/978-1-4842-8261-8

G.1.3. ISO 27000

ISO 27000[iii] is a family of standards published by the ISO (International Organization for Standardization) for information security management systems. Figure G-1 shows the ISO/IEC 27000 family of requirements, guidelines, and standards.

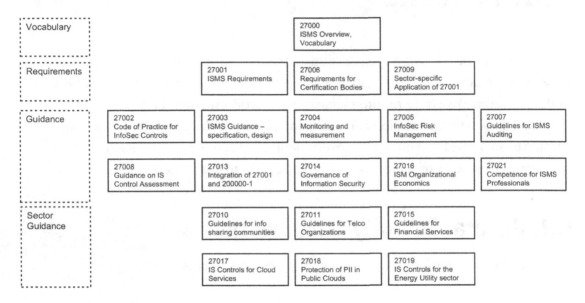

Figure G-1. *ISO/IEC 27000 ISMS Standards Family*

Each of the standards/guidelines in the diagram may be purchased from ISO. A certified, independent auditor is required to verify compliance with the framework controls. After an audit of an organization's evidence of compliance, a report is issued for the audit period stating if the controls were met. Organizations that pass the audit can place a certificate seal on their website.

G.1.4. PCI DSS

The PCI DSS (Payment Card Industry Data Security Standard)[iv] was created by the payment card industry. Any vendor processing credit card data is expected to be compliant with the PCI DSS standard. It also applies to other systems that can impact the security of systems subject to PCI DSS.

G.2. US Frameworks

The following frameworks are applicable to the United States. They may be applicable to private sector organizations or applicable to government agencies and those doing business with them. Even if they are not mandatory for your project, a lot can be learned about best practices by studying the requirements, which may be useful in preparing for an audit or future requirements.

G.2.1. CJIS Security Policy[v] – Criminal Justice Information Services Security Policy

In the United States, the Criminal Justice Information Services (CJIS) Security Policy governs the protections which must be provided for the handling of personal data related to criminal justice, including fingerprints and criminal background records.

G.2.2. FFIEC Information Technology Examination Handbook and Cybersecurity Assessment Tool[vi]

The US Federal Financial Institutions Examination Council (FFIEC) unifies standards and principles and provides security guidance for financial institutions. The FFIEC has published the *Information Technology Examination Handbook* which consists of 11 booklets including one on Information Security. It has also published the Cybersecurity Assessment Tool which includes principles and standards in the Examination Handbook. The Cybersecurity Assessment Tool can be used as a self-assessment tool to prepare for an examination or audit.

G.2.3. FISMA – Federal Information Security Management Act[vii]

FISMA requires each US federal agency to develop, document, and implement an agency-wide program to provide information security for the information and information systems that support the operations and assets of the agency, including those provided or managed by another agency, contractor, or other sources. The FISMA standards include NIST publications FIPS-199, FIPS-200, and the NIST 800 series.

G.2.4. FedRAMP – Federal Risk and Authorization Management Program[viii]

FedRAMP defines a process for the evaluation, authorization, and monitoring of the security of cloud service providers used by US federal agencies. FedRAMP approval is required before a cloud service can be used by a federal agency (with a few very limited exceptions).

G.2.5. GLBA Safeguards Rule[ix]

This portion of GLBA (Gramm-Leach-Bliley Act) requires financial institutions to have measures in place to protect personal data, including names, addresses, social security numbers, bank account, and credit card information, as well as credit and income history.

G.2.6. HIPAA[x]

In the United States, the Health Insurance Portability and Accountability Act has a security component known as the HIPAA Security Rule. This rule establishes standards for the protection of electronic personal health information. This includes personal data related to healthcare, health status, and payment for healthcare.

G.2.7. HITECH Act[xi]

In the United States, the HITECH (Health Information Technology for Economic and Clinical Health) Act governs the adoption of technology for managing electronic health records. Subtitle D of this act covers the security and privacy of electronic health information.

G.2.8. NIST[xii]

The National Institute for Standards and Technology in the United States is a government body that publishes standards. The NIST cybersecurity framework is a voluntary framework of standards, guidelines, and best practices for cybersecurity. This framework references the NIST 800 series of publications which provide guidelines and technical specifications for cybersecurity.

G.3. SOC(Service Organization Control)

G.3.1. SOC1

A SOC1 report focuses on a service organization's controls that are likely to be relevant to an audit of the entity's financial statements. Control objectives are related to both business process and information technology. SOC1 reports follow the Statement on Standards for Attestation Engagements (SSAE) 18 standard.

G.3.2. SOC2

Service Organization Control 2 is a set of controls against which a company is audited, related to security, privacy, confidentiality, processing integrity, and/or availability. The specific set of controls for SOC2 is defined by each company. As the SOC2 assessment is not based on an open standard set of controls, information on the company-specific controls is included in the SOC2 report, prepared by an auditor, after a SOC2 compliance audit. The SOC2 report was created in part because of the rise of cloud computing and business outsourcing of functions to service organizations. These are called user entities in the SOC reports. Liability concerns have caused an increase in demand in assurance of confidentiality and privacy of information processed by companies and organizations.

G.4. Notes

    i.   www.cisecurity.org/controls/

    ii.   https://cloudsecurityalliance.org/star/#_overview

    iii.   www.iso.org/isoiec-27001-information-security.html

    iv.   https://www.pcisecuritystandards.org/

    v.   www.fbi.gov/services/cjis/cjis-security-policy-resource-center

    vi.   www.ffiec.gov/cybersecurity.htm

    vii.   www.dhs.gov/cisa/federal-information-security-modernization-act

viii. www.fedramp.gov/

 ix. https://www.ftc.gov/business-guidance/resources/ftc-safeguards-rule-what-your-business-needs-know

  x. www.hhs.gov/hipaa/for-professionals/security/index.html

 xi. www.hhs.gov/hipaa/for-professionals/special-topics/hitech-act-enforcement-interim-final-rule/index.html

xii. www.nist.gov/cyberframework

Index

A

Y. Wilson and A. Hingnikar, *Solving Identity Management in Modern Applications,*
https://doi.org/10.1007/978-1-4842-8261-8

Printed in the United States
by Baker & Taylor Publisher Services